For
Bill
with kind regards!

P—

jan 78

Literature in the Marketplace

Per Gedin

Literature
in the Marketplace

Translated by George Bisset

Faber

Three Queen Square

London

First published in Great Britain in 1977
by Faber and Faber Limited
3 Queen Square London WC1
Originally published in 1975
under the title Litteraturen i verkligheten
by Bokförlaget Prisma, Stockholm
Printed in Great Britain by
Western Printing Services Limited, Bristol

© 1975, Per Gedin
Translation © 1977, George Bisset

British Library Cataloguing in Publication Data

Gedin, Per
    Literature in the market place.
1. Book industries and trade
I. Title II. Bisset, George
301.16'1   Z278

ISBN 0-571-11053-3

Contents

Note for the English Translation

My main reason for writing this book has been to demonstrate how similar the development of the industrialized western European countries has been, both from an historical point of view and in its present trend. Needless to say, there are differences but a study of the book market as one specific feature clearly shows similarities.

Sweden provides a most illuminating starting-point, as it is both economically and culturally a kind of pilot country. The trends in the Swedish book market indicate this very clearly when compared to the situation both in neighbouring countries such as Denmark and more distant European countries such as Germany and Britain.

A few quotations from *The Euromonitor Book Readership Survey* of 1975 might well have been taken from a German, French or Swedish survey: '...books are becoming another form of mass media and entertainment and they are losing their individual appeal...', '...a growing percentage of people now do not seem to read at all.' 'The desire of the British to be told what they want to read has aided the growth of the mail order business; ...a good deal of the success of book clubs over the recent years lies in the passive role adopted by the reading public.'

This book constitutes an effort to give an idea of the development of the book market—publishers, booksellers, authors and the reading public—and to show why it is now heading towards very profound problems and serious changes in the whole structure of the market.

The publication in English of *Literature in the Marketplace* is due entirely to my publisher Matthew Evans' warm interest in and understanding of these problems and to his encouragement. I would also like to thank George Bisset for his personal commitment and for the excellent way he has carried out the sometimes rather complicated task of translation into English.

8

Preface

The point of departure for this book was originally the publishing crisis in Sweden. It revealed, with a suddenness that surprised even the various representatives of the book trade, profound problems in publishing, and especially in the publication of serious fiction. A reduced title-output, rising prices and shrinking editions accorded badly with the rapid social development through which Sweden had passed since the end of the war, a development that had brought a considerable improvement in the living standard, in the level of education, and increased leisure time—all factors that should have been advantageous to the book market.

It soon became clear that the crisis was not a unique Swedish phenomenon, but that it had begun to make itself felt in all the industrialized countries of Western Europe and even in the USA. All evidence indicated that it was not merely a question of a temporary faltering economy but a structural crisis, which was obviously an outcome of a change in the societies of the West and in their cultural patterns.

In order to understand one's own times it is necessary to have an historical perspective. I have therefore begun with a survey of the book market's development, that is to say how books have become part of an organized economic market where writers, publishers, printers, booksellers and the reading public are part of the system. Although it sounds like a declaration of the obvious to say that books are produced within an economic and social reality, it is a fact to which literary historians and cultural critics continue to pay little heed, particularly in current debate.

It has also been necessary to describe the society we live in, and more especially the society towards which we are heading. In doing so it is impossible to avoid a certain simplification, but I have consciously emphasized those features which I believe will be increasingly dominant in what I have chosen to call the mass or service society.

It has become clear then that the traditional book market of the western world is a product of the bourgeois society that is moving more and more towards a mass society with a completely different cultural pattern. This change influences all sections of society of course, but it would appear that the book market in its traditional form will have extraordinary difficulties in adjusting to it. I believe that the type of book most vulnerable to the change is the novel, and this is perfectly natural since the novel was the special literary form of bourgeois society. Therefore I have devoted two chapters especially to the novel's form, its substance and its importance to the economy of the book market.

It should be emphasized, however, that when I write about the novel I frequently use it as a generic concept for 'the general book', that is to say also biography, travel books and essays or quite simply, books for persons with cultural and intellectual interests. However, I do not include in this definition news-stand literature and the simplest entertainment books.

The most important aspect of this work has been to try to give a coherent picture of the book's situation today, and in looking at that I hope we may understand something of its future. I have therefore attempted to show as many facets as possible, such as the situation of avant-gardism, the position of the critic, the future of the traditional book trade, and the economic and social predicament of the writer. I have tried to put all this into a comprehensive picture, which alas has prevented a greater in-depth treatment that would doubtless have been interesting.

The overall picture is, however, more important in the present context. I consider the book's problem in our advanced society to be a problem that in one way or another affects our whole cultural situation. If the problem is clearly defined then it should be possible to find a solution to it. If this work can provide a cause for discussion and further development of its themes then it has fulfilled its purpose.

In order to draw this overall picture I have used a number of sources within various fields of science such as economics, cultural and social history and sociology. I have chosen to quote fairly extensively direct from these sources to show clearly the facts and ideas upon which my analysis is based. As some of the sources are not easily accessible, I hope my quotations and notes will increase the value of the book as a reference work.

A book such as this, whose ambition is to describe the reality in which we live, cannot be written without the help and encouragement of a great many people. During the two years it has taken me to complete it, I have discussed the problems and have throughout made full use of many of the views of friends and colleagues. It would be impossible to name them all here, but many will certainly recognize the arguments. I would, however, like to name a few who have been especially helpful: Märta-Stina Danielsson, who was first to read the manuscript and gave me much wise advice; Adam Helms, who, in addition to his enthusiasm, placed his unique library on publishing history at my disposal; my Scandinavian colleagues, Brikt Jensen and Jarl Helleman, whose understanding of the problems supplied me with the necessary perspective; my Swedish publisher Gösta Åberg, who has seen to it that the book has the proper disposition; Göta Gorisse, who succeeded in deciphering and clean-typing the manuscript; and last but not least my family, who constantly provided me with interesting and exciting suggestions, opinions, and ideas.

The Reading Public and the Book Market

During the eighteenth century the foundations were laid for what was later to be called 'the reading public'. The invention of the printing press in the fifteenth century provided the technical pre-condition for a much wider dispersal of the written word, but it was not until the period of blossoming capitalism in the eighteenth century that the aristocracy's exclusive privilege of education was finally broken. This occurred primarily in England where a new upper class, composed of wealthy merchants and industrialists, came more and more to replace the hereditary nobility and courtiers. Wealth and ownership of property—even by the newly rich—became more important than 'blood'. The privileges of noble birth were continually reduced—more rapidly in England than elsewhere since only eldest sons inherited titles, while their younger brothers were not rewarded with any special advantages. However, the decisive criteria for membership of the ruling classes were now, besides wealth, education and knowledge.

The reading public developed initially through the publication of newspapers and magazines. The first attempts at this, made near the end of the seventeenth century, were a failure. England's first daily newspaper, *The Observer*, was started in 1681, but it was not a success and soon closed down. In 1702, however, *The Daily Courant* began publication and became an immediate success. But the real breakthrough for a new type of literature came with *The Tatler*, of Addison and Steele, in 1709, and *The Spectator* in 1714. By this time a new public had appeared that was to form the nucleus of the bourgeoisie in the nineteenth century. This public was composed of merchants, barristers, politicians and such who usually met in London coffee houses where they drank the new, fashionable drinks, coffee and tea, smoked their pipes, talked, and read the newspapers. And Addison's and Steele's success was assured because they had managed to achieve the proper 'bourgeois pitch'. The papers provided relaxation, advice and 'observations on life and manners' with a mixture of news, articles and general reading.

The size of this new public increased rapidly. Addison himself calculated the number of readers of *The Spectator* at approximately half a million (twenty readers per copy), or slightly less than 10 per cent of the population. This was obviously an early example of a publisher's exaggeration, but it has been estimated that the regular readers of newspapers and books were around 80,000 by the end of the eighteenth century. And most of these readers were to be found among the new bourgeoisie. In 1812, *The Edinburgh Review* maintained that: 'In this country there probably are not less than 200,000 persons who read for amusement and instruction, among the middling classes of society. In the higher classes there are not as many as 20,000.' In 1844 the same source gives the contemporary estimate of the reading public as 300,000 and 30,000 respectively.[1] By the turn of the century nearly 400 books a year were published, and many of these in very large editions even by later standards. As early as the year 1700, Daniel Defoe wrote a verse pamphlet in support of William of Orange that brought him £1,000 and sold 80,000 copies within a few days, and a religious pamphlet broke all previous records in 1750 with 100,000 copies. The collected essays from *The Spectator* were also among the great publishing successes. The first edition consisted of 9,000 copies, and over a period of twenty years, eleven editions were published.[2]

The vast majority of the reading public lived in the cities. Poverty and illiteracy prevented a large section of the population from reading, but there were also other difficulties such as overcrowded housing and poor lighting, the latter because taxation was based on the number of windows in a house and wax candles were very expensive. Nevertheless, the number of readers increased even among the petty bourgeoisie, such as hand craftsmen, shopkeepers and clerks, and the number of women readers particularly increased at all levels of the bourgeoisie.

This group had not, of course, been among the original coffee-house public, but towards the turn of the century they had gained greater freedom and, even more important, more leisure time. For wealthier women it was a new and pleasant way to pass the time, especially since they were excluded from male occupations such as politics, business, and hunting. Ian Watt cites a letter from Lady Mary Wortley Montagu to her daughter in which she lists some novels she would like to have sent to her and upon which she comments in terms oddly familiar even to our own times: 'I doubt not that at least the greater part of these are trash, lumber, etc. However, they will serve to pass away the idle time....' But there was an interest in books at a lower level too. Mrs. Thrale recounted that by her husband's orders she 'was not to think of the kitchen' and explained that it was as a result of this enforced leisure that she was 'driven ... on literature as [her] sole resource'. City dwellers had more leisure than ever before and this was true even of the common people, such as the wives and daughters of craftsmen and other members of the petty bourgeoisie. Rising industrialism had freed women from a number of traditional household duties like candle-making, brewing beer, spinning, weaving, and the making of soap. Watt quotes a Swedish traveller, Pehr Kahlm, who, in 1748, was surprised to find that in England 'one hardly ever sees a woman here trouble herself in the least about outdoor duties,' and indoors 'weaving and spinning is also in most houses a rare thing.'

Although people had much more leisure, and in consequence read more, a serious barrier to widespread reading still remained: the high price of books. During the latter half of the eighteenth century an ordinary worker earned about 10s a week while a shopkeeper or craftsman earned £1; Defoe's *Robinson Crusoe* cost 5s and Fielding's *Tom Jones* 13s 6d. It is interesting to note, however, that the prices were set in accordance with the social differences in reading habits. Novels sold at far lower prices than other literature, which both in design and content was addressed to the upper classes whose tastes, as Arnold Hauser has observed, were still primarily classicist and who preferred 'intellect and wit ... clarity of thought and purity of language' to the vulgar novels of the middle classes.[3] Pope's *Iliad*, for instance, cost six guineas, or the same as twenty-five novels of the size of *Robinson Crusoe*.

As a result of the high price of books, the first lending libraries were started in the middle of the century. Membership fees were generally a guinea a year or less. The idea of the lending library spread quickly and this perhaps was one of the major reasons for the rapid growth of a reading public. In 1761 an English magazine maintained that 'the reading female [!] hires her novel from some country Circulating Library which consists of about a hundred volumes.' The lending libraries in urban areas had much more to offer, such as William Lane's Minerva Library which certainly contained 10,000 volumes already in the eighteenth century. The literature of the lending libraries consisted largely of short romantic tales and the first English novels. It was in fact the same type of literature that had first been published in the burgeoning number of newspapers and periodicals, usually as short stories or in serial form: *Robinson Crusoe* first appeared in a newspaper that came out three times a week. Novel-reading grew rapidly in the middle of the nineteenth century and half of all the books borrowed for instance from the Sheffield Public Library were novels. Towards the end of the century this figure had risen to 65–90 per cent.[4]

Reading very soon became an accepted part of daily life and by the beginning of the nineteenth century 'reading is already one of the necessities of life for the upper classes, and the possession of books is . . . just as much taken for granted in the circles described by Jane Austen as it would have caused surprise in the world of Fielding.'[5]

It is remarkable how strictly the reading public was confined to the bourgeoisie: aristocrats bought the classics largely to fill their bookshelves; it was 'the middling classes' who read. The lower classes did not, despite the oft-quoted diary entry of London bookseller and publisher, James Lackington, in 1791:

> The sale of books in general has increased prodigiously within the last twenty years. The poorer sort of farmers, and even the poor country people in general who before that period spent their winter evenings in relating stories of witches, ghosts, hobgoblins etc., now shorten the winter nights by hearing their sons and daughters read tales, romances etc., and on entering their houses you may see *Tom Jones, Roderick Random*, and other entertaining books, stuck up in their bacon-racks etc. If John goes to town with a load of hay, he is charged to be sure not to forget to bring home *Peregrine Pickle's Adventures*, and when Dolly is sent to market to sell her eggs, she is commissioned to purchase. *The History of Joseph Andrews*. In short, all ranks and degrees now read.[6]

Probably it was the incredible success of Lackington's bookshop that motivated these enthusiastic diary notations (he initiated book sales and is said to have sold 100,000 volumes of 'reduced price' books per year during the whole last decade of the eighteenth century) rather than an objective analysis of the facts. There was, however, one group of people among the lower social orders who definitely belonged to the new reading public. These were the vast army of domestic servants employed in the homes of the bourgeoisie. They had the time, adequate lighting, and the books, as well as a very strong desire to emulate the habits of their employers. Watts points out that this particular occupational group was probably the largest one in the whole country and that its members' influence was important both as readers and as literary prototypes, and thus in the development of literature itself. Watts writes that Pamela, in Richardson's novel, 'may be regarded as the culture-heroine of a very powerful sisterhood of literate and leisured waiting-maids. We note that her main stipulation for a new post . . . was that it would allow her "a little Time for Reading".'

During the nineteenth century the new bourgeoisie established its position in society ever more firmly, especially in Britain, the land of its origin, but also in France and Germany, and somewhat later in Scandinavia. The members of this new middle class exhibited remarkable similarities to each other regardless of their nationality. This was true most of all perhaps, in their ideas of taste and culture. Members of this new class, whatever country they happened to inhabit, listened to the same music, admired the same plays and read much the same books, and these in turn influenced their whole life-style.

The social order established at this time remained fundamentally unchanged until World War I, after which it continued on through a period of dissolution and final disappearance by the beginning of World War II. During this period the importance of the aristocracy diminishes to insignificance and bourgeois taste and the middle-class way of life come to dominate society entirely. Indeed, Hauser maintains 'that there is no massive (literary) public apart from the middle class. But as soon as the emancipation of the middle class is accomplished, the struggle of the working class for its rights already begins.' And thus began the intense class conflicts that were to influence the whole form and structure of our culture up until the present day.

The transformation from an aristocratic, court-dominated society to a middle-class capitalistic society meant the creation of a *market* for culture. Works of art, musical compositions, books, and dramas were no longer commissioned by rich patrons for their personal use and paid for with a previously agreed sum of money. The artist, writer, or composer had to fight on an open market for whatever income he could get. There arose a theatre public, a concert public, an exhibition public, and a reading public. It had become a profession to be an artist, writer, or composer, and the practitioners of these professions created works, in the beginning, in perfect conformity with their new public, but soon, and, to an ever-increasing degree, their work ran counter to prevailing public taste.

The economic structure of the book market in the western world, as it is today, was first developed during the eighteenth century and then solidly established in the nineteenth. It was composed of the following elements: publishing houses, booksellers, newspapers and magazines, libraries, independent writers and, as we have seen, the reading public. Magazines, especially in England, led the way in the creation of this market.

The successful introduction of periodicals such as *The Tatler* and *The Spectator*, whose reasoning and moralizing were directed specifically at a middle-class public, was quickly followed by the appearance of a large number of similar publications, and it has been estimated that altogether there were as many as 800 during the whole of the eighteenth century. Many of them achieved wide distribution, like *Gentleman's Magazine*, which was founded in 1731 and had a circulation of 10,000 fifteen years later.[7] This particular journal, which was richly illustrated with woodcuts and copperplate engravings, developed a style of design and content that was widely imitated by others and also gave us the term 'magazine'. *Gentleman's Magazine* continued publication until 1907 and was still, at that time, read by the same predominantly middle-class public.

The first daily newspapers were also started in Britain. The most famous of them all, *The Times*, began publication in 1785. Already in the 1780s there was a total of 14 million copies of daily newspapers sold per year; by 1793 this figure had risen to 17 million. But France was not far behind and during a brief spell just after the revolution there were as many as 350 different newspapers published in Paris. The subscription rate was high, eighty francs per year, and copies could only be bought in this way. Those people who could not afford copies of their own could read the papers in the cafés. In 1824 there were 47,000 subscribers in Paris, in 1836, 70,000 and 200,000 by 1846. The enormous increase in the number of subscribers was largely the work of Emile de Giradin, a prolific writer and journalist who founded the newspaper *La Presse* in 1836. He lowered the subscription rate to forty francs and to make up the difference he initiated the idea of *réclame:* editorial notices, mostly of books, that were paid for by the publishers. Newspapers also ran regular advertisements, but most important was a third factor that accounted for the phenomenal success of these dailies: the serial story. As noted above, the printing of serializations occurred in Britain as early as the eighteenth century, but it was a sporadic affair directed at a less sophisticated audience and consisted primarily of simple short stories or longer tales that had previously been published as books—reprinted often without payment to the authors.

Now, however, the serial had become essential to increased circulation of the papers and a decisive factor in enlarging the readership of the new novels. It also played an important part in the literary development of writers and, no less important perhaps, it improved their finances immensely. Serialized novels replaced for a time virtually all other written entertainments, such as travel stories, natural history articles and essays and became the predominant feature of most publications. The serial gave new life to the picaresque novel, with its endless tales of adventure and crammed dramatic incident, but also—and this was something new—it had a solid foundation in contemporary social problems. It may seem paradoxical, as Hauser points out, 'to hear a very largely bourgeois public waxing enthusiastic about the "noble labourer" and storming furiously about the "cruelties of capitalism"', but in this way an author was able to capture the easily engaged sympathy of the newly rich middle class as well as the fellow feeling of the lower classes.

The serial novel came to represent an important aspect of the life's work of many writers. Successful writers were in great demand and highly paid, and the constant need for new material from competing journals often resulted in great prolificacy. When *La Presse* began publication, its first serial was one of Balzac's novels. At the time, Balzac also agreed to deliver one novel a year to the paper over a period of ten years, from 1837 to 1847. During this period *La Presse* also published most of the work of Eugène Sue. A rival paper, *La Siècle*, engaged Alexandre Dumas, who wrote *The Three Musketeers*, which proved to be an enormous success both for Dumas and the newspaper. Writers could earn tremendous sums. Dumas made 200,000 francs a year and Sue was paid 100,000 per novel, while Lamartine amassed 5 million francs between 1838 and 1851. The serial novel was also in fact of decisive financial importance to many newspapers. A serial by Dumas, for instance, increased one newspaper's circulation from 3,600 to 20,000.

While the serial story formed the pattern of publication for most continental newspapers, a slightly different method of issuing novels developed in Britain. This had, however, the same effect as the French serial: to lower the price of novels and gain a broader public for them. In Britain novels were published in monthly pamphlets, which meant that the cost was lowered to a third of the price of the finished novel, and, secondly, the instalment system made the purchase of novels easier. Charles Dickens was the writer who benefited most by this system. *The Pickwick Papers* was written for publication in this form and 40,000 copies were printed in the booklet edition, and a later novel, *Master Humphrey's Clock*, came out in an edition of 70,000. Dickens' earnings were, of course, commensurate. Trollope's career was launched by a publisher of these monthly instalments. This author was paid £1,000 per novel, issued in editions of up to 90,000.

The book trade began the moment Gutenberg's invention of movable type made possible the production of books by hand press. Until the eighteenth century, however, the printer himself generally sold his own products. It was at the beginning of the eighteenth century, with the birth of a reading public, that the differentiation between printer, publisher, and bookseller first occurred. The two latter functions were, for some time to come, frequently carried out by the same person or company, and publishers as important as Thomas Longman and Samuel Fischer continued to refer to themselves as booksellers until late into the nineteenth century. In Denmark the tradition lives on to this day where a publisher is described as *Forlagsboghandler* (publisher-bookseller).

With improved communications in the nineteenth century a need arose for a wider geographical dispersal of booksellers, and in the industrialized countries of the West a system of book merchandising was instituted that remains much the same to this day. Booksellers received their stocks from publishers on a commission basis, on approval, as it were, with full return rights since it was impossible for them to know all the latest books published, and because their assignments of books could take weeks to arrive. In return, the publisher required the bookseller to accept the books sent, that there should be a 'full assortment'. This system began in Germany and the first booksellers' association, *Börsenverein des Deutschen Buchhandels*, was formed there in 1825. This organization became the prototype for similar affiliations in other European countries, particularly in Scandinavia.

The publishing business, as such, began cautiously. Previously, printers had printed books paid for by patrons and therefore ran no financial risk themselves. In the beginning of the eighteenth century they began to turn to the developing, anonymous reading public. Usually they employed the subscription method of marketing their wares; that is to say, the printer would take orders for a book before he printed it. In order to reduce further the financial risk a number of printers would often share the costs and the responsibility of publication. A printer could buy a third, fourth or even a seventh share of a book. With the expansion of commerce and industry in the eighteenth century, development in this field was extremely rapid, especially in Britain. A typical example of the time was the bookseller-publisher, Bernard Lintot, who opened a small shop in Fleet Street at the beginning of the century. In 1711 he bought a seventh share of *Captain Cook's Voyages* for £7 3s, but within only a few years he was to pay Pope £1,200 for his translation of the *Iliad*, a sum that was later increased to £5,000 owing to the book's enormous success. The *Odyssey* was similarly successful and earned the translator almost as much, which would have been unthinkable only a few decades earlier. (Shakespeare was paid £10 for *Hamlet* and Milton £5 for the first printing of *Paradise Lost*.) Lintot was able to retire in 1730, a wealthy man.[8]

Money brought social status and by the middle of the century several successful bookseller-publishers were no longer simply skilled craftsmen or lower-middle-class artisans but accepted members of the rising bourgeoisie. Jacob Tonson, a contemporary of Lintot's and also Dryden's publisher, became secretary of the famous Kit-Cat Club. Robert Dodsley started out as a footman, but made a successful career publishing the works of Defoe and Dr. Johnson. He was described by a contemporary as 'a delightful, serviceable, bourgeois personality'. Another publisher, Thomas Longman II, left £60,000 —a considerable fortune at the time—when he died in 1797, although his firm was only a small affair with five employees.[9]

Profits rose at the same rate as the number of readers. Smollett's *History of England* earned his publishers £10,000 in the 1760s, and another financial record was established when Thomas Longman paid Thomas Moore a £3,000 advance on a poem he hadn't even begun to write. It was a romantic oriental fantasy and when it came out in 1817 under the title of *Lalla Rookh* it went into six printings in the first year. The author also noted with satisfaction that 'there has seldom occurred a transaction in which trade and poetry have shone so satisfactorily in each other's eyes.' Lord Byron's début epic *Childe Harold* sold 13,000 copies within the first three days after it was issued in 1812. A typical example of optimism for the future and the belief of the new publishers in a greatly expanding market is shown in a conversation between Sir Walter Scott and his publisher, Archibald Constable, in 1825:

> Scott doubted whether any laird within ten miles spent ten pounds per annum on the literature of the day. 'No' said Constable 'there's no market among them that's worth one's thinking about. They are contented with a review or magazine, or at best with a paltry subscription to some circulating library fourty miles off. But if I live half-a-dozen years, I'll make it . . . impossible that there should not be a good library in every decent house in Britain. . . . I have now settled my outline of operations—a three shilling or half crown volume every month, which must and shall sell, not by thousands or tens of

thousands—ay by millions! Twelve volumes in the year, a halfpenny of profit upon every copy of which will make me richer than the possession of all the copyrights that ever were ... twelve volumes so good that millions must wish to have them, and so cheap that every butcher's callant may have them, if he pleases to let me tax him sixpence a week.'[10]

These plans were never carried out, however, and history shows that Constable was perhaps by nature a little over optimistic, since a year later he went into bankruptcy with debts approaching a quarter of a million pounds—a sum which also reveals the proportionate growth of the publishing business at the time.

Those publishers who had better luck were extremely successful financially and advanced upward socially in consequence. True, publisher John Murray found it necessary to remind Lord Byron 'that he forgot in writing to his publisher that he was also addressing a gentleman'. But he was also able to write with pride:

I am in the habit of seeing persons of the highest rank in literature and talent, such as Canning ... Walter Scott, Madame de Staël ... Lord Byron and others; thus leading the most delightful life, with means of prosecuting my business in the highest honour and emolument.[11]

It is apparent from this quotation that writers as well as publishers had advanced to at least equally elevated financial and social positions. As early as the beginning of the eighteenth century a few writers had already achieved great financial and social success, but this notoriety was gained largely through the political aspects of their writing. Their fame rested on their politics rather than on their talents as creative artists. Both Defoe and Swift wrote political pamphlets, and even their most famous books, *Robinson Crusoe* and *Gulliver's Travels* were admired not so much for their qualities as literature as for their tendentious moral and educational ideals and social satire, respectively.

It was only in the role of political writer that an author could, in the early part of the eighteenth century, rise to a singularly high social position. Addison marries a countess, Congreve becomes a member of the Kit-Cat Club and Granville becomes Minister of War. The next generation of writers was to take its place again among the petty bourgeoisie. Goldsmith and Sterne lived in considerable poverty. Richardson was forced to earn his living as a printer. A statement by Lord Camden during a parliamentary debate on copyright in 1774 illustrates what the aristocracy still felt about the profession of writer, and how they yet could regard the bookseller-publisher (although certainly it was also a partisan statement opposing the idea of payment for copyright):

> I speak not of the scribblers for bread, who tease the press with their perishable trash. It was not for gain that Bacon, Newton, Milton and Locke instructed and delighted the world; it would be unworthy of such men to traffic with a dirty bookseller. When the bookseller offered Milton five pounds for his *Paradise Lost*, he did not reject it and commit it to the flames, nor did he accept the miserable pittance as the reward for his labour; he knew that the real price of his work was immortality, and that posterity would pay for it.[12]

During Dr. Johnson's lifetime, interest in, and respect for, knowledge and education increased greatly and with it there was also a new respect for writing and other artistic pursuits. (Joshua Reynolds, who was a member of Johnson's circle, was knighted, although in his capacity as head of the Royal Academy.) With the dawning of the Romantic period writers were accepted as fully-fledged creative artists. Certainly this did not mean financial success for all writers and even many of those writers who became famous failed to sell their books—Robert Burns' first collection of poems sold only 350 copies, while Dr. Johnson, as we know, lived most of his life in relative poverty, until George III awarded him a pension of £300 a year. Despite this, Dr. Johnson was considered to have been well paid when he received a remuneration of up to £100. In the eighteenth century writers often shared in the publishing of their books and thus in the profits, if there were any, or they were paid a few pounds and given forty or fifty copies of the book. Shared ownership of published works was possible in Britain because laws had been passed very early on to protect authors' rights. The first of these laws was passed in 1709, the Copyright Act of Queen Anne. Similar laws were not passed in France until 1793, in Austria in 1832, and in Germany in 1835. By the middle of the nineteenth century the royalty system had become more and more common, but there were still five principal ways of paying authors:

1) Publishing in accordance with the commission system, in which the author paid all costs of publishing including the printer-publisher's losses, but received in return all profits, if there were any. The printer-publisher received a certain commission for his work. (This method is still used in many countries when an author signs a so-called distribution contract with a publisher.)

2) A system whereby author and publisher shared profits, usually equally, after all costs had been paid.

3) The publisher bought the copyright outright at a fixed price.

4) The publisher bought the copyright for a certain number of years and an agreed number of editions, after which the copyright reverted to the author.

5) The royalty system, the newest means of payment, which established itself slowly during the nineteenth century.

By the middle of the nineteenth century the buying and selling of copyrights was very common—Dickens, for instance, did this many times—and could mean considerable speculative risks for both author and publisher. It should be noted, however, that publishers did not always try to pay the absolute minimum. Archibald Constable, the somewhat eccentric bookseller-publisher, is an interesting example: he insisted that every writer who contributed to his paper, *The Edinburgh Review*, in the 1820s should be properly reimbursed. He did this in a conscious effort to see that 'men of letters' would be firmly established within the ranks of the bourgeoisie. By providing professional authorship with high financial rewards, and thereby greater social status, he hoped to ensure a similarly elevated social position for his own profession.

Generally speaking, however, writers occupied a rather insecure financial and social position from the middle of the eighteenth century on through the first decades of the nineteenth. This was due in part at least to the gradual disappearance of the patronage system. Oliver Goldsmith was able to write: 'At present the few poets of England no longer depend on the great for subsistence; they have now no other patrons than the public.' And Dr. Johnson expresses the same belief—although he himself was still being supported by Lord Chesterfield: 'the patron of letters was being displaced by the multitudinous personage called the public.'

During the same period the subscription system virtually ceased to exist. It had, however, provided a certain security for both author and publisher and had allowed authors to be their own publishers. Again, Dr. Johnson has something illuminating to say on the subject, having grown wise through his bad experience with his edition of Shakespeare: 'He that asks subscriptions soon finds that he has enemies. All who do not encourage him defame him.'[13]

The free marketing system for the sale of books, that still exists today, was thus first established at this time. The writer no longer wrote at the behest of a patron but rather for an anonymous public, the new reading public. Hauser characterizes this change thus:

The patron's place is taken by the publisher; public subscription, which has very aptly been called collective patronage, is the bridge between the two. Patronage is the purely aristocratic form of the relationship between author and public; the system of public subscription loosens the bond, but still maintains certain features of the personal character of the relationship; the publication of books for a general public, completely unknown to the author, is the first form of the relationship to correspond to the structure of the middle-class society based on the anonymous circulation of goods. The publisher's role, as the mediator between author and public, begins with the emancipation of middle-class taste from the dictates of the aristocracy and is itself a symptom of this emancipation. It forms the historical starting point of literary life in the modern sense, as typified not only by the regular appearance of books, newspapers and periodicals, but, above all, by the emergence of the literary expert, the critic who represents the general standard of values and public opinion in the world of literature.[14]

When at last the book market really began to operate in an organized way, in the 1830s and 40s, then it did so with unexpected force. The following description of how publishers sold their books to booksellers, and their close cooperation, gives some idea of the atmosphere within the book trade in the middle of the nineteenth century, and also an inkling of the size and importance of the book market (which was perhaps never again to be repeated):

> The closeness of relationship was typified in the ancient custom of the Trade Dinner.... At the beginning of every season each publisher invited the leading booksellers to a good dinner, with rare wines and Havana tobacco, with music and with songs. Among the guests would be the principal authors, whose books the publishers was about to issue, and they would be distributed prudently among the men of affairs. When the dessert was on the table, the manager of the trade department brought in samples of the new books and piled them before the host, who proceeded, after a few words of preliminary commendation, to hand them round among the company. Obviously the booksellers were at congenial disadvantage. There was their host, as it were, in the rostrum, hammer in hand, 'Well Mr. Hatchard, how many copies may I book to you?' And if Mr. Hatchard was sitting next to the author he could hardly choose but plunge, Mr. Shaylor could remember as many as 19,000 copies of Smith's *Principia* being sold over the walnuts and wine in ten minutes, while orders for a new book by Samuel Smiles were registered to more than half that number. This was the Ercles vein of bookselling indeed, a genial harmony of hospitality and adventure.[15]

Those authors who succeeded acquired both fame and fortune within a society where social position was equated with one's income. We have already mentioned Dumas, Sue and Dickens. The latter could write in 1867—despite the fact that he continued to desire ever greater wealth for himself—'My worldly circumstances (such a large family considered) are very good. I don't want money. All my possessions are free and in best order.' Among writers it was primarily novelists who, from the middle of the nineteenth century, were able to sell hitherto undreamed of numbers of books and earn fortunes for themselves and their publishers. George Eliot was paid a £10,000 advance for a novel, and Anthony Trollope's combined earnings from writing have been estimated at £70,000.

Sir Walter Scott's financial success is well known. Before he began to write he earned £1,300 a year as a barrister, which was considered a good income at the time. As a writer he occasionally earned as much as £20,000 a year! He once received an £18,000 advance for a biography of Napoleon, and the sale of his novels in America was so huge that he should have earned as much as half a million dollars —if there had been copyright laws in that country. As things were, the American publishers withheld most of the profits for themselves. Scott was able to lay out £80,000 for his castle, Abbotsford; he was knighted in 1820 and lived in the grand style until five years later when faulty speculative investments brought financial ruin. Here is an enlightening contemporary description of the popularity of Scott's novels. It was written by his publisher, Archibald Constable—always a man of irrepressible enthusiasm—on the publication of one of Scott's lesser-known novels, *The Fortunes of Nigel*:

> So keenly were the people devouring my friend *Jingling Geordie*, that I actually saw them reading it in the streets as they passed along. I assure you there is no exaggeration in all this.... The smack *Ocean*, by which the work was shipped, arrived at the wharf on Sunday; the bales were got out by one on Monday morning, and before half-past ten o'clock 7,000 copies had been dispersed.[16]

Other impressive sales were *Guy Mannering*, which sold 2,000 copies on the first day of publication in 1815 and reached a total of 50,000 by 1836; and *Rob Roy*, which sold 10,000 copies during the first two weeks after publication in 1818 and 40,000 by 1836.

Not only were some authors knighted, but writing had now become an accepted profession both within the aristocracy, with Lord Byron as the most famous example, and among successful politicians, such as Prime Minister Benjamin Disraeli. The latter was one of Longmans' writers and wrote very successful historical novels. His best known perhaps is *Endymion*, for which he received an advance of £10,000—a record sum for a novel at the time.

The fact that writers had become independent creators of books in an open market made them also the single most important asset of their publishers, and in some cases the essential factor in the rapid financial expansion of certain publishing houses—a development, of course, that reflected the greatly increasing economic expansion of the whole industrial society. By the middle of the century very close relationships had grown up between many authors and their publishers: Dickens and Chapman & Hall, Sir Walter Scott and Constable, Byron and Murray, and Thomas Moore and Longmans. Even if fiction did not always represent the predominating business of the publishing trade, the initial investment was small, it was relatively risk-free and could earn quick and large sums of money for the publishing house.

'Half a dozen popular writers will build a publishing house,' wrote an American publisher, Walter Hines Page in 1905. And another American publisher, Robert Sterling Yard, used almost the same words a few years later: 'I'd no idea publishing was so profitable! Half a dozen novels is all you need.'[17]

Typical of the rapid development was the progress of Longmans, which by the middle of the nineteenth century had become the largest publishers in Britain. In 1851 this company issued 216 titles, almost 10 per cent of all the books published in Britain, including novels, travel books, histories, biography, poetry, children's books, school books and reference books. This type of diverse publication must have been profitable since Thomas Longman III left £200,000 when he died in 1842, and twenty years later his son built a house in the country that was described as 'that gabled monument of Victorian opulence'. The expansion of this firm was typical for the larger publishing companies throughout Europe during the nineteenth century, a remarkably stable development based on a method whereby novels provided large, quick profits and standard works gave long-term security. An English grammar, to which Longmans had acquired the rights in 1799, was still in print and selling at the outbreak of World War I. The first edition of Roget's *Thesaurus* came out in 1852 and although it has gone through many editions it is still in print today. Most incredible of all perhaps is *The Annual Register*, which was started by Edmund Burke in 1758 and is still very much alive. The great new interest in education and knowledge and the national heritage is reflected in the enormous success of Thomas Macaulay's *English History*. First published in 1848, it was issued in five volumes and sold 140,000 copies within the next few decades. It continued to be a standard work for a long time, until it was replaced and surpassed in sales by the equally famous *English Social History*, published in 1844 and written by G. M. Trevelyan, a descendant of Macaulay's. Macaulay received a cheque for £20,000 in advance for Volumes III and IV alone. The publication of his history was considered an important social event and the review of the work in the *Athenaeum* was twenty-seven columns long.

It was precisely this stability, and the interest in sustaining it, that provided the basis for the publisher's thriving backlist which thus often laid the foundation for financial security. Another example of a book with a long life was the verse cycle *The Ingoldsby Legends*, which was first published in 1840 and sold at a price of ten shillings. It was issued in almost eighty editions, totalling 450,000 copies by the end of the 1880s, and returned the publisher a profit of over £15,000. A popular cook book, *The Cook's Guide*, was issued in the 1860s and 64,000 copies had been printed by the turn of the century. (The publication of this book provides a good example of the trade in copyrights—see p. 24—which still occurred at the time. The author agreed to publication on a shared profit basis. After two years, when the book had sold 8,000 copies, the author sold all future rights and profits for a fixed sum of £600, a transaction that later proved to be a great mistake.) The value of popular novels can be seen in the reaction of the heirs of Mrs. Wood, who, when they were offered £40,000 for the rights to her extremely successful works, demanded double that amount.[18]

Another aspect of the social development of the time that strongly influenced the progress of publishing houses was the veritable explosion of knowledge. Compulsory education was established in most of the industrialized countries by the middle of the nineteenth century. In France, general education was made compulsory in 1833 and in Britain in 1870, but by this time literacy was fairly general because of the many schools already in existence. A number of publishing houses built up a stock of school textbooks of which new editions could be issued at regular intervals to one generation after another. William Collins typifies this sort of publishing house. This company began as a publisher of the Bible and religious tracts and eventually succeeded in publishing school books for the whole of Scotland. By 1875 William Collins had 1,200 employees and were selling 300,000 Bibles per year. During the 1860s the sale of school books became an important factor in publishing, and in the following ten years Collins sold 70,000 copies of each of its thirty-one titles, a total of approximately 2.3 million books. An arithmetic textbook was still selling after World War II and had sold at the time over a million copies. The second William Collins, like his colleagues Longman and Murray, became a typical Victorian magnate: he owned a town house, a country house and a steam yacht.[19]

The expansion and development of publishing and the book trade in Britain formed, as did commerce and industry generally, a pattern that was followed in most other countries in Europe. Germany, France and the Nordic countries developed in conjunction with the industrial revolution and saw the emergence of a bourgeoisie—and with it a reading public—and a similar growth in the book trade to that of Britain.

The major reason why the continental countries were behind Britain in many respects was that industrial development was so much slower in the rest of Europe. Neither Germany nor France had anything like the trade and commerce of the British Empire, with its far-flung activities, nor did they possess the natural resources, such as coal, upon which the expansion of industry was based. France was, however, far richer than Germany, which was poor and divided until the 1860s. The bourgeoisie did not become the predominant social class in France until the 1830s, and in Germany somewhat later. A consequence of this was that bourgeois literature, especially the novel, developed later also. However, English novelists were much read in France as early as the latter part of the eighteenth century, the most popular being Fielding, Sterne and Richardson, who had all been introduced in France by Diderot. In the early part of the nineteenth century the flow of English literature into France continued but now consisted largely of sentimental novels and gothic thrillers, such as Mary Shelley's *Frankenstein*, which were more in line with French romantic traditions and formed, at least partly, an influence on the novels of writers like Victor Hugo.

But the bourgeois novel, properly defined, did not appear in France before 1830 when, with the July revolution, censorship was abolished and a degree of liberalism was established. All of a sudden important novels were being written of such varying character as Stendhal's romantic *Le rouge et le noir* (published in 1831) and the passionate love stories of George Sand (1832 onwards). Balzac's first novels were published in the early 1830s, while Dumas' first work, a play, came out in 1829.

Modern French publishing began then with the July revolution and followed in principle the British pattern thereafter. It was not, of course, novels only that were responsible for the growing trade in books, there was an enormously increasing need for textbooks also.

The French publishing house Hachette is a typical case of the development within the French publishing industry; today it is the largest distributor and publisher in the country. In 1826 Louis Hachette, then twenty-six years old, bought a small publishing business that consisted of a stock of six marketable titles, of which one was a translation of Goldsmith's *The Vicar of Wakefield*, and a few school books. He began by pursuing these parallel lines, first with a four-volume novel, a Greek–French dictionary and a broad selection of Greek and Latin classics: Cicero, Horace, Tacitus, Homer, Sophocles—the choice was great and the competition small.

During the 1830s came the change in the French school system and all books were to be produced new from the start. The young Hachette was given a unique order from the Ministry of Education for 500,000 ABC books, 100,000 readers, 40,000 mathematics books and an equal number of other textbooks on geography and history. After this the publishing house grew very rapidly. In the first year of business Hachette grossed 7,000 francs. By 1833 the firm had five employees and a total turnover of 100,000 francs. By the end of the decade it had increased its income and number of employees three-fold, and when Louis Hachette died in 1864 his company was the largest publishing house in France, with 165 employees and a gross annual turnover of one million francs.[20]

The number of titles increased of course with the growth of the firm, but what is interesting is that the backlist, as with British publishers, came to comprise three-quarters of all the books published. During the decade beginning in 1840 the firm published 471 new titles and 666 new editions, whereas in the following ten years 527 new titles and 1,497 new editions were published. The perpetual reprinting provided the publishing house with the solid financial security that was typical for the successful nineteenth-century publishing houses. Those books which were successful could be counted on to bring a profit for years to come. The Greek–French dictionary, one of the first books published by Hachette, was issued in thirty-eight editions, consisting of a total of 200,000 copies, the last appearing in 1913. A similar Latin dictionary survived for a hundred years and approximately 450,000 copies were printed.

In the 1850s Hachette also began to publish novels on a large scale, especially in the form of novel-libraries. He got the idea in England when he visited the International Exhibition in 1851. He learned of W. H. Smith's success with railway bookshops, begun three years earlier. On his return home he sought, and was granted, sale rights to sell books and newspapers on a number of French railway lines. Before long he had built up a network of bookshops and sales outlets that comprised thousands of kiosks and shops, many of which the company still controls. The French railway system expanded sixfold during the twenty years between 1850 and 1870, and in doing so provided a unique opportunity for similar growth in the distribution of books. Like Smith did, Hachette tried to supply his many distributors with suitable books, and he imitated the former again by creating 'railway library' editions which sold in large numbers at low prices. The names are familiar: *La Biblio-thèque Rose, La Bibliothèque des Chemins de fer, La Bibliothèque Romans Etrangers*; all published by Hachette and issued in very large editions. One hundred and seven titles were published the first year in the railway library series and sixty the second year! A total of 500 titles were eventually published in this series.

Also, the choice of books was similar to W. H. Smith's, with Dickens in the forefront with twenty-eight volumes and *David Copperfield* the single most popular book, selling 100,000 copies, while *Oliver Twist* sold 83,000. Many of the great English and French novelists of the day were included: Thackeray, George Eliot and Emily Brontë, Victor Hugo and George Sand. The size of the market can also be seen by the number of children's books sold. During the 1860s the enormously popular *Malheurs de Sophie*, by the Comtesse de Ségurs, sold 40,000 copies per year at two francs each, its total sales eventually reaching 1.7 million.

After the establishment of the Third Republic in the 1870s the house of Hachette, along with the whole of France, entered a period of peace and success—'La Belle Epoque'. Hachette continued to be a strictly family firm but grew into a vast enterprise, publishing general literature, school books and magazines, and distributing these through their huge network of shops, which now included outlets in Algeria and Turkey.

At the outbreak of World War I the firm had an annual turnover of 60 million francs. After the war, however, the house of Hachette was no longer able to continue exclusively as a family company. Huge amounts of stock had been destroyed and new capital was needed. Hachette was restructured and became a limited company, just another large company among many, with thousands of shareholders. 'They change into a public company and an unfortunate change of atmosphere develops', writes the company's biographer.

Among the larger industrialized countries of Europe, Germany was the slowest to develop a reading public. Though there was a rapidly growing bourgeoisie from the eighteenth century onwards, its members lived strictly in accordance with Lutheran ideals. Reading was to be restricted to what was true and *erbaulich* or *nützlich* and therefore moralistic and practical books predominated.

There was a certain number of novels published as early as the beginning of the eighteenth century, their themes usually taken from heroic tales of chivalry, but they were not read generally by the new middle class who looked down on this type of literature. More typical for the time was a 'Frauenzimmerbibliothekchen' begun in 1705 and containing books such as *Unterwiesene Köchin, Garten-Lust, Haus-Vater* and *Frauen-Zimmer-Apothekchen.* As late as 1732 a translation of *Paradise Lost* was forbidden, as it was considered too dangerously romantic.

However, a combination of pietism and rationalism eased the rigid morality of the times and toward the middle of the eighteenth century a reading public gradually emerged. Not surprisingly perhaps, it was the translations of English books that broke the first ground. *Robinson Crusoe* was published in Leipzig in 1720 and five editions were printed the first year. There was, of course, a stroke of luck in this choice since the book was considered to be both 'true' and morally edifying.

Addison and Steele's periodicals were also imported to Germany and met with some success from 1710 and through the following twenty years under the names *Der Vernünftler* and the un-Addison-like *Der Patriot,* selling at times as many as 5,000 copies. However, it was not until the second half of the century that the novel gained a general readership. During the decade beginning in 1740, approximately 150 novels and collections of short stories were published; by the first decade of the nineteenth century this figure had reached 2,000![21] But despite this undeniable quantitative success the novel did not achieve the same popularity in Germany as it did in Britain during the same period. The more successful writers such as A. H. Lafontaine or von Kotzebue were closer in spirit to the writers of horror stories and tales of chivalry than they were to the authors of bourgeois novels, nor were they able to create a readership and market for the novel as their British and French counterparts did.

On the other hand 'literary' writers like Goethe were never popular—with the exception of his *Werther.* When his collected works were published between 1787 and 1790 there were only 602 subscribers! One of the reasons for this was almost certainly the later industrialization of the country—the middle class had not yet attained a sufficiently strong economic and social position to establish their own culture.

Germany experienced a cultural decline after Goethe's death and booksellers and publishers concentrated their activities mostly on the distribution of textbooks and non-fiction—there simply were no bourgeois novelists of the stature of Dickens and Balzac in Germany. It can be safely said that the modern book market in Germany began in 1876 when the government ruled that all books whose authors had been dead more than thirty years would not be covered by copyright. This caused a tremendous increase in the demand for, and publication of, the classics, which were soon to grace the bookshelves of a bourgeosie that was now well enough established to see cultural activities as an important part of their lives. A bookseller in Berlin describes these years of the classics in the following manner:

> The book trade offers much that is new and splendid for this year's Christmas table, and for the first time for those of us who are less privileged; it is a real joy to see the extent to which the classics are being purchased. We ourselves order Schiller, Goethe, Lessing, always by the hundreds and sell them merely by setting them out in the window. Many publishers of such cheap editions *have sold, within a few days, stocks of 500,000* [my italics].[22]

The publication of the classics gave rise to a reading public—the organization and technical competence for the publication and sale of books already existed. There were a large number of bookshops throughout the country and in 1850 the first machine-bound books were manufactured. All that was lacking were good German-language writers.

When Samuel Fischer started his firm in 1887, and formed the pattern for future literary publishers in Germany, one of the first things he published was Ibsen's drama, *Rosmersholm*, which was considered a daring thing to do at the time. He published books by Zola and Tolstoy the same year. The six titles he published the first year comprised dramas and short stories exclusively. But in Germany too the novel soon became the greatest source of income for publishers. A contemporary colleague of Fischer wrote to one of his authors: 'The person who wishes to make money today must have saleable goods in stock, but dramas and poetry are unsaleable goods for which you cannot earn money. The poetry of money lies in prose! Write prose and I shall pay you rich rewards!' Fischer himself gained rapid success and published a large number of novels in a variety of editions with names such as *Nordische Bibliothek, Collection Fischer, Zeitgenössische Romane* and *Gelbe Romane*. These were more or less the same type as had existed in Britain for a long

33

time and they also certainly provided the pattern upon which the 'Yellow Series' of novels published by Bonniers in Sweden and Gyldendals in Norway were based.

Translations came to play an important part in Fischer's publishing activities, first, because German literature was still very limited—particularly in regard to the novel—and secondly because the time had arrived for an internationalization of the book market. S. Fischer very soon became a large literary publisher. Authors such as Dostoevsky, Ibsen, Björnson, Herman Bang, Schnitzler, Bernard Shaw, Franz Werfel, Thomas Mann and Hermann Hesse were on their lists of writers. The same steady trend is apparent here too: continual reprintings, increasingly large editions and occasional vast first-year sales of new books. Ibsen's collected works were issued in a 'People's Edition' of 20,000 copies and totalled 110,000 by 1930. Hauptmann's *Die Weber* was printed in 270,000 copies and Schnitzler's *Reigen* in 107,000 copies. *Buddenbrooks* started slowly, it was considered too long and awkward in two volumes, but was a great success when it came out in one volume on thinner paper! It was published in 1902 and had gone into twenty-six editions three years later, totalling 36,000 copies by 1906, 185,000 by 1929 and 1,324,000 by 1961, without ever once being published in a pocket edition. Gerhart Hauptmann's collected works were published altogether in 90,000 copies. Hermann Bang had little success in the beginning, but in 1919 35,000 copies of his collected works were sold and one or two single books sold as many as 70,000 copies.[23]

S. Fischer can be regarded as the prototype for serious bourgeois publishers on the continent, as can Gyldendal in Denmark and Bonniers in Sweden. These publishing houses went through a similar pattern of development until the outbreak of World War I and then many of them continued along much the same lines between the wars. There was a likeness in the type of books written and published and they were produced for a homogeneous reading public that remained unchanged through the years.

In America, however, we find an interesting divergence from this pattern. Again, the publishing business reflects the development of society in general. The relatively late, but considerably more explosive build-up of the American economy coupled with a strong optimism about the future lends a special character to development in that country. A whole continent was to be structured from the ground directly into a modern industrial society.

There was a great enthusiasm and feeling for culture among those who saw industrialism as a means to economic, technical, and social progress. Emerson wrote at the time: 'Poverty shall be abolished; deformity, stupidity and crime shall be no more. Genius, grace, art shall abound.' And in the first issue of *Harper's Magazine*, in 1850, one writer maintained that: 'Literature has gone in pursuit of the million, penetrated highways and hedges, pressed its way into cottages, factories, omnibuses and railroad cars, and become the most cosmopolitan thing of the century.'

It was easy to start a publishing company in America. All one had to do was import printed sheets from British publishers or simply copy British books, and those who did it paid the writers insignificant sums or nothing at all. As I mentioned above, Sir Walter Scott should have been paid approximately half a million dollars in royalties for the sale of his books in America but for one novel he had to be content with £25. In 1827 he received the highest royalty payment any British author had been paid up to that time by an American publisher, £250, for his biography of Napoleon, which was printed in an edition of 12,500 copies. This irregular relationship between publishers and authors gave the publishers vast profits, and their often tough attitude towards the authors is well illustrated by an anecdote concerning the publication of the novels of the famous Swedish writer, Fredrika Bremer. During her travels in America she published a few books under the aegis of George Putnam. He was an honest man who paid his writers the fee that was agreed upon, as he was a supporter of copyright laws. It was then discovered that Harpers were already publishing Fredrika Bremer's books without a contract of any kind. Putnam, together with the author, appealed to Harper to pay 'out of courtesy'. Harper answered: 'Mr. Putnam, courtesy is courtesy and business is business,' and refused to pay a penny.

Harpers was founded in 1817 and exemplifies the explosive and often ruthless development of the American book trade. The two Harper brothers were printers by trade and in 1817 they opened a small printing shop and published a few books on their own. The first of these was Seneca's *Ethics*, and a year or two later they came out with Locke's *Essays Concerning Human Understanding*. They worked hard, successfully and unscrupulously. 'Their prosperity was largely founded on the lack of an international copyright law, and they were from first to last opposed to the enactment of such a law,' wrote one historian. What they did instead was fix their prices for pirated British novels at one quarter of the price in Britain and then sold them in very large editions. By 1830 they had become the largest printers and publishers in the country. Along with novels they published dictionaries, Bibles and school books—for a market that grew at record speed and where a great deal of money was to be earned in a short time.

Between 1825 and 1850 the number of American libraries, for instance, increased three-fold. By 1850 Harpers had become the largest publishing house not just in America, but in the world. In 1853 they had 750 employees, sixteen buildings and a backlist of 1,549 titles, of which 722 were newly published and 827 were new editions—a level of activity they sustained for the next twenty years. The company was now sufficiently well-off to pay for copyrights, and in doing so they hoped to stop other publishers from pirating their books. Writers were, however, paid very little—Dickens received a fixed sum of £250 for *Little Dorrit*, while the most he was ever paid was £2,000 for *Edwin Drood*. Harpers refused, however, to pay non-English language writers at all, right into the first decade of this century.

During the same period Harpers began to publish magazines. The first issue of *Harper's Magazine* (it is still published today) came out in 1850. Its first-year circulation was 50,000 and three years later it was up to 130,000. When the sixteen buildings burned down in 1853, stock and other inventory were valued at one and a half million dollars. The company was quickly rebuilt and Harpers rode a floodtide of increasing readership and growing wealth. Their presses printed twenty-five books per minute, ten hours a day, the year round, and the company could note triumphantly in 1857 that the need for books represented 'an unparalleled demand . . . increasing at an unprecedented rate; when presses were working day and night'.[24]

Contrary to the European industrialized countries there was not a bourgeoisie in America that supported the publishing of books. Instead there was a large population where anyone could be a potential buyer of books, if only they had the money and could be reached. This meant that neither publishers interested primarily in serious literature, nor booksellers of the European type, developed there, and that in consequence there was no homogeneous book market. The development of publishing in America was characterized by the same factors that governed other business enterprise: to reap as great a profit as possible in an extremely competitive market. The important thing was to sell books in the largest editions possible; the content of the books and the method of marketing them was of secondary importance.

After the Civil War America became more than ever the land of opportunity—that is, the land of unimagined economic possibilities. A whole continent was to be built up from the ground, industrialized, educated, settled; millions of immigrants were to come there to seek their fortunes. Or, in the words of Morison and Commager: 'Men hurled themselves upon the continent with ruthless abandon as if to ravish it of its wealth. . . . Never before had wealth been more irresponsible . . . never before had wealth been more ostentatious.' Madison, who quotes these lines, claims that publishers differed from the robber barons: 'They sought financial success, of course, but as gentlemen.' But publishing too became part of the violent thrust and competition within the society and the gentlemanly ideal was only adhered to when the publishers could afford it. Fortunes were made and lost and there was little place for the European literary publishing house. 'The minimum turnover should be 200,000 dollars to give a profit and 400,000 are necessary for prosperity,' wrote publisher Robert Sterling Yard in his memoirs at the turn of the century.[25]

The printings were often enormous and the books could be sold in every conceivable way, in bookshops, department stores, by mail order and from door to door. Lew Wallace's *Ben Hur*, published in 1880, sold a million copies initially, while an additional million were sold to the mail-order house of Sears, Roebuck thirty years later. Children's books too, were published in very large editions, for instance Laura E. Richards' *Captain January* which sold 300,000 copies.

In America, as in Europe, it was the novel that was published in large editions and produced the greatest profits at little risk. There were, however, other books which also sold in huge numbers. A handbook on surgery sold 40,000 copies in a short time and the *Encyclopaedia Britannica*, in twenty-four volumes and at 125 dollars per set, sold 45,000 sets—which, symptomatically perhaps, was four times the number sold in Britain.

Book publishing then became big business and as such, the object of considerable interest by the great financiers of the day. Harpers, because of its rapid expansion and the cut-throat competition, had fallen into financial difficulties and was saved from bankruptcy by J. P. Morgan. Other financiers and bankers entered the business at the turn of the century. These men insisted on even greater commercialization of the trade, which, in the words of Robert E. Spiller, contrived to 'put publishing, like other business, under the control of finance capitalism, with the result that the banks and investment trusts, which supplied it with capital, insisted on greater efficiency in the interest of surer profits'.[26]

There were, of course, publishers of the European type: the old Boston firm of Houghton Mifflin, for instance, with its close relationship with New England writers such as Longfellow and Emerson and with Walt Whitman and Mark Twain. It was also near Harvard University and its researchers and academicians. In 1915, Alfred Knopf started a publishing house that published largely translations of the best of European literature. But these houses were exceptions within American society.

The American book market was as different from its European counterpart as American society in general differed from European society. With its vast, socially undefined population, its poorly organized dispersal of bookshops, and advanced sales methods—(ideas such as 'price-cutting' and 'loss-leader' were introduced in America as early as the nineteenth century) and with the competitive prices that were an unavoidable part of the commercial pattern, where every means was used to create a bestseller market, America provided the image to which the European book trade would adhere during the period after World War II. The newly formed American Publishers Association tried in 1901 to introduce fixed book prices, but in a long court case between this association and Macy's department store the Supreme Court, after thirteen years, ruled that fixed book prices were irreconcilable with the anti-trust laws. America became the image of the future in another respect, in the publication of cheap editions, and this too reflected social trends and the dominant forces of commercialism. I shall return to this matter in Chapter 2.

During the latter part of the nineteenth century England and France, and Germany after Bismarck came to power, enjoyed a period of rare stability. To quote Hauser's summation:

> The nineteenth century, or what we usually understand by that term, begins around 1830. It is only during the July monarchy that the foundations and outlines of this century are developed, that is to say, the social order in which we ourselves are rooted, the economic system, the antagonisms and contradictions of which still continue, and the literature in whose forms we on the whole still express ourselves today.... From Stendhal to Proust, from the generation of 1830 to that of 1910, we are witnesses of a homogeneous, organic intellectual development. Three generations struggle with the same problems; for seventy to eighty years the course of history remains unchanged....[27]

(It should be mentioned here that Hauser wrote this in 1940—the book was published in 1951 and must have had a long gestation period. When he writes 'today' he does not mean 'now'—one of the central themes of my work is the high degree of social and cultural change that has occurred since the end of World War II.)

This stability was the pre-condition for the thriving success of the publishing houses that were founded during the nineteenth century —generation after generation could expand their businesses with ever increasing lists of books that could be reprinted time and time again.* For S. Fischer an edition consisted of 1,000 copies, but the number of editions could well run to two figures. The profits earned could be reinvested in the firm—there was little tax to speak of and inflation was an unknown word—and the devaluation of the currency amounted to no more than 1 or 2 per cent per year. The public was loyal and unchanging; the ownership of books carried a certain social status, while reading them was a self-evident habit of the whole bourgeois class. There was not yet any apparent difference between a serious work of literature and a bestseller. Thomas Mann and Ibsen were at least as successful as Courts-Mahler. Culture had a definite market value. S. Fischer describes the situation in 1911 with considerable satisfaction:

> The choice of literary production can therefore not be decided upon a business basis alone; it is the result of the work's aesthetic value. . . . The book's incalculable worth puts it in a different category, in a business sense, than a product that has a materially measurable value. . . . While many of the activities connected with publishing, such as all the technical aspects of printing and production, have become industrialized—newspapers and mass-products for immediate consumption—*the basic form of the book trade has remained fundamentally the same for almost a hundred years* [my italics].[28]

World War I brought an end to the long years of stability.

* Of the publishing houses founded in the eighteenth and nineteenth centuries many are still active and important today. In Britain there are Longmans (1724), John Murray (1768), William Collins (1819), Macmillan (1843); in France, Hachette (1826), Plon (1854), Flammarion (1884); in Germany, Brockhaus (1805), Bertelsmann (1835), Ullstein (1877), S. Fischer (1886). In America a large number of the major houses were founded during the same period: Wiley (1807), Harpers (1817), J. B. Lippincott (1836), Little, Brown (1837), Scribners (1846), G. P. Putnam (1848), E. P. Dutton (1852), Rand McNally (1868), Dodd, Mead (1870). The same longevity holds for Scandinavian publishing houses founded at this time: in Sweden, Norstedt (1823), Bonniers (1837), Almqvist & Wiksell (1839), Wahlström & Widstrand (1884); in Denmark, Gyldendal (1770) and Jespersen & Pio (1865); in Norway, Cappelen (1829) and Aschehough (1872); in Finland, Werner Söderström (1878) and Otava (1890).

Following it, the western world was plagued by one crisis after another—chaos and inflation in Germany during the 20s, the Wall Street Crash, unemployment and fascism during the 30s. And in conjunction with these crises came the beginning of the disintegration of the bourgeoisie and increasing demands by industrial workers for improved and more humane living conditions. Insecurity, a hectic tempo and rapid change characterized the years between the wars. But the period before the outbreak of World War II was all too brief to enable the fundamental changes taking place in Europe to produce a thorough-going effect. 'The general air of confidence continues also for the first few years after the First World War, and the atmosphere within the ranks of the bourgeoisie, except among the lower middle classes who must battle against frightening odds, is in no way hopeless,' Hauser writes, still from the perspective of the 30s and 40s.

In the publishing world the pattern of almost a hundred years gradually changes and American methods appear in the form of cheap editions and the launching of bestsellers; and among the mass media, such as radio, the weekly press, films, increase in influence. S. Fischer, who, in 1911, could look into the future with complacency towards the unfluctuating development of a stable and secure society, describes a totally transformed publishing environment in an essay in 1926, indicatively entitled *Bemerkungen zur Bücherkrise* (Viewpoint on the Book Crisis):

> When the history of our times is told people in the book trade will pay special attention to the year 1926. It is the high point of the economic crisis and there is a dreadful calm on the book market. It would be easy to blame this on the state of the economy. Considering all the symptoms, however, one must conclude that the evil runs deeper than this. A relaxation in the economic crisis will certainly bring about a thaw in the frozen book market, but books play far too small a role as a product of trade to be dependent on the crisis in economy in the country as a whole. This means the part played by the book crisis has a still greater importance for our cultural standard of living. *It is therefore symbolic that the book now is an object that can be most easily dispensed with in our daily life.* We indulge in sports, dance, spend our evenings by the radio or at the cinema; after the day's work is done we are all too busy and have no time to read books. . . . *The lost war and the American wave of culture have transformed our way of life, changed our taste. . . . It would seem that the bourgeois class that remains after the cataclysm and which before the war comprised the cultural and economic leadership of the country, is in a state of disintegration* [my italics].[29]

40

Fischer's words were prophetic, but their truth was not apparent until after World War II. As I mentioned above, the years between the wars did not represent a period of economic catastrophe for publishers. On the contrary, this new epoch brought about an expansion of the market and some books were issued in huge editions, but Fischer had understood that radical changes were taking place in society and that the book market would change accordingly. In the same essay he calls attention to this change: 'our book market has been weakened by the decline of *a regularity of interest* by a broad consumer group; the buying of books takes place now in *irregularly occurring explosions*' [my italics]. Fischer himself had experienced the first 'bestseller', a term that did not yet exist in the German book trade, in 1913. One of the firm's authors, Kellermann, had written a novel *Der Tunnel*, dealing with the construction of a tunnel, which sold 100,000 copies the first year. This constituted a record in the German book trade and would not be repeated again until 1928, with Wassermann's *Der Fall Maurizius*. By 1931 *Der Tunnel* had sold a total of 338,000 copies. In 1929 Fischer was to witness a 'sales explosion' of hitherto undreamed-of proportions. Ullstein's publishing house published Erich Maria Remarque's *All Quiet on the Western Front*. A million copies of the book were sold that year. Fischer had rejected the book despite the fact that he suspected its potential. This negative decision caused a considerable amount of thoughtful concern, and one wonders perhaps if it wasn't made owing to a certain reluctance to face the new epoch, with its frenetic pace, its mass media and its commercialization.

The majority of the older publishing houses not only survived between the wars but actually grew larger owing to the strength gained through their former development. They were in possession of valuable copyrights and the new, dynamic market gave them an opportunity to reach new readers through book clubs, cheap editions, and collected works. The venerable firm of Longmans is a case in point: the new epoch that began between the wars had not yet managed to influence the traditional structure of this publishing house. At its 225th anniversary in 1949, the firm's historian maintained that there was no need to write the history of the company beyond 1842. Longmans had established its future structure by that time: 'Those who have controlled the business during the last 107 years have provided no *new* answers; the interesting thing is that, in themselves and in their policies, they have provided the old answers over and over again under new conditions and with changing problems.'[30]

The lack of most materials and intellectual matter during World War II provided the traditional publishing houses with an extension of time to live on in their old ways. During the war it was possible to sell virtually everything that was published. Great changes came rapidly, however, in the 50s and 60s, changes that began between the wars and which reflected the deep transformation taking place in the whole of western society.

The old family firms, like their counterparts outside the publishing world, became either limited companies or were bought up, or closed down. Longmans provides an example. The last Longman died in 1972, but long before this, in 1947, this house had become a public company. The family firm, with a gradual but steady growth—turnover had increased from £175,000 in 1906 to £350,000 in 1939—had been transformed into a huge concern with world-wide interests when it was merged in 1968 with a large finance group. Two years later this new company bought, in its turn, Penguin Books. The old firm that had 'provided no new answers' for 107 years had become within two decades, a vast concern with an annual gross turnover of almost £20 million. After seven generations of Longmans it had now become just another impersonal company among many.

S. Fischer suffered a similar fate. This publishing house went through a period of great expansion following World War II. In a country where people had burned their books and in which great destruction had been caused by the war, there was an enormous need for literature, and the old copyrights to the works of Hesse, Mann, Werfel, and so on were virtually priceless. Guaranteed success, however, marked the beginning of the end of this company as a family firm. Fischer's son-in-law, who had run the firm after S. Fischer's death, decided in 1965 to withdraw from the business and sold it to the Holtzbrinck group, a large financial group whose nucleus is one of Germany's largest book clubs. According to the family, the reason for selling was: 'The difficulty of financing a company that is forced to expand, in an atmosphere of increasing competition and requiring constant infusions of investment capital; capital which it no longer seemed reasonable, as had previously been the case, to supply from the family's own resources.'[31]

This development is typical of the situation throughout Europe. The Holtzbrinck group has also purchased a number of other German publishing companies. Ullstein is now part of the Springer concern and Rowohlt is partly owned by Time-Life. Bertelsmann, a small publishing house for more than a hundred years that published mostly religious books, has grown into a huge financial group and has bought up a number of other publishers. In Britain, Cassells has been purchased by the large publishing group, Collier-Macmillan, while Secker & Warburg has been bought by Heinemann, which in turn is owned by a finance group. Jonathan Cape, Bodley Head, and Chatto & Windus are all partly owned by Granada Television, and Michael Joseph by the Thomson group, and so on. Certainly there are still a few small publishers left and new ones appear from time to time, but these will never again be able to rise to dominant positions in the publishing world. Within the three decades after World War II, a tradition that developed over 150 years has been broken, a tradition that resulted entirely from the growth of a bourgeois society. The transformation of this society into the post-industrial, service society of today has brought about fundamental changes in every aspect of the book trade among writers, publishers, booksellers, and the reading public.

2

The Disintegration of the Reading Public*

In the preceding chapter I have tried to underline the traditionally homogeneous quality of the book trade. The reason for this was that its activities were directed towards a homogeneous public—the bourgeoisie.

There was, of course, some variation within the group we have called the reading public. Right from the beginning—the first years of the eighteenth century—there was a kind of 'popular market' in which large editions of broadsheets, political pamphlets and religious booklets were sold. In Britain there were ballads for a halfpenny or a penny, booklets with abridged tales of chivalry, crime cases and such. They usually consisted of twenty-four pages and were called 'chapbooks' because they were sold by chapmen (pedlars). There were also cheap papers with versions of tales that had been printed first by some other newspaper. These publications could sell tens of thousands of copies. Swift's *Conduct of the Allies* (1711), for instance, sold 11,000, and Price's *Observations on the Nature of Civil Liberty* (1776), 60,000. Bishop Sherlock's *Letter from the Lordbishop of London* (1750) was printed in an edition of 105,000, but its wide circulation seems to have been at least partly due to the fact that many copies were handed out free. Another means of taking advantage of the popular market was shown by a bookseller who, after the Battle of Trafalgar, printed 50,000 copies of a brief biography of Lord Nelson and sold them for six pence each.

For the most part, however, this popular literature was directed at the people who bought the more expensive books. The homogeneity was fairly self-evident during the eighteenth century, since readership was limited and the books published few—again this refers to Britain, the precursor for the rest of Europe in the field. There was a total of 100 to 200 titles a year published during the eighteenth century. Most of these were of a religious nature. Novels

* I have taken this term from Q. D. Leavis's interesting study *Fiction and the Reading Public*.

44

published numbered, on the average, seven per year from 1700 to 1740, twenty a year for the next three decades and approximately forty a year for the remainder of the century. In the year 1800, 400 new titles were issued and by 1822 almost 600. By the middle of the century the figure abruptly rose to 2,600 new books![1]

The number of novels published increased rapidly, but there were hardly more during the first half of the nineteenth century than could be read by all people in the same social class. Because of this, writers maintained a close and meaningful contact with their readers, so much so that it is not an exaggeration to say there was an absolute identification between the writer and his readers. Edwin Muir wrote of Walter Scott: 'In his stories the public got the upper hand of the novelist, and it has kept its advantage, with few set-backs, ever since,' and of Dickens, 'of whom one could not say whether he led his public or was led by it'.[2] And when Sherlock Holmes died in his unhappy duel with Professor Moriarty, the gentlemen of the City tied mourning bands round their tall hats. Sir Arthur Conan Doyle received many letters of outrage and among these one correspondent addressed himself to the author with these words: 'You are a brutal cad.' This commitment—or rather this reciprocal exchange—became even more finely tuned through the publication of novels in serial form. Writers such as Dickens, Dumas and Balzac were able to follow public reaction week after week and month after month. As is well known, *The Pickwick Papers* changed character under public pressure. The original idea was that Dickens should write a text to illustrations of a collection of sportsmen involved in a series of varied activities. Despite the fact that from the beginning Dickens wrote more text than was agreed, the first numbers sold badly. It wasn't until Sam Weller appeared, in the fifth issue, that sales began to rise and Dickens developed the comic line in the story, not at all as it had been planned at the start. Similarly, Dickens allowed *Great Expectations* to end happily, contrary to his original intentions, when a friend and reader asked him to.

Taste varied, of course, even in the nineteenth century. Well-educated readers preferred George Eliot and Anthony Trollope to Dickens, but they read him also, and conversely, the broader public who read Dickens had no difficulty in reading the favourites of the educated if they wished to do so.[3] The distance separating different tastes was not so great, as can be seen from the following comment of an upper-middle-class Victorian: 'We began on Jane Eyre one winter evening, mildly irritated at the exaggerated praise we had heard and fully determined to be critical. But as we read we forgot both praise and blame, we lived completely with Jane in all her adversities and married, at last, Mr. Rochester at four o'clock in the morning.'

The novelists of the middle of the nineteenth century express those two characteristics that were the distinguishing feature of the new bourgeoisie: sentimentality and realism. And out of this emerged the harmonious relationship between author and reader. But in the development of this society and consequently in these novels there lay also the seeds of discontent and schism. Industrialization had brought riches and culture to a new class within the society, but also it had created a new lower class: the industrial worker, the urban proletariat.

The conflict was already formulated in Balzac's work. He writes for a bourgeois audience, he himself is a member of the bourgeoisie and yet, at the same time, he shows the misery inherent in this progressive world. Towards the end of the century the conflict deepens, especially in France, and many writers become committed to social change and begin to criticize bourgeois values. Erich Auerbach discusses the situation of these writers and points out its paradox. The Goncourt brothers no longer enjoy a happy relationship with their public. On the contrary, they attack their readers in the preface to *Germinie Lacerteux*, a novel about the ruin and degradation of a serving maid:

> We must ask the public's pardon for giving it this book, and for warning of what it will find there. The public likes false novels: this is a true novel. It likes books which pretend to move in society: this book comes from the street. . . . The public further likes innocuous and consoling reading adventures which end happily, imaginings which upset neither its digestion nor its sincerity: this book, with its sad and violent distraction, is so made as to go against its habits and be injurious to its hygiene. Why then have we written it? Is it simply to shock the public and scandalize its tastes?

'No', the writers assure us, the reason is that the novel has a great social task to perform, it has even, they claim, partly usurped the role of science, and therefore it becomes the duty of writers to show people the suffering and misery that exists all around them.

But it should have been obvious just from the tone of this attack on bourgeois readers, and there were no other kind, that it was launched not from the outside but from within their own ranks. The authors simply presupposed that it was precisely this bourgeois audience that would read their book. In the preface they did pose

46

the question: 'Why should the lower classes not have the right to "The Novel"?'; but they meant novels written *about* the lower classes rather than for them. Auerbach claims that the writers could risk attacking their public in this fashion because it was 'anonymous and not clearly defined'. In fact, it is perfectly clear from the Goncourt brothers' preface that they had no intention of breaking away from their bourgeois public, but merely wished to challenge it. Their books, like those of Emile Zola, sold extremely well.[4]

The brothers Goncourt may well symbolize the schism which appeared between a number of the leading novelists of the day and their public. This does not mean that their novels were read less, but it is the first indication that a divergence of interest was taking place within the novel genre, a divergence that became more and more marked during the twentieth century. Novels that attack the established society, usually the society represented by the readers of these novels, were balanced against novels whose intention was to provide relaxation, entertainment and escapism. Between these two extremes there was, of course, a whole spectrum of other books, not least among them the psychological novel which, at another level, showed the first signs of the alienation of the bourgeoisie from the society they themselves created. The harmony that existed between the novelist and his readers during the middle of the nineteenth century vanished. This did not, however, hinder the audience from growing larger and larger up till World War I. There remained a positive reciprocity: the public loyally continued to read its authors even though it was attacked by them.

Another reason for the growing audience was the availability of books and a lowering of prices. Novels commanded lower prices than the classics already in the eighteenth century, since, as was mentioned before, the latter were published predominantly for the private libraries of the aristocracy. Contemporary novels such as Richardson's *Clarissa* or Fielding's *Tom Jones* cost 3 shillings per volume and slightly less than £1 for six volumes. Books were still, however, so expensive that buyers were pretty much restricted to the middle classes.

The price of the novel rose slowly during the nineteenth century to 16 shillings per volume, while 31s 6d was the price for a 'three decker', the three-volume novel. These prices remained unchanged until the 1890s, but after the middle of the century publishers began to issue new editions of many of the earlier successful novels in single volumes at 6 shillings. Mass production and mass distribution had begun. The rotary press had just been invented. This was a press constructed in Germany at the end of the nineteenth century that printed 128 pages at a time in folded sheets and this provided the means to vastly increased production to fill the burgeoning market that was opening up with the spread of new railway lines. People had time to read when they travelled and bookstalls were soon opened in all railway stations.

The increasing competition and the broadening of the bourgeois public—the number of doctors, teachers, office clerks, and so on in England were approximately 357,000 in 1851, thirty years later there were 647,000—brought about further reductions in book prices, and there were protests over those books which still remained relatively expensive, especially the three-deckers. When *Endymion* was issued in this form in 1880 a rival publisher wrote to *The Times* protesting that the book should have been printed in an edition of 500,000 copies, to sell at 2s 6d. The correspondent claimed that American publishers would certainly have done this if the book had been published there. *The Times* considered the suggestion sufficiently important to take it up in an editorial where it advised against such a rash enterprise. The paper maintained that although the public could be unusually large, because of the fame of the author, it would be absurd to consider so large a printing. The edition comprising 10,500 copies was also shown to be more than adequate. A cheaper edition that came out a couple of years later, at 6 shillings, did, however, sell 25,000 copies within two years.[5]

The high price of the three-deckers could be partly explained by the large advances paid to authors and by the fact that many books were bought by the private lending libraries which, from 1840 on, played a very important part in the spread of reading, especially of novels, throughout England. The largest of these was run by C. E. Mudie, a bookseller who had 25,000 subscribers who read up to forty books a year for an annual fee of one or two guineas. He bought a record number of 3,000 copies of *Endymion*. For these libraries low book prices meant a disturbing form of competition. Three-volume editions were therefore increasingly used as library editions, with cheaper editions selling more widely to the general public. Three-deckers virtually disappeared during the 1890s because of the competition from cheaper editions, while at the same time the private lending libraries diminished in importance.

Another reason why cheap editions began to come out in ever greater numbers was that in Britain in 1842—as later in Germany— new copyright laws were passed that limited copyright to seven years after an author's death, or forty-two years from a book's initial publication. By the end of the century then, there were a whole series of works that had become free from copyright.

One of the houses that led the way in the publication of new, cheap editions was Collins, a publisher with considerable experience in issuing large, inexpensive editions of the Bible. For this sort of production, the company used the new rotary presses. At the turn of the century they issued the series, Collins Handy Illustrated Pocket Novels which later became Collins Illustrated Pocket Classics and which included works by Sir Walter Scott, Dickens, George Eliot and Thackeray. The attractive design of the series and the low price were surprising even by the standards of the time. *David Copperfield* was printed on 867 thin pages with sixteen illustrations and bound with 'full gold back'; it cost 1 shilling. The secret behind the production of this book was simply that the company had for decades published a Bible in the same format that sold for less than a shilling—all they had to do was continue production with different contents.

These cheap series were an enormous success: within two years fifty titles had been published and three years after starting, in 1906, 400,000 copies had been sold. By the end of the 1940s Collins had sold 25 million books.

The development of this line of publishing illuminates the homogeneity which continued to characterize the publishing trade on into the twentieth century up till 1918, and in some cases until the end of World War II. In 1911, 660,000 copies of this Collins' series were sold and 1948 sales amounted to exactly the same figure. Virtually nothing changed in the publication of these books. The price rose slowly to two shillings in 1922 and remained so until 1939! The greatest change in the outward design of the books came in 1936 when the hitherto dark-red cloth in the binding was enlivened with other colours and the title-page was changed. The titles remained much the same as they had always been. The most important of the original classics were retained and the series was supplemented during the years with living authors such as H. G. Wells and Walter de la Mare. The five most-sold books up until 1939 were all by nineteenth-century authors; in order of sales they were: *Wuthering Heights, David Copperfield, A Tale of Two Cities, Vanity Fair* and *Jane Eyre.*[6]

A comparable example of continuity, low prices and high standards is to be found in Germany, in the famous Reclam series. Leipzig publisher Anton Philipp Reclam published a two-volume edition of Shakespeare which cost 1½ taler, equivalent to 1s 6d then.

This was half the price of previous cheap editions of Shakespeare. Six reprints were issued the first year. By comparison, Macmillan's Globe Shakespeare edition in 1864 cost 3s 6d. Reclam was encouraged by this success to begin a general series modelled on British editions and in 1867 came out with Goethe's *Faust*, at 20 pfennigs (about 4d) per copy. The series was rapidly expanded with novels, essays, poems and plays. The price, cover, and title-page remained unchanged until 1917. After a period of seventy-five years, in 1942, 8,000 titles had been published and the number of printed copies approached 275 million. Henrik Ibsen was among the most popular authors and his *Peer Gynt* led the field with 719,000 copies, followed by *A Doll's House* with 584,000 and *Ghosts* with 544,000. Plato and Kant were printed in almost 1 million copies each and the works of Schopenhauer in 860,000 copies. Among translations English authors predominated, and Shakespeare especially whose collected works had sold 6.4 million copies up to 1942. Dickens' books sold 1.5 million, Walter Scott 424,000 and Oscar Wilde 401,000. American authors were well represented too: Mark Twain 776,000, and Edgar Allen Poe 455,000 copies. Soon the series was supplemented with twentieth-century writers including Galsworthy, Conrad, Jack London, E. M. Forster, Hemingway, and Somerset Maugham.[7]

I have mentioned previously the writers who criticized society and used the novel as a weapon to attack social injustice, often with considerable success. But at the time there was a growing need for relaxation and entertainment. One of the reasons for this was the increasingly marked difference between work and leisure, and the market forces that were released by the new distribution potential of the cheaper series tended to see a greater financial exploitation of this leisure.

The spread of popular literature was made easier by the new distribution outlets, the most important of which were the railway bookshops. Britain again led the way since the railway network was built up there more quickly than anywhere else in the world. (Between 1850 and 1870 railway mileage there increased from 1,000 to 24,000 kilometres; in France from 3,000 to 17,000; in Germany, from 6,000 to 20,000 and in Italy, from 500 to 6,000 kilometres.) W. H. Smith acquired a monopoly on railway bookstalls in 1848 and began to publish his own series of 'Yellow Backs', consisting of reprints and superficial novels written especially for the series. The bigger publishers also took advantage of this new potential and issued a large number of cheap editions such as Routledge's

Railway Library and Longman's Traveller's Library. These were a great success and also, incidentally, provided the prototype for the 'news-stand' literature of today.

The simple romantic novel had appeared in Britain as early as the eighteenth century as successor to the works of Richardson, Smollett and Sterne. Interest in the novel increased greatly even during this period and encouraged many writers to attempt the genre. The first thrillers or 'gothic' tales began to appear; works like Hugh Walpole's *The Castle of Otranto* and the novels of Ann Radcliffe (the precursors of modern-day bestselling novels by Daphne du Maurier and Victoria Holt); and exotic novels and moralistic novels of greatly varying quality. Clara Reeve, herself a successful writer of romances, criticized the superficiality of the genre in her book *The Progress of Romance* (1785) where she said 'the printing presses groaned under the burden of novels that sprouted anew like weeds each year,' and that 'every work of any value gave rise to many sequels that presented a danger to the society since, through bookshops and lending libraries, they were available to virtually anybody.'

These romances became the source of 'working-class literature' which a number of publishers specialized in during the 1820s and 30s. Rapid urbanization formed the basis of the need for relaxation and escapism of the growing urban proletariat. During this period there were a number of private organizations in Britain providing broad educational programmes for the poor. This produced a new, general literacy that certain publishers were quick to take advantage of, issuing editions such as The Poor Man's Gothic Novel—a 36-page booklet with a blue cover costing six pence. These booklets contained abridged versions of classic thrillers, simple romances or famous murder cases such as *Full, True and Particular Account of the Murder of Mr. Weare by John Thurtell and his Companions*—said to have sold 250,000 copies—or *The Gypsy's Prophecy*, or *The Feast of Blood*.

An interesting variation on this type of publishing was the spreading plagiarism, especially of the works of Dickens. Publisher Edward Lloyd printed a whole series of slightly altered titles like *The Penny Pickwick*, *Oliver Twiss* and *Nickelas Nicklebery*.[8] This type of publication did not, however, pave the way to better reading among the lower classes, on the contrary: the plagiarizing of Dickens shows that not even this writer reached the working classes undiluted, but rather in a false and vulgarized form. This sort of publishing reached considerable proportions intermittently but was completely separate from bourgeois publishing—the publishers themselves were regarded with contempt by 'real' publishers, nor did they usually last long. In fact, this kind of publishing represents the beginning of news-stand literature and the popular press, and was by no means part of the bourgeois book trade.

But even in this field there was an increasing need for entertaining literature, partly at least to utilize the greater production facilities and fill the growing distribution apparatus. The case of Edward Bulwer-Lytton provides an interesting example of how effectively, over a long period, the book market functioned at that time. In 1828 Lytton published *Pelhams, A Novel of Fashion* in an ordinary three-decker format at 31s 6d; it was not much of a success. Twenty-five years later Routledge published it in his Railway Library series at 1s 6d and sold 46,000 copies in five years. Later the book came out in a variety of cheap editions and by 1890 had sold a total of 200,000 copies. Lytton later wrote a series of popular novels (the best known being *The Last Days of Pompeii*, which sold 125,000 copies in America alone) that grew increasingly superficial, according to Mrs. Leavis, in an effort to pander to public taste:

> Lytton had discovered how to exploit the market.... And this lowering of the level of appeal makes Lytton the first of modern bestsellers, with Marie Corelli and Gilbert Frankau as his direct descendants.... Lytton's inflated language means an inflation of sentiment, and his pseudo-philosophical nonsense and proposterous rhetoric carry with them inevitably a debasing of the novelist's currency.... To make a useful generalisation, bestsellers before Lytton are at worst dull, but ever since they have almost always been vulgar.[9]

Thus the simple commercial literature of entertainment grew alongside the classics, the good new novels, and popular science books. The market was, however, still dominated by good literature, despite the lengthening inroads of popular literature, and managed to hold its position between the wars. But by the 1950s the two forms of literature had definitely gone their separate ways. Or as Hauser formulates it:

> But in Dickens' day, as in our own, there are two groups of people interested in belles-lettres. The only difference between that age and our own is that the popular light literature of that time still embraced the works of a writer like Dickens and that there were still many people who were able to enjoy both kinds of literature, whereas today good literature is fundamentally unpopular and popular literature is unbearable to people of taste.[10]

World War I had the same effect as a revolution, socially, economically, and culturally. The bourgeois establishment was seriously shaken by it, especially from a moral and social point of view. The powerlessness of the aristocracy was at last confirmed and the working classes could begin to harvest the fruit of their long battle for better living conditions.

But it takes time for revolutions to transform society. The period between the wars was too brief to allow for the achievement of absolute social change. It was a process that had begun during this period but had not been completed, but its influence was considerable in the shaping of the culture. We have seen how the traditional patterns of the book trade remained relatively undisturbed—inflation was moderate, book prices were virtually unchanged, the bourgeoisie still harboured cultural ambitions—but at the same time new forces arose: social schism and insecurity, a mass media producing for a mass market, and mass commercialization.

In the quotation I have already given (p. 41), S. Fischer expresses anxiety over the 'explosion' of the book market in 1926, the 'shallowness of the intellectual and spiritual life that is in danger of turning into a grave apathy. If this situation continues for long it will bring about a coarsening of taste, a defeat of the spiritual and moral forces in our land.' Bourgeois society had become a 'great, anonymous, unorganic whole'.

Mrs. Leavis too describes the period beginning in 1930 as 'the age of cinema and mass production'. Bestsellers and the weekly press compete for people's reading time, and these are 'designed to be read in the face of lassitude and nervous fatigue' and 'the reading habit is now often a drug habit'. She tries to show in her study how popular writers are influenced by big business to ever greater efforts to write so that the public will buy their books, while serious writers tend to isolate themselves. One of the writers she interviews—he sells a million of his books in America and Britain per year—claims that he has studied how films are made and learned what the public wants. He goes on to explain, obviously without considering his attitude particularly cynical, that:

> The general public does not wish to think. This fact, probably more than any other accounts for the success of my stories. . . . I have evolved therefore, a type of fiction that may be read with the minimum of mental effort. . . . A great many professional people enjoy my books *because they offer the mental relaxation which they require of fiction* [my italics].[11]

The success of the detective story is another indication that many people regard reading only as a form of relaxation. 'Virginia Woolf?

53

Why, you can't read her unless your mind is absolutely fresh!' is considered fair comment, and Mrs. Leavis quotes another writer of romances and popular novels who describes his readers as average middle-class 'scientists, priests, lawyers and business men'. Collins' Crime Club attracted 20,000 members in its first year, and this company has begun to sell American-imported Westerns also.

From the perspective of the 1970s the years between the wars seem like a period of vital literary activity, particularly in regard to the novel. Writers such as Steinbeck, Hemingway, Faulkner, Gide, Undset, Hamsun, and Graham Greene were working then, many of them at their peak. But the contours of the divergence between the two mainstreams of writing, serious and popular, become ever clearer and writers operating in either stream become more and more isolated from each other. It may be of interest from the historical point of view to note that Mrs. Leavis considered this development already complete in the 1920s:

> We realize ... that the general public—Dr. Johnson's common reader has now not even a glimpse of the living interests of modern literature, is ignorant of its growth and so prevented from developing with it, and that the critical minority to whose sole charge modern literature has now fallen is isolated, disowned by the general public and threatened by extinction.[12]

With the beginning of change in the European societies the American influence becomes ever stronger. This is especially true of the media market, films, the weekly press, and books. We have seen earlier that the American book market differed from the European market in its more frenetic commercialism, its poorly developed network of bookshops, and considerably stiffer competition. This was because America had a different social structure from Europe's, with no bourgeois class to suppport a broad publication of books generally and novels specifically. It was necessary then to use every means available, and this was true even in the nineteenth century, to attract a public: low prices, appealing titles, stories suited to the lowest common taste and ruthless marketing practices. There was no given public and this meant that it was necessary for publishers to use every means of persuasion available to gain an audience for those books they believed could become bestsellers.

The 'hard' American book market has been studied by an American researcher who investigated the financial state of 138 books published by the distinguished firm of Scribners between 1880 and 1882. He shows that only a third of these books were issued in editions of more than 1,500 copies. Barely 15 per cent rose to 2,500 copies and only two of these books were printed in more than one edition. Henry Holt, another publisher, wrote in 1907 that over a period of forty years he had published only two books that had made him a profit. In 1901 *Publishers' Weekly* maintained that of the 1,900 titles published during the preceding year, a maximum of 100 had sold more than 10,000 copies.[13] Profits, and in some cases they could be huge, were thus earned on vast printings of a very few books. Unlike Europe, where a broad base was the deciding factor, in America it was the peaks that were decisive to earnings. In the final decades of the nineteenth century 'bestseller' had already become a generic term. While a novel would go on selling year after year in Europe and a backlist of books provided security for the future, those books that sold well in America usually did so the first year and were published in very large editions, but the popularity of such a book was often short-lived. As early as 1872 *Publishers' Weekly* complained that the public was only interested in books published that year, 'nine out of ten queries are for this year's books', and in 1904 the same journal claimed that even the best books would certainly be 'crushed to death' by the new books that were piled on top of them.

On the other hand, those editions that sold over a short period, if the book was a bestseller, were considerably larger than similar editions in Europe. *David Harum*, a book about horses which is unknown today, sold 400,000 copies in fourteen months in the 1890s. Following the success of *Ben Hur*, Lew Wallace's next book came out in an edition of 50,000 at one dollar and fifty cents and eventually sold over a million copies. When publisher Robert Sterling Yard writes about bestsellers round the turn of the century, he means editions of 100,000 sold in the first year. His colleague, Walter Page, writes at about the same time: 'The first and obvious way is to secure books that have an enormous popularity. This is the effort of nearly all the publishing houses today. If a novel reaches an edition of 100,000 copies, there is a good profit.'

The most important market for general literature after the American civil war was, of course, the market for low-priced books. America led the rest of the world in the establishment of this market, and more than any other it was greatly influenced by stiff competition and profit-seeking. As early as 1840 American business men realized that there was money to be made in 'the emerging market for popular fiction', and 'publishers of books and periodicals turned to cutthroat competition as a means to outsmart their rivals'. Small booklets began to come out in America as they had in Britain.

They contained mostly copyright-free English novels and sold first at fifty-five cents each until the stiff competition drove the price down to twenty-five cents, then twelve and finally six cents, while regular novels cost from one to two dollars. Publication of these booklets ceased after a year or two when the prices had been reduced too far to earn a profit. It was not until 1860 that cheap books returned to the market, this time in a form that was exclusively American: 'the dime novel'. In Britain inexpensive books had been published in small, bound volumes that were suitable for the book-shelves of the bourgeoisie, while in America the competitive prices, the different methods of distribution and the fact that books were published for a different public, forced or allowed publishers to issue paperbacks. The novels contained therein were no longer imported European works, but largely original stories about the hardships of new settlers in the West.

With this the modern mass-market book was created in more or less the same form it retains to this day: a paperback pocket book with a low price—10 cents then—and with an illustrated cover and the series' insignia—they were all orange-coloured to begin with—and distributed through news-stands. The type of novel was much the same too as they are today: romantic or violent stories, written to order and to a specific length. The first book in the series published by Erastus Beadle was called *Malaeska, The Indian Wife of the White Hunter* and was 128 pages long; still an ideal length for the presses when a large printing is planned. Success was immediate, a specifically American public had been discovered—a mass-market public—and along with it, the books it wished to read. If the European novel was bourgeois, the Western was definitely non-bourgeois: 'The dime novel not only idealized and promoted the spirit of adventure and individualism in good Jacksonian fashion, it also exalted the humble man as opposed to those born with a silver spoon in their mouths.'[14] During the first five years alone four million of these books were sold, but, it is interesting to note, editions of each title were usually not more than between 35,000 and 80,000 copies. In contrast to European series these books were not reprinted year after year but were distributed and read immediately, and then forgotten. They were specifically American and uniquely suited to the American market, and when Beadle tried to introduce the books into Britain he was forced to give up after issuing only sixty titles.

Beadle's series were quickly followed by other similar ones. The stories themselves presented no problem. A 'writers' factory' was set up and writers were commissioned to write books of 75,000 words and were paid between 200 and 700 dollars per book. The famous 'Nick Carter' and 'Horatio Alger' books were produced in this fashion. The ruthless competition brought with it the usual over-production and by the 1880s publishers' storerooms were filled with millions of books. Many of these books were destroyed, but one of the largest of the publishers, George Munro, succeeded in selling 3 million of his surplus books to a soap manufacturer who gave away a book with each cake of soap he sold.

Regular publishers also saw the potential in this market. Walter Page wrote: 'A novel-reading democracy ... is a new thing. . . . It made new and big markets, and we all rushed after it. Cheapness and great editions became the rage. Writers wrote for the million; publishers published for the million.' The publishers issued cheap series of their own best sellers. In the 1890s the price of these books was fifty cents, or a third of the hardcover original. In conjunction with this there were also cheap series of original stories such as Harper's Half-Hour Series and Library of Select Novels with prices between fifteen and twenty-five cents. These series included both novels and non-fiction. They were not, however, all that successful, the price and standard were perhaps too high. On the other hand, there were publishers who established themselves at the turn of the century by specializing in cheap editions. They bought the rights to original books and often rented the plates from the original publisher. This aspect of the business became more and more important for the regular publishers and eventually accounted for much of their income. 'There are houses whose whole business is to get a secondary sale of novels,' Yard writes.[15]

Although the American book market evolved under completely different social and economic conditions from the European market, by the 1920s and 30s it began to exert an influence in Europe. Beadle's methods had failed in Britain in 1860, but in the years between the wars the same methods made a great deal of headway in Europe. Those changes were beginning to take place in European society that brought it ever closer economically and culturally to the American society, so that after World War II the influence from across the Atlantic had become decisive. In the final analysis the American influence did not, of course, dominate European development, but many of the social and technical factors present in Europe today had their origins in America. Both the service society and the mass culture began there and their effects are being felt to an increasing extent in Europe. It is quite natural therefore that the American book market would affect the European market. 'Bestsellerism', large editions in preference to broader sales, and news-stand books did not eliminate the sale of bound, hardcover books between the wars, but they were introduced in Europe during this time and finally flooded the market during the 1950s and 60s.

Mrs. Leavis too points out the influence of American magazines between the wars. Here are the instructions of a press agent to British writers who hoped to be published in the American press:

> Just a Little Friendly Advice. If you want to be a successful writer for American Publications, where high prices are paid for really first-class matter, bear in mind that American fiction, in the main, is not *pessimistic* nor is it *lewd* or irreverent, neither is it *red* nor *un-American*.
>
> Avoid *morbidity*. The Americans don't want *gloom*, but something that will brighten life. The sun must always be shining. Treat *sex* reverently, and avoid its unsavoury aspects. Don't be *vulgar*. Remember that serious thought is not looked for in the majority of American magazines.... Leave *social* and *political* problems to take care of themselves. Remember that America is a young and prosperous country, and there is nothing on God's earth to equal it.[16]

The disappearance of the homogeneity of the European reading public tended to make it more and more like its American counterpart. Readers in Western European countries are no longer part of a clearly defined class, but rather a large mass of people who are influenced by the mass media and who occupy their leisure time by using and consuming the increasing number of material things that surround them. If they read, it is for relaxation or because a book has achieved a 'mass media effect', won the Nobel Prize, been filmed or shown on TV, or because the writer has acquired notoriety in some other connection. There is a latent interest in reading a 'great book', but this must compete with a variety of other interests. Books are no longer a self-evident part of the way of life of a particular class, but represent only one of many possibilities. It is this public's time and money that the book trade must compete for in the future.

3

The Development of the Book Market in Denmark, Norway and Finland

One gains a clear picture of how small and homogeneous bourgeois Europe was during the nineteenth century, and up until World War I, if one examines the development of publishing houses in the Nordic countries. Both Denmark and Sweden follow the pattern set by Britain, France and Germany. Norway, in turn, has been greatly dependent on the progress of publishing in Denmark. And although development in Finland followed much the same lines, it had a late start because of the historical background of the country.

Denmark was the recipient of these new economic and cultural impulses before Sweden because of its geographical closeness to the rest of continental Europe; Germany was most influential in this respect. Around the beginning of the nineteenth century a new merchant class began to develop, and together with academics and government officials, they came to form a bourgeois reading public. The power and importance of the aristocracy diminished—neither in Denmark did this group play an important part in the cultural life.

Denmark did not possess a strong culture of its own until the second half of the nineteenth century. Before this time people read the same writers that were read in Britain and on the continent. *The Tatler* and *The Spectator* were translated as early as 1720 and inspired similar domestic publications. The first great English novels by Fielding, Smollet and Richardson were introduced and met with considerable success. They were followed in the nineteenth century by Walter Scott—from 1822 on, thirty of his novels were translated into Danish at a rate of about two per year—then Dickens, Victor Hugo, J. F. Cooper, Balzac, George Sand, Eugène Sue, and so on.

The reading of novels predominates in Denmark too, and the following few lines by author and critic J. L. Heiberg, from 1827, have a familiar ring. He complains that no one has time for great literature and most people 'read only to pass a free hour, in a word: they are the clients of our lending libraries, these countless male readers and even greater numbers of female novel readers'.

As is obvious from this remark, the lending libraries played an important role in attracting a reading public around the middle of the nineteenth century, just as they did in Britain and France. The first library opened in 1725 and by 1840 there were twenty-two private lending libraries in Copenhagen, a city with a population of 120,000. The books to be found were exactly the same as in the aforementioned countries, but they were soon supplemented with a few Nordic titles. One library, for example, had 55 novels of Dumas, 53 of Eugène Sue, 25 of Bulwer-Lytton and 28 of Swedish novelist Emilie Flygare-Carlén.

That these were fairly large operations is shown by the fact that Gerhard Bonnier, father of publisher Albert Bonnier, ran a library containing 13,000 volumes at the beginning of the nineteenth century.

The serial system was imported from Paris and had the same positive sales results for the new daily papers in Denmark as it had in France. And, of course, the same authors reappear: Jane Austen, Dickens, and Victor Hugo! *Berlingske Tidende* had a circulation of 1,100 in 1838 that rose, with this new reading public, to 8,000 by 1859. This was little, however, compared to the success of the magazine—also modelled on the British pattern—*Illustreret Familie Journal* (Illustrated Family Magazine) which began in 1877. Seven years later it had a circulation of 72,000 and by the turn of the century over 200,000. Two years later a similar circulation was achieved by a rival magazine called *Hjemmet* (The Home).

The new novels were distributed in booklet form as well as through newspapers and magazines, again like their British predecessors. Gyldendalske Boghandel was the largest and most important of Danish publishers and it soon issued a number of series under the titles 'Gyldendals bibliotek', 'Roman og Novelle' and 'Moderne Verdensliteratur', thus ensuring the Danish reading public access to serious literature in different editions and at varied prices. By 1870 the total number of titles available in Danish amounted to approximately 11,000, of which about a fourth was fiction. (Britain had at that time no more than a total of 14,000 titles available in the bookshops.) The stocks were kept up to date by continual reprinting, a fact that is made clear by the nickname given to the warehouse by Gyldendal's staff: they called it 'Eternity'.[1]

During the latter half of the nineteenth century a national literature began to appear in the form of plays, poetry and novels, often selling in very large editions. Here, too, it was the consistently steady demand that inspired the large editions. J. P. Jacobsen's *Niels Lyhne* was issued in four editions between 1880 and 1914 and sold a total of 7,000 copies, whereas his collected works sold 40,000 copies during the same period. Holger Drachman's most popular novel sold 22,000 copies in his lifetime, while his early poems sold 7,000 copies. A popular edition of H. C. Andersen's fairy tales, in two volumes, was issued in 150,000 copies. Again, the publication of school books was very important in providing long-term security and stability. Gyldendal's *Bibelhistorie* (The Bible Story), for instance, went through fifty-four printings of 20,000 copies per year, and Gerhard Bonnier sold 18,000 copies of a Reader in two years.

It is important, however, to realize the limitations of the book market in Denmark: in 1912 the total net financial turnover for books in Denmark was estimated at 3 million kronor.

The same European pattern was followed in regard to reading public, writers and publishers: a bourgeois public who read the books by writers who deserted the patronage system for subscription publishing and then, from about the middle of the nineteenth century, left the publishing of their books to the established publishing houses. And these publishers in Denmark, Gyldendal particularly, became rich and powerful; wealth and power gained essentially through the publication of fiction. Fredrik Hegel, head of the house of Gyldendal, owned both a town house and a country house and behaved with all the arrogance of a *grand seigneur*.

The years between the wars represented change in Denmark too. From the secure publication of reprints year after year and volumes of collected works, the bestseller suddenly began to dominate. Sally Salminen's *Katrina* sold 100,000 copies in 1937. A. J. Cronin's *Hatter's Castle* sold 78,000 and Remarque's *All Quiet on the Western Front*, 75,000 copies.[2]

After World War II Gyldendal, rather as Longmans, Collins, Hachette and S. Fischer had, ran into serious financial difficulties. It has subsequently adjusted to the new social structure of the present day, become a public company, and its main sources of income are from its school book department and its large book club, while the regular publishing of serious fiction would hardly seem to be sufficiently profitable to be worthwhile without large editions of a few bestsellers, which overshadow the publication of other general books.

Development of the book market in Norway took a considerably longer time. Norway was a poor country, politically dependent on

Sweden and linguistically bound to Denmark, and because of the inaccessibility of much of the countryside, industrialization had a late start. The difficulties of communication and poverty stood in the way of the development of a literary public. When a new 'golden generation' of writers appeared in the middle of the nineteenth century, the four greatest of them, Björnstierne Björnson, Henrik Ibsen, Jonas Lie and Alexander Kielland, were published by Gyldendal in Denmark. There was simply no publisher of comparable size or importance in Norway at the time and the country was, on the whole, dependent on the import of books from Denmark. The situation in the middle of the nineteenth century was described by a contemporary newspaper:

> There is something which must astonish almost everyone here, that serious literature is to be regarded in our Fatherland as an article to be imported, and this, despite the many attempts to emancipate our Norwegian language. Not only have we imported *en masse* all the Danish novels and short stories, we have even been forced to order all our translations from Swedish, German, French and English belles-lettres from Denmark.[3]

An association of Norwegian publishers was formed in 1875 by four publishing houses, Aschehoug, Cammermeyer, Cappelen and Malling, partly in the hope of persuading the better Norwegian writers to return to Norway, but in this they failed. The present Norwegian publishers' association was founded in 1895. At the time there was not yet a general reading public in the country. The few Norwegian publishers that existed were all very cautious about fiction and had rejected both Ibsen and Björnson. There were in fact no important Norwegian publishing houses and this extraordinary caution was the reason for it, good novels were decisive in ensuring a successful publishing business. The Danish dominance was so great that it was not until 1870 that more books were produced in Norway than were imported from Denmark. Most of this output consisted of school books and such, but by the 1880s Aschehoug, under William Nygaard's leadership, began to compete fairly successfully with Gyldendal.[4] (By the 1920s Aschehoug was larger, with a turnover of 3 million kronor in 1925, almost double that of the Norwegian branch of Gyldendal.) It was not until 1925 that Norwegian interests took over the Danish-owned Gyldendal in Oslo and in so doing created a modern Norwegian publishing business.

Norwegian writers, once they established themselves, had considerable success. *Magnhild*, a novel by Björnson, was printed in

8,000 copies in its first edition in 1878. His collected works were printed in two volumes and came out in an edition of 10,000 in 1872, an equal number the following year and 10,000 copies per year between 1881 and 1891. Ibsen's plays were also a great success in book form. *Enemy of the People* was published in two editions of 10,000 each in 1877, its first year of publication, and *A Doll's House* during its first year of publication in an edition of 14,000 copies.[5]

Demand for works by these authors did not diminish over the years. In 1907 a new popular edition of Björnson came out consisting of 65,000 copies, and in 1932, seventy-five years after he was first published, a new twelve-volume, 75,000-copy edition of his collected works was issued in Norway. A lot of money was at stake. In 1906 Björnson had received 200,000 kronor (approx. £25,000) for his collected works, a sum that was later to be considered scandalously small.

Once again we can see how publishers could survive on their older copyrights and how financially important fiction was to them. Gyldendal Norsk Forlag was bought from its Danish owners in 1952 for a little over 2 million kronor. Seven years later profits from the sale of Björnson's collected works alone were equal to the purchase of the whole publishing house.[6]

The slow development of publishing in the country was well compensated for by the success of Norway's Gyldendal during its first thirty years under domestic ownership. Everything that had been ignored earlier through an overcautiousness was now accomplished in a very short time by Gyldendals. Other publishers such as Aschehoug concentrated largely on reference books and school books. The emphasis at Gyldendals was on *belles lettres*. During its first five years as a Norwegian company, 58 per cent of all the books published were fiction and up to the outbreak of World War II more than half the publishing list consisted of fiction. Certain individual books were issued in large editions, such as Knut Hamsun's *The Vagabond* in 30,000 copies, but it was the collected works of great national authors that were tremendously successful.

I have already mentioned Björnson. Jonas Lie's collected works sold 57,000 copies, Ibsen's 90,000 and Kielland's 80,000. During a period of twenty-five years, up to the end of World War II, over 2 million copies of Hamsun's books were sold in various series. Then too there were 'mixed' series like The World's Best Novels in eighteen volumes, Norway's National Literature also in eighteen volumes, and Poets of Our Time in twelve volumes.

This publishing business was built up over a period of thirty years, whereas in other European countries it had taken a considerably longer time for most houses to achieve the same importance and stability. But the great changes occurred at approximately the same time, after World War II. In Norway, as elsewhere, it is fiction that loses most ground, Norwegian books as well as translations from other languages. Evensmo notes that there is 'a strange contrast' in the fact that during the years of economic crisis between the wars Gyldendals published every year a number of Norwegian novels that sold over 10,000 copies and still more that sold between 5,000 and 10,000, simultaneously many of the novel-series mentioned above were issued in editions of 15,000. Even during the period immediately after the war some Norwegian novels sold in editions of 30,000 to 50,000, but after 1948 the size of the editions was radically reduced. A study in 1953 showed that during these five years only two Norwegian novels had been published in editions of over 10,000. Ten others were issued in printings of 5,000 to 10,000 and forty-four between 2,000 and 3,000. The Norwegian Authors' Association characterized the situation thus:

It is a fact that Norwegian literature has had a difficult time competing in the sale of books in the last few years, both at home and on the world market. Fifty years ago the largest part of most writers' incomes were earned abroad, while at the same time the translations of foreign books did not represent very serious competition at home. Today it is only the exceptional Norwegian book that is translated into languages other than those of our neighbouring Scandinavian countries. In conjunction with this is the fact that translations now account for the greatest number of sales on the Norwegian book market....*New publishing and sales methods in most countries favour bestseller literature to the disadvantage of serious literature, and Norway is not the only small language area wherein the state of serious literature is precarious* [my italics].[7]

The reduction in sales, however, applied even to translations. The percentage of fiction published by Gyldendal, in relation to total output, during different periods was as follows: 1925–29, 39 per cent Norwegian, 19 per cent translations, totalling 58 per cent; 1945–49, 30 per cent Norwegian, 22 per cent translations, totalling 52 per cent; 1971–73, 15 per cent Norwegian, 5 per cent translations, totalling 20 per cent.[8] The publication of serious Norwegian books remains relatively high because of the important publishing subsidy that exists in the State's 'purchasing agreement'. This has been in force since 1965.

The reduction in the sales of the novel resulted in serious financial

64

difficulties for Gyldendal, after twenty-five successful years under Norwegian ownership. Book sales fell during these years (1950–63) and it was the weekly magazines that saved the company's finances; during these years three-quarters of all profits were earned by the company's magazines. Under such circumstances the importance of fiction from a financial point of view is strongly reduced, and it is entirely probable that this type of literature, during this period, brought net losses rather than profits. Despite the fact that Gyldendals is by far the most important publisher in Norway especially of fiction, the basis of its finances is now founded upon the publication of school books, reference books and a mail order business dominated by part ownership in several book clubs.

The book market developed more slowly in Finland than in the other Scandinavian countries. This was caused by a number of contingent circumstances: the geographical distance from the predominant European cultural areas, political dependency on Russia and Sweden, and bilingualism. Publishing did not really begin, in the modern sense, until the middle of the nineteenth century. In 1844 there were only 95 Swedish and 37 Finnish books published— a figure that rose gradually to 880 titles by the turn of the century.[9]

The distribution facilities were also modest—in 1880 there were a total of thirty-eight bookshops in the whole country—and editions usually consisted of no more than a couple of thousand copies. One exception to this rule was Johan Ludvig Runeberg's bestseller *Fänrik Ståls Sägner* (Ensign Stål's Sagas) an epic poem on the Russian–Finnish War in 1808–9, written in Swedish. The first part was published by the author himself when his publisher backed out at the last minute. Two thousand copies were printed in 1848 and 1,000 more in the 1850s. But when the second part was issued in 1860, five editions were published the first year, totalling 25,000 copies. The first Finnish language success was Z. Topelius's *The Book of Our Country* which was published in sixteen editions in the Finnish language between 1875 and 1899 and sold a total of 200,000 copies.

It was not until the turn of the century that the same sort of series of novels that had been published earlier in the other Nordic countries began to be issued in Finland too. The largest publisher in Finland at the time, G. W. Edlund, published translations of Dickens, Thackeray, Scott, Maupassant, Tolstoy, etc. The publishing houses were still relatively small, however, and there was no broader-based continuity until the Finnish language publishers became

65

established at the end of the nineteenth century. Finnish then began to gain more and more importance as the cultural language of the country. In 1895 there were 400 books published in the Finnish language and 250 in Swedish. Sixty years later the number of new titles in Swedish was no more than 411, while new Finnish books numbered 1,717.

The dominance of the Finnish language in the cultural life of the country began around the turn of the century and was the prerequisite for the establishment of the, now, two largest publishers in Finland, Werner Söderström OY and Otava. Both companies developed rapidly during this century, as within a brief span of time literature in the Finnish language had to be added to the culture and educational system. For this reason the books published were predominantly school books and reference books rather than serious fiction. This type of publishing still plays a decisive financial role in the business in Finland, unlike Sweden and Denmark. Examples of the most common type of publishing are: a variety of dictionaries, Finland's history, cultural historical works in a number of volumes, series of geographical books. In the 1930s Werner Söderström OY, the country's leading publishers, was able to sell a medical book for laymen and a housewife's dictionary in editions of 100,000, and during the 1960s they sold 60,000 copies of a 22-volume world history. Otava and Tammi, Finland's second and third largest publishers are still able to sell 30,000 to 60,000 copies of a multi-volumed dictionary over a period of a few years.

It is interesting to compare this type of publishing in Finland with publishing in Denmark and Sweden, where the book market was thriving fifty years earlier and where it is considered virtually impossible to sell encyclopedias today. There is now some anxiety in Norway that the market for this particular type of literature is diminishing there too. Recently the two largest Norwegian publishers of dictionaries and encyclopedias, Gyldendal and Aschehoug, agreed to stop competing with each other and publish a dictionary jointly. It was believed that the market was not sufficiently large to absorb two such works. A similar development must be predicted for Finland too, and this could also result in serious financial difficulties for Finnish publishers in the future.

4

The Swedish Book Market

The publishing business, in the modern sense of the term, began much later in Sweden than in the Anglo-Saxon countries, continental Europe and Denmark, but earlier than in Norway and Finland. The publication of books in Sweden in the seventeenth and eighteenth centuries was irregular and of modest dimensions. The books were sold by printers and bookbinders and were mainly of a religious nature. Popular prayer books could sometimes achieve impressive sales—*En Christens Gyllene Clenodium eller Siäleskatt* (A Christian's Golden Treasure or, Treasure of the Soul) was printed in an edition of 50,000 copies near the end of the seventeenth century —while the serious literature available was probably read by no more than a few hundred people. The leading baroque writer, Georg Stiernhielm, was completely dependent on a royal pension and the famous Swede, Olof Rudbeck, published his *Atlantica*, the best-known historical-mythological work of the time, himself in 500 copies; it sold very 'sluggishly'.

A decisive step forward was made in the history of the Swedish book trade when printer Lars Salvius forced through a ruling in 1752 that allowed printers themselves to sell the books they printed, not only in paper-bound sheets but hardcover as well. Previously bookbinders alone had the right to sell bound books. In 1757 these rights were enlarged to include books printed by other printers and Salvius opened the first 'universal bookshop' the same year. This had no particular practical value at the time since other printers were reluctant to deliver their products to a rival printer. His business was largely confined to the sale of those books he produced himself. By the end of the century, however, printers and bookbinders were forced to cooperate in the sale of each other's books through the bookshops. The bookshops had begun to appear when the demand for books necessitated such a service.

The establishment of freedom of the press in 1810 represents the next important stage in the development of a book market in

Sweden. With this law, censorship was abolished and writers retained the rights to everything they wrote: 'Every written work belongs to the author or is the property of its legal possessor.' But progress was slow; there was still no reading public that could stimulate a more rapid growth of the book market. In 1826 there were twelve booksellers in Stockholm and by 1847 this number had been reduced to eleven. The situation was still worse in the provinces. The railway network had not been constructed and books were sent out by horse-drawn carts to commission agents. These latter were frequently teachers and priests and sold books to earn a little extra income. Here is how magazine publisher J. E. Rydquist describes the book trade in Gothenburg in 1830:

> In many places, and even in Gothenburg—the country's second city— there are no open shops for the sale of books. If you desire a book you must be lucky enough to find the bookseller at home; sometimes you will certainly seek him without success; and if you are travelling, the book you wish must be greatly coveted or indispensable if you would make further attempts to possess it. And so prayer books, school books, almanacs and such necessary articles are the only books sold in the country towns. Uppsala is the exception; in general half of all the books sold in the provinces are sold there, in the same way as Stockholm sells as many books as are sold in the rest of Sweden together.[1]

A German traveller in Sweden wrote a description of the country around 1820 in which he claimed that most books in the land were published by the authors themselves or were sponsored by the State. A countryman of his, journeying through Sweden ten years later, noted one of the great differences between this country and the continent: 'Sweden is certainly a poor country, but this does not explain why one fails to find a single bookshop of any importance.'

Publishing at the time reflects the underdeveloped book trade in general. True, Lars Salvius published a 72-page catalogue in 1771, but the majority of books listed in it were scientific, by such as Linné, Kalm, and Chydenius, and were aimed at a very limited readership. Writers of fiction and poems could not support themselves by their pens. One historian has pointed out that he has not heard of a single case from this period where a poet received any direct payment for his work from a printer.

Of course Sweden was in touch with the blossoming literary development in England and France, but the semi-feudal society of the time was not able to absorb the bourgeois literature from those countries. Those attempts that were made failed time and again and left little trace in the country as a whole. This was especially true of efforts to build up a book market and create a reading public. That great precursor of bourgeois literature, *The Spectator*, was, of course, the main source and prototype of the magazine *Den Sedolärande Mercurius*, but this periodical, published in 1730-1, aroused little interest. Olof von Dalin's similar publication *Den Svenska Argus* was a considerable success but survived only two years. There were a number of other attempts at publishing this type of journal but they all ended in failure.

Fielding's *Tom Jones* was issued in Sweden in 1765, sixteen years after it originally appeared in England, and an additional fourteen years elapsed before the translation of *Joseph Andrews* was published, in 1780, almost forty years after the original. Sterne's *Sentimental Journey* suffered a similar delay. It was published in Sweden in 1790, at least two decades after the original. About the same time several of Richardson's novels were published. To judge by a contemporary newspaper notice they seem to have been fairly popular in certain circles. The paper complains, true to the academic taste of the time, of the general lack of taste. Good writers are ignored, but 'on the other hand you may find Pamela, Clarissa and Grandison in every bookshop, whereby the owner betrays his lack of learning and taste for literature.'

This complaint must have imitated foreign criticism though, since the notice was printed in 1777, some years before Richardson was translated into Swedish and the number of people who could read English in Sweden at the time would have been very limited.

Sentimental German novels also had a brief period of success in Sweden. There was *Werther*, of course, but there were also petty-bourgeois novels by such writers as Kotzebues and August Lafontaine, of which fifty or so books were translated. These failed, however, to exert much influence on either the book market or literature in general. At the beginning of the nineteenth century the novels of chivalry and adventure, mainly imported from Germany, achieved some popularity in Sweden. During the first two decades of the century these stories were admired even by educated people, the first to exhibit bourgeois tendencies, and they could be found reading books with titles like *Rinaldini*, *The Monk*, *The Terror of Spain*, *The Black Fritz*, and *The Monster of France*: leading Swedish romantic writers such as Atterbom, Tegnér, Almqvist and Stagnelius read and were influenced by novels like these, but their popularity was short-lived and they soon drifted down to 'the lower classes' and 'petty-bourgeois ladies'. In 1840 a contemporary story names 'a seamstress, a cook, a housemaid, a laundry maid, a kitchen maid' to be among the readers of novels of chivalry.[2]

It was the lending libraries rather than the publishers and bookshops who profited by these novels of chivalry. The libraries that had such books on their shelves were assured of success—they were forced occasionally to limit the borrowing of these books to just one a day—while there was no demand for serious Swedish or foreign literature. Apparently not even Sir Walter Scott's novels were really successful.

By the 1830s it began to look as though Sweden was about to acquire publishing facilities and a book market similar to that in Britain and France. The beginnings of industrialism turned Sweden towards England and reduced its dependency on Germany. In 1833 Lars Johan Hierta, with considerable foresight, began publishing translations of foreign novels in booklet form modelled on French publications: 'A Reading Library of the Latest Foreign Literature'. In his autobiography he writes that his goal was to introduce 'the best foreign authors of serious literature'. The enterprise was successful 'beyond our expectations'. The first works he used were by Washington Irving, Walter Scott, Edward Bulwer-Lytton and Fenimore Cooper, and they were in such demand that they had to be reprinted and 'gave a good profit for many years'. Three weeks from the time Hierta announced his publishing plans he had 1,000 subscribers in Stockholm and 1,500 in the provinces. The Reading Library was issued during three years in forty-five volumes. This was followed by The New Reading Library (1836–43) in fifty-five volumes, and finally two additional series (1844–53) which included most of the great European novels of the time: works by George Sand, Dickens, Eugène Sue and Alexandre Dumas.[3]

Hierta's example was followed by N. H. Thomson, who had opened a printing business in Stockholm in 1831. In 1835 he issued The Cabinet Library of Latest Literature and then later The New Cabinet Library of Latest Swedish and Foreign Novels 1845–6. Translations were now mixed with Swedish novels. Finally he issued an exclusively Swedish series of novels called The New Swedish Parnassus which included works by virtually all the few contemporary Swedish novelists: August Blanche, Emilie Flygare-Carlén, C. J. L. Almqvist, M. J. Crusenstolpe and C. F. Ridderstad (who was influenced by Eugène Sue and had no less than ten novels in the series). Among the foreign novelists one finds all the great names that were missing from Hierta's series: Victor Hugo, Balzac, Marryat, and Pushkin. Altogether, Thomson published over 200 novels, usually in 96-page editions. Hierta published almost as many and there were a number of smaller publishers who printed similar weekly publications.[4]

Neither Hierta nor Thomson had any lasting success, however, and other publishers had been sceptical from the beginning. 'The attempt to sell a complete library, at an untried low price, of good novels in Swedish translation was regarded by experienced publishers as absolute madness', Hierta wrote. The few booksellers there were, also reacted negatively, probably because the majority of these books were sold by subscription, from publisher direct to the subscriber. Both Hierta and Thomson became wealthy men—Hierta had his private yacht and Thomson retired in 1856 with a considerable fortune—but neither of them built up a lasting publishing business based on the publication of novels.

The reasons for the slow development of the Swedish book market must be seen against the background of the country's social structure in the nineteenth century. Sweden had long been a poor, largely agrarian land, with strong traditions of class founded on the aristocracy and public office. This was not conducive to the growth of a bourgeoisie, which, as I have shown earlier, was a prerequisite for the development of a modern book market. In the year 1800 only 10 per cent of the population lived in cities, and half of all these people lived in Stockholm. Urbanization was a slow process: in 1870, 72 per cent of the population still lived on the land, by 1890 this figure had sunk to 60 per cent.

The slow process of industrialization began during the middle of the nineteenth century. Building projects in the larger European countries had created a market for Swedish wood products. A large timber industry was built up between 1850 and 1870. At about the same time new technical methods for the processing of iron were developed, thus creating the necessary conditions for the establishment of the first iron works such as Kockums, Bolinders, and Motala. Improved communications were also essential to economic development. An important step in this direction was achieved with the completion of the Göta Canal, which joined the Baltic and North Seas, in 1832.

The building of the railways came later. In 1860 there were only 525 kilometres of track in the whole country and it was not until the 1870s that serious extension of this network began. By 1880 the total track distance had grown ten-fold, to 6,000 kilometres.

The modernization of Sweden really started in the 1870s, and the industrial revolution in the country stems from this time. During this decade the development of the manufacturing industry could be characterized as 'explosive'. There was a severe slump during the 1880s again, with a calamitous agricultural crisis that helped to stimulate mass emigration to America, but in the 1890s there was an upswing and the break-through toward a modern Sweden was an accomplished fact. Basic industries doubled their production many times and the same was true of manufacturing industries. It was at this time that enterprising industries were first founded, often based on a single great invention, as in the case of ASEA (electrical equipment), Separator (milk/cream separation), and L. M. Ericsson (telephones). Consumer industries, producing furniture and textiles, were also started during this period.

The social changes were reflected in the transformation of the parliament (formerly elected from among the upper hierarchy of the society, members were now publicly elected to two houses), compulsory education and the establishment of the first *folkhögskolorna* (people's high schools) in 1868, but here too progress was slow. Eighty per cent of Sweden's male population still did not have the right to vote at this time. During the decade, industry's share of the GNP rises for the first time above that of agriculture, and the wages of industrial workers, far below those in England and Germany, increase rapidly so that by the turn of the century they are the second highest in Europe. Within only a few decades Sweden has been transformed from one of the poorer countries in Europe to one of the richest.

During the first two-thirds of the nineteenth century the tardy development of Swedish literature illustrates the slow progress of society before the arrival of the industrial revolution. We have seen how foreign novels had brief periods of success in Sweden but failed to induce an atmosphere of continuity. Neither had the impulse from the great novelists of the day stimulated the creation of equivalent fiction in Sweden. An example of how underdeveloped the Swedish book market was is provided by the fact that Swedish writer Fredrika Bremer was in greater demand in Germany, England and America than she was in Sweden, if her royalties and the interest of publishers are any indication. Her English publishers, Chapman, Hall & Virtue, demanded the right to publish a book of hers before it was published in any other country (this demand was connected with protection of copyright). Brockhaus in Germany tried to insist on the same condition. Publishers fought over her works in America (see p. 35) and she herself wrote that 'the English publishers are the only ones abroad who pay me really decent royalties (even more than in my home-land).'

The following description, by a Commissioner of the Publishers' Association in Växjö in 1851, gives some idea of the size of the reading public at the time. (It is also reminiscent of Archibald Constable's comment, quoted earlier, from the 1820s.)

My reading public . . . consists largely of country people, the majority raw farmers, of whom most could not read freely the contents of a book in ordinary Swedish, or so-called Gothic, style, let alone novels and such, printed in the Latin style. . . . Well, what of the few land-owners and gentry? They are best occupied with the growing of potatoes and distilling of schnapps, etc., . . . and read little between times . . . preferably a deck of playing cards. . . . Of countrymen there are still the priests: must they then read a great deal more? Of these it is almost entirely the curates who buy books the most on credit and now and then an assistant preacher: the rectors you never see at all, for once they . . . have gained a parish . . . they neglect, as no longer necessary, all the extra trouble that reading entails.[5]

The odd book could be printed in fairly large editions, but it was usually a practical book such as *Cajsa Warg's Cook Book*, which went through fifteen editions between 1755, when it was first published, and 1849. The last few editions consisted of 2,000–3,000 copies each. Tegnér's *Fritiof's Saga* came out in nine editions from 1825 on totalling 25,000 copies in his lifetime. The number of school books show the progress of education during the middle of the nineteenth century. Between 1825 and 1890, 150,000 copies of a nature study textbook were printed and books on 'country housekeeping' could sell as many as 50,000 copies.

A few writers were able to support themselves by their pens in the 1830s and they were novelists, such as Crusenstolpe, Flygare-Carlén, Blanche, Braun and one or two others, but they were excep-tions. As late as 1877 a Danish traveller could write that 'the Danish middle classes generally have a more developed feeling for reading than their Swedish counterparts and certainly spend more on the purchase of books than do Swedes', and Rinman, who quotes this letter, adds: 'This is in line with observations we made previously: the relatively illiterate character of the Swedish middle class. . . . As is well known, Denmark had at this time, to a much greater extent than Sweden, a thriving domestic literature and a readership that was responsive to it.'[6]

The Swedish Publishers' Association, founded in 1843, represents the first attempt to organize the book market in Sweden, and concentrated on the arrangement with wholesalers and commission agents. But without a reading public the book market developed very slowly during these years.

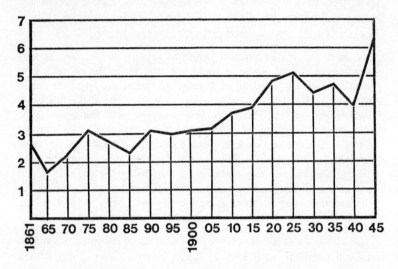

Swedish book production 1861–1945 shown in titles per thousand of population.

The publishing of books was therefore very cautious and far from expansive right up until the 1890s. As is shown by the curve of book sales in relation to population, the publication of books was proportionately no greater in 1885 than it was in 1861. It was around 1890 when the publication of books began to increase—parallel to the great expansion of the Swedish economy. Up until this time there were two main categories of books published besides school books, serious fiction and the humanities on the one hand and theological on the other. In 1865 there were 196 titles published in the first category and 82 in the second. In 1880 the situation is much the same, with 222 titles in the 'literary' category and 177 theological works—18 and 14 per cent respectively of all the titles published that year.

Up until the late nineteenth century then, there was little exciting or stimulating literature being published, and publishing at the time was still deeply rooted in a Swedish society that was very largely influenced by academic and official authority. The country was also affected by a certain insecurity in the area of change between the old society and the new. Karl Otto Bonnier's description of the

1860s and 1870s shows that there was a need for general economic expansion before a new atmosphere of creative cultural activity could develop (even though his conclusions are the opposite of mine):

> But 'the bourgeoisie', which increased very fast and soon usurped both the parliament and the monarchy, had also a dark side: it had killed literature. Little had been added to it during the fifties and one can but conclude that during the sixties, especially true of *belles lettres*, literature died completely. 'Utility', 'Practicality' became the slogans of the day and publishers, the servants of literature, were forced to obey this injunction. These useful books came to take the place of the missing serious literature. The record of Swedish publishing during these two decades is mostly then, a listing of many excellent practical publications and a fairly large number of reprints of older Swedish writers, but new Swedish writing is only represented by a very few, and in quality it is an extraordinary meagre product.[7]

The development of Albert Bonnier's publishing house runs to a great extent parallel with the development of the modern Swedish book market. Albert started his company at the age of seventeen, in 1837, but it was not until the 1860s and 1870s that it became one of the larger publishing houses in the country. Albert built up his business slowly and carefully within an area of publishing ignored by other larger publishers. Beginning with modest publications of the type *The Little Home Medical Book*, *Book of Ballads*, and *How to Bring up Young Girls*, he worked his way up to serious literature by two routes, partly with the publication of *Svea* in 1844, an annual anthology with contributions by younger Swedish writers, and partly by competing with other publishers such as Hierta, in the publication of a series of novels starting in 1846. Actually this latter was more like a weekly magazine and was called *European Serial, Magazine for Fictional Literature*. Not surprisingly, the first number contained a novel by Eugène Sue. Unfortunately there is no record of the number of sales, but it seems unlikely that it would have been published in larger editions than 2,500. Publication of this journal ceased during two years in the 1850s, but *European Serial* continued on after this interval until 1910.

During the 1850s other Swedish publishers withdrew more and more from the publication of foreign novels, which is, of course, another indication that the public was very limited for this type of literature, and Albert remained alone in the field. Although this area of publishing did not, at that time, yield any great financial success it provided for steady sales and a permanent contact with new European fiction. Virtually every great name in European literature appeared in the *Serial* during its more than sixty years of publication: Dickens, George Eliot, Victor Hugo, Thackeray, Daudet, Zola, Flaubert, Tolstoy, Dostoevski, Anatole France, Thomas Hardy, Thomas Mann, H. G. Wells, Bernard Shaw, and so on. The *Serial* increased its circulation during the 1860s and 1870s and at times reached 4,000–5,000 copies.

There are other sales figures that also reveal the slow development of the book market. A Bellman edition published by Adolf Bonnier in 1855 sold 3,000 copies, 'a very major success'. Explorer Charles John Anderson's *Lake Ngami* sold 2,000 copies the following year, and Renan's *The Life of Jesus*, published in the 1860s, sold 6,000 copies, 'almost unique at the time'.

The company continued to grow steadily and in 1865 the printing house and publishing offices were moved to a larger building, but until 1880 the publishing offices consisted still of only three rooms. It was during the 1870s, however, that Albert Bonnier became one of the two largest publishing houses in Sweden (the other is Norstedts) and remains so to this day.

During this decade Bonniers began increasingly to dominate publishing in Sweden and the size of book editions grew considerably. The new improved living conditions in Sweden influenced the book market. Translations in serial form were published in even larger editions. A book such as Stanley's *Through the Dark Continent*, for example sold 5,000 copies in 1878. It is obvious that editions of this size were profitable since Albert Bonnier paid Nansen 30,000 kronor in advance in 1897 for *Across the Polar Sea* (this was approximately £1,500, a huge advance for the time in Sweden). This book sold 6,000 copies and was regarded as a great success. Victor Rydberg's translation of *Faust* was published in 1876 and sold 3,000 copies in an illustrated version that cost 18 kronor for the paperback edition and 27 for the hardcover edition. In the late 1890s, 5,400 copies of Sven Hedin's *A Journey through Asia* were sold in two volumes at 25 kronor.

The breakthrough comes forcefully in the 1880s in conjunction with the general economic progress. It is no longer unique, as it was a decade before, for a book to sell more than a few thousand copies. Karl Otto Bonnier gives the figures for those books that sold best during the 1880s: Victor Rydberg's *Poems*, 8,500 copies (compare this with the sales of Stanley's book a few years earlier: a collection of poems that sells almost twice as many copies as a world-famous book on exploration!); Weber's *World History*, 6,000; Rosander's

The Knowledgeable Schoolmaster, 10,000 copies; Topelius' *Field Surgeon's Tales*, 30,000 copies.

One can compare these figures with those of the first weekly magazine to be launched in Sweden, *Svenska Familje-Journalen* (The Swedish Family Journal), in 1864. In the beginning it had a circulation of 5,000; by 1871 this figure had increased to 35,000, and by the end of the decade to 70,000.

Economic progress generates cultural development. Suddenly there was a book market in Sweden of a type similar to that which had existed for a couple of generations in Britain and France, and for a somewhat shorter time in Germany and Denmark. This in turn brought with it a new development in Swedish literature: a bourgeois literature which, after years of stagnation, replaced the academic literature of the past. The 1890s were the years of greatest influence for the bourgeoisie and they also represent one of the most fertile periods in the history of Swedish literature, with writers such as Heidenstam, Fröding, Selma Lagerlöf, Levertin, and Ola Hansson. They were all published by the house of Bonnier, since, as we noted earlier, this was the only Swedish publisher that concentrated on the publication of quality fiction. The size of the editions increased during this and the next few decades to printings that are considered remarkable even today. Heidenstam's *Karolinerna* (tales of Charles XII's war against Russia) was printed in 8,000 copies and the author was paid 16,000 kronor. Selma Lagerlöf's books sold in even greater numbers: in 1900 *En Herrgårdssägen* (A Manor House Saga) sold 10,000 copies, and two years later *Till Jerusalem* (To Jerusalem) sold 15,000 copies within a few months, 'a singular record for new Swedish literature'. The record was beaten, however, by her *Nils Holgersson*, which sold 40,000 copies in 1906 in the regular edition and 100,000 in the school edition the following year. By 1957 it had sold a total of 745,000 copies.

The company did, of course, publish other books than novels, but novels occupied the main focus of their activities and a central place in their finances. They published everything there was that was proper to a newly awakened bourgeois culture: encyclopedias, general history, art history, travel books. In 1898 Bonniers published Becker's *World History* in seven large octavo volumes, with 2,000 illustrations and maps in colour, in an edition of 10,000 copies.

These large editions meant that writers who were successful could now earn their living by their profession. I have already mentioned Heidenstam's royalties for *Karolinerna*. Strindberg had perennial money problems certainly, but in 1912, the last year of his life, he earned 200,000 kronor for his collected works, about the same as Disraeli received for *Endymion*.

The development of the book market in Sweden from the end of the 1880s onwards is shown most clearly by the turnover of the two largest publishers, Bonniers and Norstedts, during these years. In 1866 Bonniers showed a gross turnover of a little more than 100,000 kronor, while Norstedts had reached 167,000 by 1862. By 1873 Bonnier's turnover was 200,000 kronor and in 1884 it rose to 364,000—this was the year that *Fältskärns Berättelser* (Field Surgeon's Tales) was published. Turnover decreased in 1886 to 221,000 only to recover again as the company approached a period of great expansion: in 1890 the turnover was 400,000 kronor and in 1898, 620,000. In the 1890s there were still only a dozen or so people employed in the publishing offices and about forty in the printing shop. In 1928 there were 500 employees. At the beginning of the century Norstedts was still larger, handling as it did much of the official printing business in the country. This house had a turnover of 1.2 million kronor in 1903 and 1.5 million in 1919.[8]

The reason for this success was not just that Sweden had become a rich country, but that in conjunction with this increased wealth it had also gained a reading public. It was during the 1880s and even more so during the 1890s that reading became a part of the way of life of the well-to-do middle classes. Those who bought and read new novels, collections of poems and travel books were not such a large group—Karl Otto Bonnier has estimated their numbers before World War I to be 'a few tens of thousands of educated people'—but, on the other hand, they read almost everything that was published. Reading became a habit that was clearly part of the bourgeois pattern. In the evenings people gathered round the living-room or dining-room table to read or to do needlework, and not infrequently they read aloud to each other.

The book market developed rapidly in the beginning of the twentieth century and this expansion was based on the homogeneous, loyal reading public. This public broadened constantly, giving rise to a bourgeois literature. There is the same homogeneity between the Swedish bourgeoisie and Hjalmar Söderberg, Bo Bergman, Sigfrid Siwertz and Olle Hedberg during the first decades of the twentieth century as there was between the English middle classes and Dickens and Thackeray a few generations earlier. In this new phase the time had come for collected works and educational literature. The sale of this type of literature was very important to Bonnier's development. In the 1930s Karl Otto Bonnier writes: '*belles lettres*, by far, do not weigh most heavily on the scales of success. . . . If I were to give but a small idea of what constitutes the main substance of this business then I should have, first of all, to draw attention to a variety of *collected works* that the company has published during this period.' Bonnier's *Encyclopedia* was published in two editions, *Bonnier's General Art History* in 100,000 copies. *Sweden's National Literature*, in thirty volumes, was published in two editions, *Bonnier's General Art History* in twenty volumes, *World Literature* in fifty volumes, *Bonnier's Illustrated Literary History* in seven volumes and finally *Swedish Lyric Poets*, an anthology of the greatest Swedish lyric poets from the 1880s onward, in about fifty volumes. It was not long before international bestsellers began to appear on the Swedish book market along with Swedish ones. (And some Swedish writers became famous throughout the whole of the western world.) Remarque's *All Quiet on the Western Front* was published in Sweden in 1929 and sold 66,000 copies the first year. The following year Axel Munthe's *The Story of San Michele* sold 27,000 copies, and the book about André's balloon voyage to the North Pole, 70,000 copies.

In Sweden too the new media and the beginning of the mass society began to exert an influence on the reading public. Karl Otto Bonnier throws some light on the situation in his comments in relation to the acquisition by Bonniers of the magazine publishing company Åhlén & Åkerlund in 1929. (His remarks are similar to those Samuel Fischer made at about the same time, see p. 40.)

I cannot deny that this development, so unlike what we older publishers have seen earlier, not only astonished publishers and booksellers, but was regarded by them with some suspicion. I and all the others in the trade who have lived in the belief that the readership in Sweden could not be widened beyond, at most, a few tens of thousands of people, did not really believe in the possibility of creating a reading public of millions. But Erik Åkerlund was right! He offered his public what they most desired: things to delight the eye and divert the mind . . . we felt though, more and more day by day, how the huge sales of weekly magazines encroached on the sales of books which in all probability, precisely because of this competition, from now on could not be extended. In other words, we had the feeling that the future belonged to the weekly press—in so far as the masses and their reading was concerned—rather than to books.

Karl Otto Bonnier had as yet only noted the beginning of the coming changes in the social structure, but he had already felt the tremor of disintegration of the reading public that was to occur so rapidly in the 1950s and 1960s. The remarkable thing is that he had also witnessed the rise of the bourgeois society and this reading public—it had not existed longer in Sweden than his lifetime.

But before the diminishing of the homogeneity of the reading public, a development occurred in Sweden that is probably unique to this country: the appearance of a working-class reading public and proletarian authors who write for it. That is to say, a situation that corresponded to the phenomenon of the bourgeois novel and its readers.

As I have pointed out earlier, popular reading has existed as long as books have: broadsheets, religious pamphlets, pirate novels and, towards the end of the nineteenth century, even some of the most typical of bourgeois novels were widely popular, often in abridged form. In Sweden we have had anthologies such as Bonnier's 'Öreskrifter för folket' (Penny Books for the People) from the end of the nineteenth century. Among these were works similar in quality to Harriet Beecher Stowe's *Uncle Tom's Cabin*. Other publishers issued 'godtköpsupplagor' (bargain editions) for twenty-five öre (1s 6d) per book which included slightly abridged versions of the works of Walter Scott, Thackeray and Swift. Occasionally one or two of the most popular of these books could be issued in large editions, but it is unlikely that they reached the masses, who did not habitually read.

During the years between the wars a number of series of novels were published. They were of mixed quality and success. The competition from the greatly expanding weekly press became more and more of a problem, particularly from a cultural point of view. During the 1930s the Social Democrats had come to power and interest in working-class culture coincided with a rising self-respect and standard of living among workers. The magazine *Folket i Bild* (People in Pictures) was founded in 1934 to counterbalance the sentimental and escapist weekly press, and it had considerable success. The time was ripe and there were writers who could write for the workers and about the realities of their lives. The book market was still dominated by the bourgeois reading public, but workers' educational programmes, improved schooling and the general rise in the living standard had changed the picture by the end of the 1930s. In 1940 a workers' publishing house was started for this new reading public with high-class fiction but at a level that suited people who were not habitual readers: 'Books for the people should tell a story, describe everyday situations, reality, historic

80

traditions, have robust humour, and be written by authors who have the talent to draw their stories with broad, clear strokes,' wrote Arne Hirdman in a study of 'Books for the People' published in 1950. To further this policy a system of distribution was created whereby agents would contact workers at their factories. Bookshops were so closely tied to bourgeois society that the question was often discussed as to whether it was suitable for workers to enter bookshops in their working clothes.

Sales surpassed all expectations. The editions that began at 20,000 copies were soon raised to 50,000 and then to 100,000. In ten years 7 million copies of these books had been sold. But then suddenly these 'Books for the People' disappeared with the same swiftness as they had come. During the 1960s they sold less and less well, while at the same time an increasing vulgarization was noticeable. They had reached a low cultural level where neither Walt Disney's books nor pornography were excluded. Society had changed. The workers no longer carried on the battle for education but were absorbed ever more quickly into the mass society and by its mass media, and as a result suffered from a lack of time and lessening interest in an active cultural commitment. The economic and social improvements also meant that it was more difficult to recruit agents in the factories— they had neither the same need for extra income nor the same motivation for ideological involvement. And finally: simultaneously with the disappearance of 'working-class readers' no new 'working-class writers' were forthcoming.

The 1940s were the last great period of traditional book publishing. Wartime shortages of most consumer products and the closed frontiers had a favourable effect on the sale of books. The war had also preserved bourgeois society—social change came to a standstill for the duration. But during the 1950s Sweden approached the new epoch more quickly than ever. The post-industrial society had begun.

The house of Bonnier could still be regarded as a typical bourgeois publisher, concentrating on good fiction, and continued to be extremely successful in the early 1950s. Less than twenty years later this company was showing losses of millions and was forced to cut down drastically on both its output and personnel. A study carried out at the company in 1959 gives a clear picture of the effect of these rapid structural changes.

First, the sales curve for books is shown in comparison to that of newspapers. During the period 1938–45 the sale of books at current prices in Sweden had increased much more rapidly than the sale of

81

newspapers. During the period 1945–58 the situation was completely reversed. Following this, a comparison is made between the price curve for serious literature and the prices coming under the heading of 'entertainment and recreation', both against the consumer price index. This shows that during 1949–58 the price of books increased twice as much as the consumer price index, which averaged 10 per cent per year, while the cost of entertainment and recreation increased slightly less than the consumer price index. An investigation of the sale of books at fixed prices showed that the sale of serious literature had stagnated, and during some years actually decreased. The sale of newspapers, on the other hand, had increased steadily.

An estimate of the number of books published presents the problem from another point of view. During the period 1945–53 the number of titles issued remained the same or was reduced; after 1953 there was a rapid increase. Falling sales were compensated for then, not only by a sharp rise in prices, but also by an increase in output. The conclusion must be that the average edition per book became smaller, and this is borne out by the study. It shows that editions were reduced in size by approximately 37 per cent during the ten years covered by the investigation.

These investigations concerned the book market as a whole. After this a special study was made of the development of publishing at Bonniers, in which, not surprisingly, the same trends were apparent. At the time Bonniers should have had approximately 30 per cent of the book market, excluding school books, while its share of the market only in general books must have been considerably higher. The influence of the mass society is obvious. During the period 1948–58 the average printings of fiction, non-fiction and children's books were reduced by 49 per cent and no less than 60 per cent during the last six years. It was the cheap editions and the book club that kept turnover high. A relatively small number of popular titles were now sold at low prices to a large number of people. Cheap books almost doubled their share of Bonnier's total sales during the period 1945–58, from 16 to 28 per cent. (Since then the same trend has continued. At the present time cheap editions—paperbacks and book club editions—account for approximately 60 per cent of Bonnier's turnover.)

At the same time as there is an increase in the sales share of cheap books the breadth of sales of ordinary books becomes smaller. A few bestsellers become more and more important. In 1958 there were 200 titles published at Bonniers including fiction, non-fiction, and children's books. *Of these, the three 'best' books accounted for no less than 29 per cent of the total sales.* (In 1956 and 1957 the figure was 26.2 and 26.5 per cent respectively.)

This development was further strengthened during the sixties, a fact shown in the material of the State Commission on Literature set up in 1968. A natural outcome of this situation was the severe financial repercussions suffered by the 'literary' publishers. Adjusment to the rapidly changing society was not made quickly enough and publishers continued to publish books for a bourgeois reading public that had gradually disappeared.

5

Sweden: the Publishing Crisis. A Case Study

Sweden's neutrality during World War II had an advantageous effect on the Swedish economy. This was particularly true of the book trade. The economic conditions were especially conducive to the sale of books, since most other consumer products were rationed during the war. This situation in the book trade continued on into the surging economy of the 1950s. If anyone had said at the time that the book trade was facing an imminent crisis, the prediction would have been regarded as an absurdity. Faulty statistics, a large reserve of resources gathered during the preceding decades and the concentration of publishing within a few large companies (Bonniers, Esselte and Almquist & Wiksell/Gebers had 60 per cent of the total market during the 1950s and today the two latter companies have merged)—all these factors contributed to the ignorance of the changing conditions in the book trade. It was these changes that were to culminate in the so-called publishing crisis in 1970 and 1971.

The first indication that there could be serious financial problems in the trade came from an outside source, in a study published by the Swedish National Price and Cartel Office in 1963.

The background to this study was the discussions that had begun on the abolition of fixed book prices, or the net book agreement. In 1953 the setting of prices was no longer controlled and special dispensation had to be sought in order to retain fixed retail prices. The Swedish Publishers' Association had been granted such dispensation, since it was generally thought that uncontrolled book prices would leap to a type of competition that would be harmful to culture. This opinion was shared in most Western European countries. The Market Court (the tribunal responsible for economic issues) expressed its anxiety over the sharp increase in book prices—an anxiety that was not, however, shared by publishers and booksellers—which was much greater than the consumer price index. That this anxiety was justified is shown by the acceleration of the trend between 1955 and 1967 when book prices rose by 130 per cent while the consumer price index rose by only 50 per cent during the same period. In the study done by the Swedish National Price and Cartel Office it was pointed out that as a result of rapidly rising prices 'the sale of books and paper at prevailing prices has certainly increased during the 1950s but that the rate of increase has remained considerably lower than that noted for the total consumption development. This situation, in conjunction with the changes in the book price index, indicates an even more unfavourable development in sales.' It is, however, significant of a generally positive attitude toward the situation of the trade that those who made the study cautiously added: 'The report is, however, impaired by a fairly high degree of uncertainty.'

The only anxiety felt in the trade was the anxiety of the privileged: the 100-year-old protective wall—consisting of control over the establishment of new booksellers, the commission system and especially the fixed retail prices—began to totter.

The publishers' five main arguments put forward to protect their privileged position were as follows and they may be of some interest from the perspective of today.

1. The cultural argument (i.e. fixed prices protect the ability of publishers to publish low-run up-market fiction).
2. The abolition of fixed retail prices could possibly give lower book prices, but at the same time the number of bookshops would be reduced. This is undesirable from the point of view of the general public, if one accepts that books are a cultural medium.
3. It was considered that an eventual lowering of prices would not appreciably stimulate the desire to read.
4. The publisher would probably earn more if fixed prices were abolished.
5. Free competition exists in the production stage. Writers are freely able to choose their publishers and the different publishers can produce their books at different prices.

The most important aspect of the debate was, of course, the cultural argument, but in an investigation carried out in 1964 it was estimated that the hard-to-sell, yet available, serious Swedish fiction accounted for 1–2 per cent of the total turnover, the same estimate arrived at in the report of the State Commission of 1968 (L68).

The publishers' sense of security in their own narrow world is also reflected in the fact that they showed no interest in compromise nor in changing their attitude. This leaves, as one of the investigators remarked, a 'completely static impression' during the years

85

between 1953 and 1965. The result was that the Government decided in 1965 that free retail prices were to be permitted from 1 April 1970.

Even though the abolition of the net book agreement was regarded as a severe blow to the trade, it was not taken as a reason for analysis or discourse on the underlying problems. It was not until 1968 that a general debate began on the possibility of a serious crisis occurring.

The development curve shown in Table 1 shows clearly a stagnation in sales from all books except school books during the whole of the 1960s, at a time when the price of books had risen sharply. While the consumer price index had doubled during the years between 1954 and 1971, the price of serious literature had increased threefold and prevailing prices rose more than did the prices of both cinema and theatre tickets. Unfortunately there are no separate statistics for school books and other books for 1955. However, if we use the ratio 1:2 that prevailed during the latter part of the 50s, we find that 'other books' sold for approximately 47 million kronor, and if we estimate a rise in prices of 130 per cent we arrive at the sum of approximately 110 million kronor. The sale of 'other books' totalled 108.6 million kronor at current prices, that is to say, that although this was looked on as a positive development, in actual fact the sale of books was somewhat reduced.

This trend was strengthened near the end of the 60s. The Government-sponsored investigation into the state of literature in 1968 (L68) estimated that the sale of general books by all the members of the Swedish Publishers' Association increased by only 22 million kronor between 1966 and 1970. This was 2.6 per cent per year, or 13 per cent for the whole period, which here too is approximately equivalent to the increase in prices during the period, with this difference: that both the rise in prices and the increase in turnover are considerably lower. The regular serious fiction *decreased* its share of total sales from 15.5 per cent to 13.2 per cent—and we know that the mass-market publishers' sales of popular fiction and romances increased during this period.[1]

Another factor that should have been recognized as a serious warning was that the number of titles published increased sharply during this period. In 1956 the total number of titles issued was 4,492 and in 1970 there were 7,709, an increase of almost 70 per cent. If the increase in turnover is entirely due to increased prices and not to a rise in volume, and the number of titles issued has increased by 70 per cent, this means a comparable lowering of the average size of the editions of the books published by an equal

TABLE I. *Sales to bookshops at prevailing prices from publisher members of the Swedish Publishers' Association. (Net prices, returns not deducted. Figures below in thousands of kronor.)*

Year	School	Others	Total
1955			70,076
1956			74,787
1957			84,090
1958	28,213	55,707	83,920
1959	30,203	59,088	89,292
1960	32,472	58,471	100,943
1961	37,266	68,244	105,511
1962	43,357	74,527	117,884
1963	53,072	83,325	136,398
1964	59,741	85,727	145,469
1965	64,027	97,848	161,876
1966	78,317	101,014	179,331
1967	96,143	108,685	204,828
1968	109,511	116,316	225,828
1969	117,533	116,974	234,507
1970	115,574	119,077	234,782
1971	125,136	123,560	248,696
1972	—	107,010*	—
1973	—	118,300	—
1974	—	113,500	—

* From this year deliveries through bookshops to the library book-binding service were discontinued. The value of this was 28 million kronor in 1970.

amount: 70 per cent. (Certain adjustments must be made because the cheap mass-market books are included in the number of titles.) Even if the publishers had not analysed the situation in this way they must have been aware of a fall in profits per published title, since one of the basic tenets is: the larger the edition the greater the profits. In fact, it would seem that they increased their output and raised their prices in order to compensate for an otherwise inevitable reduction of turnover and threatening losses. With this the vicious circle closed.

Serious fiction suffered particularly since the number of titles did not increase after 1964—the main increase was in non-fiction. While the number of titles published which could be described as *belles-lettres*, was 945 in 1965, the figure for 1970 was 805 and only 704 in 1972. This reduction was divided between from 5 to 10 per cent for the original Swedish titles and 30 per cent for translations. This decline is also reflected in a growing unwillingness to publish new writers. In 1965–6 the number of new authors published was 158; six years later there were only 118.

Publication of classics, another culturally valuable field, was also reduced. The investigators found that the study had, 'with great clarity, documented the serious shortage that exists in the availability of both Swedish and foreign classics. This does not apply only to ancient classics, but also to works, generally acknowledged to be classics, from the twentieth century.' No statistics concerning the changes during the 60s were presented, but the investigators write: 'What is especially ominous, however, is the development that began in the latter half of the 60s but did not reach its full force until 1970–1 when it began to affect inventories and the issuing of editions of the classics.' It was pointed out that in 1970 and 1971 alone, the number of available titles had declined by approximately 100, but even more important, that between 1971 and 1972, through bargain sales, no less than a third of the titles had disappeared from the catalogue covering books in print. It was also pointed out that practically all the series of classics, both Swedish and foreign, had been discontinued.

At the same time as all forms of serious fiction and poetry suffered from a reduction in publication and sales there was a sharp increase in the publication of technical and other non-fiction books. There was a total increase of 70 per cent in the number of titles issued between 1956 and 1971. During this period fiction (novels, poetry, drama) increased by only 38 per cent while the number of non-fiction books, including school books, increased by 90 per cent. Fiction's share of the total books published had already declined from the period between 1941 and 1945, when it was greatest at 29.5 per cent, to 18.3 per cent in 1969.

The difficulties in the business have centred on the ambitious literary publishers whose sales have been predominantly through bookshops. This is shown clearly in one of the investigations in the L68 studies. Thirteen publishing companies were included in the investigation and in 1966 these thirteen together accounted for half of the total financial turnover of books in the country. They were also responsible for 90 per cent of the serious fiction sold through bookshops, 60 per cent of the non-fiction books and 70 per cent of the children's books. It was shown in the investigation that almost half the serious fiction published was printed in editions of less than

3,000 copies and that despite these small editions, 50 per cent of these books sold less than 1,000 copies. Of the slightly more than 1,000 titles published only twenty-five of these were printed in editions of more than 25,000 copies, and although these represented a mere 2.4 per cent of the total number of titles, they accounted for 17.4 per cent of the total number of books printed.

These figures show that a very small number of books financed the major share of the costs of publishing all the books, and also that it could not have been very rewarding to be a publisher under such circumstances. The investigation also concluded that during the period 1965–70 the thirteen publishing companies together were run at a loss of approximately 1.5 per cent of the total turnover. And these losses were incurred despite the fact that the 60s were generally regarded as a time of expansion and profit 'during which, for most of the period, publishers pursued an optimistic publishing policy'. The investigation of profitability for the years 1968–9 and 1970 showed that 'the total business results for the thirteen companies had deteriorated badly during this period.' And although 1968 showed a gross profit of 5.2 million kronor, losses for 1970 amounted to 4.5 million kronor.

The sharp increases in book prices not only helped to conceal this negative development but also contributed to the decline in sales. During the 60s people began to complain more and more that books were too expensive. (An editorial in a leading newspaper in 1968 warned that with the current rise in prices there would be 'a paperback market with ordinary hardcover prices and a luxury market with hardcover books at luxury prices'.) This was emphatically denied by virtually every representative of the trade. What is obvious, however, is that some time during the 50s the price of books rose to the level where they were more often bought as gifts for other people than for the purchaser's own use.

Sweden has led the way in the raising of book prices. Not only did prices rise more quickly than those for consumer goods, but during the 60s book prices in Sweden became the highest in the world. This too should have worried publishers, but it made no more impression than the argument that books had become luxury articles. The comparative prices in Table 2 provide a graphic example of the level of prices. One should keep in mind, certainly, the varying burden of VAT, where Sweden leads with 17.5 per cent and Britain is exempted. This, of course, is of little interest to the customer.

If this development seems dismal for 'traditional' publishers, the

TABLE 2. *Book prices in four countries, 1971*

	Sweden	Finland	England	West Germany
Baldwin: *Tell Me How Long the Train's Been Gone*	51	31	22	38
Charrière: *Papillon*	62	27	22	36
Heyerdahl: *Ra*	60	32	44	39
Knef: *The Gift Horse*	46	31	28	39
Puzo: *The Godfather*	56	25	22	38
Rattray Taylor: *The Doomsday Book*	60	27	26	33
Segal: *Love Story*	29	15	16	26

The prices are in Swedish kronor (£1 = Skr 7.80) and are for hard-covers. VAT is included with 11 per cent for Finland, 17.65 per cent for Sweden and 5.5 per cent for West Germany.

situation is quite different for so-called mass-market publishers or other special publishing businesses. The increase in sales between 1966 and 1970 amounted to a total of 6 per cent per year, of which the share for members of the Swedish Publishers' Association was 2.6 per cent (see p 86). At the same time 'other publishers' (those who publish mostly news-stand literature or sell books by instalment) increased their sales by 20 per cent per year, or 41 million kronor, during the period 1966 to 1970. This result is reflected too in the fact that the eight largest publishers, six of which are members of the Swedish Publishers' Association, together experienced a reduction in their share of the market, from 63 to 55 per cent in 1970.

The categories of literature that increased most during the latter part of the 60s were cheap hardcover and mass-market books. They have shown an increase in sales of no less than 50 per cent in five years. 'Popular' literature (romances, westerns, and crime books) had increased its share of the total number of fictional books published during the period 1965 to 1972 from 33 to 43 per cent. Sales of cheap hardcover books, mainly through book clubs, showed an increase of approximately 23 million kronor.

In 1966 the sales of ordinary serious fiction were about the same as cheap hardcover books: approximately 40.5 and 43 million kronor respectively. By 1970 the sale of ordinary fiction had risen insignificantly to 43 million kronor, while cheap hardcover books showed a turnover of 66 million. As I mentioned above (p. 87), the publication of Swedish literary books has declined sharply and translations even more so. In the L68 investigation it was estimated that the number of titles issued by the five largest 'quality publishers' had declined during the latter half of the 60s from 1,500 to 1,115, whereas the number of titles isued by the mass-market publishers had risen from 974 to 1,235. B. Wahlström, the largest of the mass-market publishers, has passed Bonniers as the leading publisher of fiction, and Wennerbergs, the second largest of the mass-market publishers is in third place ahead of Norstedts. The situation is demonstrated vividly if one considers that Bonniers issued 352 fiction titles in 1965 and only 199 in 1972, or slightly more than half as many. The figures for B. Wahlström are reversed, from 170 to 341 titles. We can infer from the rising turnover that B. Wahlström has not merely survied the economic doldrums at the end of the 60s but has also enjoyed large profits. In 1958 it was still a relatively small company, best known for its inexpensive children's books. It had at the time a turnover of almost 6 million kronor, which slowly increased to 8 million by 1963. Then, during the years of the publishing crisis, its turnover increased to 12 million kronor in 1968, 15.6 million in 1970, and 20 million in 1972. It is safe to assume that this company's turnover for 1974 was at least 30 million kronor.

In the L68 investigation the radical restructuring of Swedish publishing that is now taking place is summed up as follows:

> It is obvious that the tendencies toward cutting down and restructuring of book publication by the leading 'quality publishers', which can easily be traced during the period 1965–70, has increased in intensity over the last two years. It is impossible to judge from the information available to what extent this has influenced the publication of quality literature. But it is a development that must be regarded as most regrettable, if, as seems likely, these publishers are concentrating to a much greater extent on 'entertainment' literature and established authors, and less on new young Swedish writers and the translation of serious foreign literature.

6

Perspective from Abroad

In general terms the Swedish publishing crisis has not attracted much comment abroad. The reason for this is probably that it has wrongly been considered a local phenomenon and of no particular interest as regards international publishing conditions, but quite clearly a similar crisis is developing in other western countries. In Denmark for instance, figures show that there is a growing stagnation in the sale of books and in fact it is just the 'bookshop sales' that have suffered.[1] The Danish bookshops sell approximately 15 million books a year, if we exclude school books, a figure that is exactly equivalent to the rapidly expanding book sales through book clubs and news-stands, 11 million and 4 million volumes respectively. The sharply rising turnover curve for books indicates price increases that are even greater than those in Sweden. Between 1954 and 1971, the turnover in books at current prices increased 500 per cent—600 per cent if we include VAT—while sales at fixed prices only increased by 100 per cent. Also, these increases occurred at the beginning of the 60s, while from 1967 turnover has levelled off. Indeed, the total number of titles issued declined by 5 per cent in 1973. It seems likely that a real decline in the value of sales can be expected in the coming years.

Just as in Sweden, representatives for the trade retain a narrow view of the problem that is marked by fear of outside competition. Hans Hertel shows that there is a dangerous concentration in the trade, especially in the publication of fiction. During the 60s between twenty and twenty-five publishing companies closed down entirely or ceased publication of serious Danish literature, since it was no longer profitable. Of Denmark's eighty established publishers only six publish serious fiction, even though one or two small companies publish some experimental literature. Primarily, the publication of serious Danish literature is concentrated in one company, Dansk Gyldendal. Of the 350 new titles and booklets issued annually in the country, 90 per cent are published by this company.[2]

The trend in Denmark is in fact the same as the trend in Sweden: fewer and fewer books carry the whole burden of sales. Only eleven books of all the serious fiction published by Gyldendal in 1970 were printed in editions of more than 5,000 copies. Only ten non-fiction books were printed in editions of between 5,000 and 10,000 copies. Of the translated books (Gyldendal does not dominate this field to the same extent) only three were printed in editions of 15,000–20,000 copies and these were entertainment novels: two books by Alistair Maclean and Segal's *Love Story*. Two more were issued in editions of 6,000–9,000, from a total of fifty-six translated novels published. Equally, an investigation into Danish reading habits revealed that half of all the Danish books read were written by ten authors, although they represented only 4 per cent of all the authors mentioned in the questionnaire.

When it came to translations, 2 per cent (ten authors) wrote 25 per cent of all the books read. Hertel summarizes to show how the book market is changing very rapidly to a mass market:

> Attention is very quickly focused on a few big names. The tendency is even greater in regard to book-club and other cheap editions; both types are based on the idea: lucrative mass production of books that everyone is talking about. . . . It is also the demand for profits that makes it difficult to market the various series of classics, and backlist sales are too slow (editions in stock are often destroyed because warehouse space has become too expensive). And with this, the older works disappear out of bookshops—and out of mind.
>
> This tendency is also strengthened by the potential of the mass media to reach a mass audience, a tendency that spreads from the commercial distribution of literature to the whole literary system (here again, a self-perpetuating mechanism). Then too, the literary material in the daily newspapers is restricted to the big names (often from the big publishing companies) that are to be reviewed for the day and greatly praised—everyone expects this—and which (almost) sell themselves by their trade mark ('Have you read the latest novel by X?'), while lesser writers (from small publishing houses) have by comparison considerably smaller chances. (Once again there is the tendency for mass communication to fortify the existing situation and attitudes. . . .)[3]

In Norway it is believed that there is no crisis. The Chairman of the Norwegian Publishers' Association and head of Gyldendal, the leading publishing house, maintains, in a comparison between the situation in Sweden and Norway, that publishers are careful not to overproduce and that the book trade is protected through freedom from VAT and the official buying rule: the State buys 1,000 copies of every new Norwegian novel published. The net book agreement and the commission system, which obliges 400 bookshops to keep all new literature in their stocks for three years, are additional guarantees. Gyldendal is losing money on fiction and most books sold through bookshops. Dictionaries and collected works are the main part of their turnover and this business is absolutely essential to the company's finances and makes it possible to publish general literature.

According to trade statistics bookshops accounted for only 48 per cent of the total book sales in Norway in 1971. Instalment buying and mail-order sales are large and profitable and are probably the main reason Norway has so far avoided a crisis in the trade. (The main Norwegian book club is the largest in Scandinavia, with over 200,000 members, and it is owned and run just by the 'literary' publishers.) As in Sweden, it is the publishers who are not members of the Publishers' Association—non-literary companies—which are expanding most. They had 45 per cent of the market in 1971. Sales for members of the Publishers' Association through bookshops declined from 87.2 per cent in 1964 to 63 per cent in 1972.

Although Norwegians spend more *per capita* on books than any other people in the world—150 kronor per year compared with 115 and 75 in Denmark and Sweden respectively—the publication of serious fiction is declining there too. The average edition of a Norwegian novel has declined from a high of 4,900 copies to 4,100, and printings of translations have also been slightly reduced. Turnover in real prices for this type of literature has diminished too. There has been a certain stagnation in the total business for member publishers of the Norwegian Publishers' Association, from 177.5 million kronor in 1972 to 174.8 million in 1973.

The situation in Finland is similar to that of Norway, where as yet no crisis has occurred. The publishing business is flourishing. It should be observed that for the past few years there have been no fixed prices for books, a change in the former net book agreement that has left no negative effects as far as the publication of serious fiction is concerned. In Finland too there has been an increase in the sale of books, outside the bookshops. The various Finnish book clubs have built up a membership within a few years of over 300,000 members. Instalment sales of books have increased from 22 per cent of the total turnover in 1963 to 26 per cent in 1972. Both these selling methods are considered very profitable. It would seem that even in Finland the successful finances of the larger 'literary' publishers have been based on sales outside the bookshops and that the publishing of serious fiction actually entails financial losses.

Although Sweden would appear to lead the way in the changes occurring in the book market, the tendency is in fact uniform, throughout the whole of Western Europe. Comparisons in depth lie outside the scope of this work, but it may be of interest to glance briefly at the situation in Germany, where a few years ago spokesmen for the trade formed a 'committee for research in the book market', in an attempt to gain some idea of future development. In a study of the economic development, the author shows that the belief in a thriving book market is as unrealistic in Germany as it is in Scandinavia.[4] And although turnover is high at the moment, it is growing at a slower rate than other forms of recreation. Up to 1966 book purchases were greater proportionately than overall private consumption, but now the situation is reversed. The area of the book market that is developing most rapidly is the educational sector. This has occurred at the expense of what is appropriately called 'the voluntary book'.

The German book trade, which once provided the prototype for the western commission system, is also operating under ever increasing difficulties. Average net profits have fallen from 3.4 per cent in 1960 to 0.2 per cent in 1973. It has been estimated that no fewer than 4,000 of the country's bookshops are run at a loss and are threatened with closure. In Germany a publishing crisis, or book crisis, is being openly discussed, despite the fact that the number of books issued has increased by approximately 2,000 titles per year. In 1951 14,000 titles were issued; in 1973 this figure had risen to over 36,000. The reality behind these figures is that fewer and fewer new editions of previous titles have been issued and that 85 per cent are entirely new, also that the majority of these are technical and other non-fiction books, issued at the expense of serious fiction. The percentage of fictional books issued has not actually decreased, but there is reason to believe that, as in Sweden, there is more popular fiction being published and fewer serious novels.

A sociological survey of reading habits in Germany shows that the position of the book has not developed at the same pace as the rest of the society, that is to say that reading, especially of serious fiction, has declined.[5] Despite the greater amount of time Germans devote to the 'media'—TV, radio, newspapers and books—the time for reading books has declined from 13 per cent in 1967 to 9 per cent in 1973. People were asked in the survey whether they would like to own more books if they could afford them and had room for them.

Forty-one per cent said that they had no wish to own books even under these circumstances—against 37 per cent in 1967. To be well-read had very little social status. It came low on the list of desirable attributes, behind being good company, being in good physical condition, and political interests.

There has also been talk in France about a book crisis, and the government has sponsored a study to 'ensure that the book will survive'. Economic demands have meant that the variety of books has been reduced and the position of books in society is threatened. It is particularly the classics, humanities and aesthetics that have been most affected, for instance, De Noël-Gonthier's series Méditations, and Garnier's Classics.

Instead, the sale of books by instalment and through book clubs has greatly increased: it has been estimated that in future 50 per cent of all books will be sold in this way in France.[6]

Two studies of the reading habits of the young have been made recently in Britain, and these too paint a pessimistic picture.[7] A comparison between these studies and similar ones made in 1940 show that the reading habit is now only half as common among children between the ages of ten and fifteen as it was then. Television is given much of the blame for this change. Sixty per cent of the children in this age group spent two hours per day in front of the television set, and 40 per cent more than three hours. The books that were read were mostly fiction, with the classics and especially Dickens predominating. The most serious aspect of these findings is that children lost their desire to read when they were fourteen or fifteen. Thirty-two per cent of the girls and 40 per cent of the boys were completely uninterested in books.

The Swedish and international publishing crisis did not occur suddenly. The figures presented here show clearly that the problems became increasingly severe after World War II, but that publishers and booksellers not only tried to ignore them but also tried to avoid all changes away from the traditional trade in books. Fixed prices and the commission system were regarded by all as the central issue, and necessary to a high standard and broad variety of books. This opinion was shared by writers, booksellers, and publishers. Independent of political or ideological persuasion, they adhered to an almost 150-year-old system and tended toward traditionally conservative views. They hoped to sustain a system of price protection, monopolies and limits on the establishment of new booksellers, all in the name of 'the cultural argument'. This is as true of Sweden as of other Western European countries. In Britain the struggle for 'the net book agreement' has been carried on with considerable energy, and in April 1974 in France 850 authors appealed to the Government with a suggestion for fixed book prices, in an effort to counteract the signs of a crisis that are beginning to appear in the French book trade.

It is obvious that the problems in the book trade are not unique to Sweden, but rather are more or less the same throughout the whole western world. To find an explanation for this development it is necessary to have a good idea about the ways society and the people who make it up have changed since the modern book market was created 150 years ago. We must learn what sort of a society we live in today and how it will look in the immediate future. It is a generally accepted fact that the economic and social development in society influences completely the pattern of our lives, in so far as our material environment is concerned. Oddly enough the same assumption is not regarded as self-evident when it comes to our consumption of culture. Obviously we cannot isolate our interest in culture and our patterns of consumption of it from other social phenomena. Our way of living, our views on the family and on our leisure time, our work patterns and value judgements—all these things have a decisive influence on the whole cultural development, and not least on the writing, production, distribution and consumption of books.

Unlike many other cultural products, books also have the marked character of 'goods'. The relatively simple process by which they could be reproduced meant that during the nineteenth century they became an economic factor around which an important trade and industry was built. In this way the book entered the economic system and in turn became dependent upon it. Despite this fact, during debates on the subject, there has often been a refusal to see the production and distribution of books as a part of the whole social development—rather, they have been treated as an isolated cultural product. Marxist writer Lucien Goldmann provides an exception to this rule; he writes: 'A book or a film is primarily a product among other products. As such it belongs to a sector of capitalist production that can only survive on condition that it is lucrative, brings a profit.'[8]

To understand the variable function of the book in society we must, though, investigate how society itself changes.

7

The Mass or Service Society

Current political and ideological debate is based to a large extent on the premise that we still live in a class-stratified society created by industrialism, which is marked primarily by the conflict between the bourgeoisie and working class. More and more social studies, however, point to changes in the economic and social realities and values which in turn transform the social and ideological pattern of the industrial state.

American sociologist Daniel Bell has coined the term 'The Post-Industrial Society' and maintains the theory that western society is going through a period of great historical change, not least perhaps in its social structure.[1] The reason for these changes is primarily the huge strides made in recent years in science and technology. One could say then that the industrial society has become a society of information and knowledge. One result of this is that technocrats have gained greater power even in the political process and that intellectual work has become more subject to bureaucracy, at the expense of culture and free research. Development points more in the direction of a new working class—or service class—composed of all those who work for a wage. This trend is reflected in the fact that white-collar workers in the USA in 1956 were equal to the number of industrial workers, but by 1970 there were 20 per cent more white-collar workers. Company owners who are very powerful during working hours no longer automatically exert influence outside the firm. Another sociologist, Ralf Dahrendorf, claims that the important thing in our society is not ownership but influence. This indicates a change in the connection between economics and politics and thereby also in the singular conflict between the bourgeoisie and the proletariat. He therefore introduces the term 'Service-Class Society', a term more suitable to the social pattern in industrial countries.[2]

André Gorz, a well-known Marxist writer, also points out how everyone who works for a fixed wage is in the same situation as the industrial worker, whether he is a technician, engineer, academic or researcher. There is no longer any place for devoted handicraft, creative work or long-term research. The owners of capital govern their lives in any case. There is a need to struggle for a 'meaningful existence', which Gorz interprets as a struggle against the capitalists. The nationalization of the means of production involves only an increase in bureaucratization; instead we should create decentralized, independent democratic institutions. Those who are occupied in doing creative work today are in the same situation as industrial workers were earlier, and they are similarly exploited:

> Industry in the last century took from the countryside men who were muscles, lungs, stomach: their muscles missed the open spaces, their lungs the fresh air, their stomachs fresh food; their health declined, and the acuteness of their need was but the empty functioning of their organs in a hostile surrounding world. The industry of the second half of the twentieth century increasingly tends to take men from the universities and colleges, men who have been able to acquire the ability to do creative or independent work; who have curiosity, the ability to synthesize, to analyze, to invent, and to assimilate, an ability which spins in a vacuum and runs the risk of perishing for lack of an opportunity to be usefully put to work.[3]

George Lichtheim, whom Bell also quotes, maintains that contemporary industrial society is increasingly 'post-bourgeoisie', which is the result of a disintegration of the nineteenth-century class structure. 'Least of all does it follow that industrial society retains a "bourgeois" complexion. There cannot be a bourgeoisie without a proletariat, and if the one is fading out, so is the other, and for the same reason: Modern industrial society does not require either for its operation.'

Bell points out that Marx, in the third part of *Das Kapital*, changed his view of capital as a 'pure' concept. The appearance of large merchant banks and corporations influenced this change of attitude. He saw that it would not be the owners of capital but rather the industrial leaders who would achieve power, which would lead eventually to an increase in office workers and administrative staff. These workers, according to Marx, would become members of the proletariat. Similar thoughts have been expressed recently by economists such as J. K. Galbraith, who introduced the term 'technostructure', meaning that it is the heads of companies who exercise control and not the investors. This means also that there is a single-minded interest in growth, apart from whether it is meaningful or not.[4]

Herbert Marcuse has also noted the changing of the class-society.[5]

Instead of freeing man from toil and subjugation, the rapid, dominant technological development would seem to have prevented every social change that could give us 'a new humane way of life'. Marcuse writes:

> At its origins in the first half of the nineteenth century, when it elaborated the first concepts of the alternatives, the critique of industrial society attained concreteness in a historical mediation between theory and practice, values and facts, needs and goals. This historical mediation occurred in the consciousness and in the political action of the two great classes which faced each other in the society: the bourgeoisie and the proletariat. In the capitalist world, they are still the basic classes. However, the capitalist development has altered the structure and function of these two classes in such a way that they no longer appear to be agents of historical transformation. *An overriding interest in the preservation and improvement of the institutional status quo unites the former antagonists in the most advanced areas of contemporary society* [my italics].[6]

Current development is moving away from the production of goods toward services and the service society.* Unlike the agrarian and early industrial societies, it is no longer muscle power which is the decisive factor in our life situation, but rather knowledge and information. The important person in the service society is the specialist, the expert, or the professional. Values have changed then from those of the industrial society in which material wealth was the essential goal, to a service society where services and social benefits such as a health service, education and recreation are the important elements.

The service society becomes a group society rather than a society of individuals. People become increasingly dependent on, and a part of social institutions. David Riesman noted this as early as two decades ago. The changes in the society have meant that the individualist and pioneer, the 'inner-directed' man has been replaced by the 'other-directed' man, shaped by social conformity, the mass media and consumer needs.[7] The conflict between factory worker and capitalist has been replaced by cooperation between organizations that represent both categories, and by institutions of society and private corporations who also can be very close to each other.

* In the choice between various terms for distributing the 'new society' which is replacing the industrial society, I have had to choose between the three designations: post-industrial society, mass society and service society. I finally stuck with the latter two, which I feel are most adequate, particularly as a description of the Swedish variant. They illustrate both the social and the economic situation.

Statistics clearly show the change-over to a service society in the USA. At the turn of the century, three out of ten workers were employed in service occupations, while the remaining seven produced goods. In 1950 there were an equal number of workers employed in either category. In 1968 six out of ten were employed in services. It is estimated that by 1980 the ratio will be seven to three.[8]

The background to this development is the centralization and shifting of power in the western democracies. The power of governments, and especially leaders of governments, has increased at the expense of parliamentary assemblies; this is true in the USA, Britain, France, Germany and even Sweden. Decision-making is accomplished more and more by parliamentary committees, extra-parliamentary organizations and bureaucracies. A Swedish MP goes so far as to claim that 'the traditional system of parliamentary representation has in reality been abrogated in both the federal and municipal parliaments.' A study was made in West Germany of the legislation passed by the German Parliament over a period of two sessions. It was found that the number of laws passed in Parliament had fallen by half, whereas ordinances imposed through the bureaucracy, which in practice had the effect of laws, were on the increase. The rapid rise of public administration is another indication of the power shift. New civil service departments and state institutions are growing up in all these countries.

It is knowledge and not possessions that brings success in the service society. Therefore a new upper class has arisen, often called the meritocracy. As a result of this society is increasingly divided into two segments: the elite—and the rest of the people. Education, which was the great dream of industrial society, is in principle available to all people today in the more advanced countries. Radical thinkers such as Ivan Illich, Niels Christie, John Holt, and Paolo Freire have come to regard it more as a threat in its present form, where school is used not only to provide knowledge but also to manipulate and standardize the students. This is true not only of the schools in the West but also in the Soviet Union, where enrolment in the best high schools and universities is open, first of all, to the children of the new upper class. This one-sided concentration of knowledge has then a negative effect in that it fortifies the prevailing injustices within the society.

There is less and less scope for the type of culture that is not included in the training for a specific profession and cannot be put to some practical use. Bureaucracy and technocracy do not promote cultural activities. Bourgeois society was built round religion and

Christian morality, and the Bible represented a central source not only of moral rectitude but also of culture; these have not been replaced by anything comparable in our time.

One can also point to the accelerating rate of development in regard to knowledge and communications and growth of the population, changing ever more rapidly the world in which we live. A few examples will provide the proper perspective: 90 per cent of all the scientists who have ever lived are still active within their fields today. As late as 1920 most scientists were convinced that the universe consisted only of the Milky Way: within the last ten years we have learned that our galaxy is only one of millions or possibly billions of similar galaxies. The dimensions of our existence change even on our own planet. Between 1965 and the year 2000 the world's population is expected to double. Just 150 years ago the vast majority of people lived in the country; today a major portion of the population of the western world lives in cities. We are more mobile than ever before, which allows us to know more people. Earlier, people knew only a few friends, their relatives, and neighbours; today we have thousands of acquaintances and know still more people through the mass media. Bell is correct in underlining the fact that this acceleration is occurring not only on a technological and demographic plane but also on a political level. The service society implies the availability of social, human, and political rights offered by a democratic society for a large number of people. These rights carry with them decisive changes of attitude, social ties, and of responsibilities, for instance, in marriage, sexual patterns, and family life.

The American journalist and sociologist, Alvin Toffler, has also noted the rising rate of change and its consequences for the society:

> For we have not merely extended the scope and scale of change, we have radically altered its pace. We have in our time released a totally new social force—a stream of change so accelerated that it influences our sense of time, revolutionizes the tempo of daily life, and affects the very way we 'feel' the world around us. We no longer 'feel' life as men did in the past. And this is the ultimate difference, the distinction that separates the truly contemporary man from all others. For his acceleration lies behind the impermanence—the transience—that penetrates and tinctures our consciousness, radically affecting the way we relate to other people, to things, to the entire universe of ideas, art and values.[9]

This accelerating pace causes, of course, great changes in people's life-style. Family life is disturbed in order to allow for the increased mobility our times require. Urbanization was the first step toward the dissolution of the agrarian three-generation family, and soon the so-called nuclear family was formed, 'a stripped-down, portable family unit' as Toffler calls it. Sociologist William Goode has described how 'the pair-family and the industrial system' suit each other. 'Geographic mobility' and 'social mobility' are favoured by the nuclear family. What is meant by this is that 'the well-endowed individual can advance socially without regard to family-ties', as a Swedish sociologist puts it. The service society requires even greater mobility. Unmarried, childless couples who live together are becoming more and more common. This is not because of a more tolerant moral attitude, but because the dissolution of the traditional family increases the economic growth rate. In Sweden the Trade Union Organization has enthusiastically supported the idea of 'a mobile work force'. In the USA, where there is no housing shortage to inhibit people from moving, 36.6 million move during a single year, approximately 15 per cent of the population. Even in Britain almost 11 per cent of the population move each year, and in France the figures are about the same.

Another important aspect of the life of modern man is, of course, the influence of the mass media. Only ten years ago the mass media were regarded as one of the great potentials for increasing people's knowledge and education, but now more and more researchers are pointing out the negative effects of the continual bombardment of words, pictures, and impressions. In an essay, with the significant title 'Over-Stimulation—A Threat to Our Quality of Existence', a Swedish psychologist warns of the negative physiological and psychological effects that an overflow of impressions can have upon us. She notes that despite our technologically advanced environment we have failed to study its negative effects. Over-stimulation implies quite simply that 'the impressions flowing in are beyond the recipient's ability to absorb'.

Certainly people have great adaptive ability, but the growing symptoms of stress, for instance, indicate that many of us are approaching the limits of this ability. The fact remains, man has a limited capacity to absorb and make use of information, 'a cognitive saturation', which also includes a reduced ability to make decisions when there is an overabundance of information upon which decisions are to be based. The most serious effects of over-stimulation, however, are probably the emotional repercussions. If people are pushed beyond their tolerance threshold, an habituation effect occurs,

which is the most effective way man has of defending himself against over-stimulation. When we are bombarded by too many, too strong or too repetitious impressions the nervous system reacts more faintly. Stimuli lose their penetrating effect and reactions are toned down. The physiological stress effects diminish in intensity and feelings of pleasure and displeasure subside. But at the same time there is a decline in feelings such as commitment, sharing, consideration and sympathy. This attrition of feeling comes furtively—without warning —since in the actual habituation process there is a certain blunting effect, a diminishing of the sensitivity and reflexes. *Overstimulation can, therefore, be a pathway toward a general passivity* [my italics].[10]

We all know that the influence of various media is increasing: there is innocuous constant music in shops, lifts and offices; the TV is turned on virtually all the time during our leisure hours and many people have more than one radio in their homes, as well as two or more gramophones; and greater numbers of people are finding it desirable to have an extra television set for the children, or for the summer cottage. Recently an advertisement appeared in the daily papers in Sweden in which a firm offered two TV sets for sale in a package deal—one large and one small. The motivation was as follows:

> Our 34 inches of screen comprise two practical sets: one 14-inch screen and an additional 20-inch screen. You will have excellent colour reception wherever you are.... You may watch Channel 1* whilst other members of the family watch Channel 2. You can take one set to your summer home.... The most sensible method of viewing colour television is to have two sets.[11]

We also know that the mass media, in the industrialized countries of the West, occupy a greater part of people's free time than any other activity. It has also been said, and not wholly unrealistically, that the hold of the mass media over Western man can be likened to a 'second industrialization'. Not only is his external environment affected, but also his inner psyche.[12] In the USA, the most advanced country in mass media output, it has been estimated that an adult person devotes 52 minutes per day to reading the newspapers. This together with advertising, signs, instructions and so on, amounts to between 10,000 and 20,000 words a day. Listening to the radio for a little more than an hour each day accounts for approximately another 11,000 words, and a few hours viewing television, aside from the plethora of images, another 10,000. The average American is subjected to 560 advertising messages per day; of these, however, he is only able to absorb 76. Even the tempo of classical music has increased. Studies have shown that Bach, Haydn and Mozart are

* There are only two television channels in Sweden.

played at a faster tempo by contemporary musicians than they were when the music was composed.[13] An important point in conjunction with this problem is how leisure time has developed in our society. The concept of free time is part of industrialism. Primitive peoples have no awareness of a separation between working hours and leisure hours, and a division of time in the agrarian society was created in accordance with the rhythm of day and night and the seasons. Industrialism brought about a new consciousness of the importance of time. A small number of people employed a large number of wage earners whose labour was measured in time, and paid for accordingly. Time acquired an economic value. (The maxim, time is money, is said to have been coined by Benjamin Franklin in 1748, in reference to the growing industrialism in England at that time.) The ultimate consequences of the economic importance of time is the industrial time study and the time clock, which have now been installed in offices as well as factory.

With the advent of specific working hours, the remainder of the day, or free time, became sharply demarcated from the work period. Among other things, it had the effect of separating culture and working life for all time. But leisure was not the same as free time. Rather than use the leisure hours to relax, this time too came to have a great economic potential, partly for the individual and partly for a whole new industry: the recreation industry. For the individual, the concentration of work to a particular time of the day meant that all other activities must be fitted in during free time— most meals, intercourse with friends and family, repairs to home, sports and so on. On top of this, people were under increasing pressure from the recreation industry to buy as many of its products as possible. This in turn required more money, and therefore it became necessary, paradoxically, for more and more people to seek extra work during their free time. It has been estimated that the work week has diminished by 31 hours since 1850, but that this increased free time has not given people any extra leisure time at all.[14] This extra work-free time has been eroded by long journeys, more work with children and in the home, greater distances from work and shopping areas, queues, waiting time and so on.

It is not just the free time people have that can be put to economic use, even the shortage of time can be utilized in various ways. A typical example of how the shortage of time can be exploited is this advertisement for a chain of hamburger restaurants, placed in a daily paper:

Our trade has been on the upswing in the past few years.... That business is good is due partly to our own efforts and partly to market development. There is a growing need for our services and what we sell. More and more people are eating their meals outside their homes. More and more people are taking pre-cooked meals home with them. Why? Because we live in a time-poor country with a high standard of living.

The mass society directs even our free time from a social point of view. A Swedish researcher, a specialist in occupational medicine, in a contribution to a study expresses society's interest in the free time of its citizens in this rather brutal fashion:

Free time can be said to have three main functions on the individual level, namely, to provide recreation, entertainment, and to stimulate personal development through a variety of social and cultural activities. *From a more general point of view one could say that free time makes possible the consumer role and facilitates the integration of the individual within society* [my italics].

Certainly modern western society has increased production, and with it the welfare of society and the individual, but at the same time increased centralization and bureaucratization have de-individualized man and made him passive. Both employer and trade-union organizations are agreed that boring mechanical work must be compensated with increased incomes and more free time. The same researcher, Dr. Bertil Gardell, comments:

It is during man's leisure that self-fulfilment and social integration shall take place. I believe this line of thought to be false.

To what extent is the intended content of free time satisfactory to various wage earners? Is it so that those who have the worst jobs are the people who can best compensate for this with an active and socially rich leisure life?

No, on the contrary. All experience shows that those people who have the most interesting and satisfying work are the same people who have the most interesting and satisfying leisure time. We know that work with low qualification requirements gives a low quota of satisfaction and therefore a low measure of self-confidence, low general life-satisfaction and an increased number of nervous disorders, and that *all these things leave negative traces in the individual's free time . . . and this is especially true of cultural and intellectual activities which require active participation* [my italics].

In the industrial countries of the West welfare has been defined as the availability of goods. Priority is given to the consumption of goods that yield the greatest amount of economic growth. In modern society, consequently, free time should be used to achieve the greatest

possible consumption. It is during free time, according to the ideology of growth, that working man is able to spend his money.
It is well known that stimulation of consumption is one of the
primary methods used for improving a country's economy. The
economic forces direct consumption, through market influences, to
those goods which produce the highest profits. Consumption takes
time, and this contributes to the paradoxical effect that although we
have more free time we have less and less time to spare.

The consumption of culture has been shown by economist Staffan
Burenstam-Linder to belong definitely to those free time activities
which are economically unrewarding and therefore of little interest
generally for the countries that have the growth ideology as their
lodestar. This is true of all industrialized western countries, independent of their political orientation:

> The pleasure derived from time spent in developing the mind and
> spirit is in fact very little dependent on goods. For this reason, such
> pursuits will be most attractive when the general level of income is
> low—although above that of a paralysing poverty. As the average level
> of incomes continues to rise, new possibilities open up. Activities that
> are enhanced by a high goods intensity become increasingly attractive.
> Time will be reallocated in this direction. Only if there is a very strong
> successive increase in total consumption time can culture time also
> increase. Even if one might think that increased time would be needed
> in which to relax *from* consumption, increasing time will in fact be
> devoted to relaxation *for* consumption.
>
> Thus there is a great risk that culture is a pursuit with a negative
> income elasticity. The cultivation of the mind and spirit is quite simply
> an inferior activity.[15]

Another principle used to increase private consumption in growth
countries is to increase the density of goods available. This implies
that the consumer is encouraged to acquire as many products as
possible. This in turn means that he has less and less time to devote
to each new consumer product. Those who have a camera, fishing
equipment, a dog, boat, piano, gramophone, have, of course, less
time left to read books. The high consumption requirement is also
accompanied by an intolerance of 'inactivity' in our type of society,
other than the forced inactivity brought on by poverty or unemployment. The effect of this is that people in poor societies have plenty
of spare time, whereas we, with our increased free time, with an
eight-hour work day and five-day week, with a month's vacation,
have very little spare time—with a numbing of the sensibilities and
symptoms of stress as a result. Burenstam-Linder quotes Swedish

author Vilhelm Moberg, writing on his childhood to exemplify the intermediate state between poverty and riches which he calls 'cultures with time welfare':

> No one in my childhood was in a hurry. They did quite a lot of work, usually very hard work, but they never gave evidence of any haste. When I left this environment in due course and returned to the home of my parents on a visit, my father observed my nervous unrest and asked: 'Why in such a hurry, boy? You'll get to your grave in time, like everyone else.'[16]

Growth has been the economic foundation of western countries which hoped to increase their welfare as quickly as possible. Burenstam-Linder claims that *economic growth causes a general increase in the shortage of time*. He supports his theory with the belief that consumption takes time, and since we live in a society of great consumption we have less and less time. Indeed, the more rapid the tempo of growth the greater the increase in the demand for profit yields from time.

It is important to note that time considered as an economic factor affects the poorest people in the welfare society most. Urbanization, the dissolution of the family and specialization in society mean that tasks that could previously be performed in the home, such as looking after the children, doing the laundry, and making repairs, must now be carried out by other 'specialists' (who in turn are forced to hire labour for similar services—who looks after the children of the day-care worker?) This has been called an 'increased economization' of society. More and more of everything must be purchased, time included. It is obvious that cultural activities, under these conditions, are relatively unimportant to society and come very low on the scale of needs.

One of the most characteristic features of the service society is therefore that it is not conducive to the promotion of cultural interests, despite palpable improvements in the economic standard, increased education, and greater free time. Stress, hectic consumption during free time, the inability to relax, the diminished importance of home and family, the tiring enervating effects of the mass media and education for production are features of this society which run counter to the improvements that the idealists of industrialism had hoped for.

Nor has the changeover from bourgeois society to the service society meant that the bourgeois ideal of education for all has become a reality. On the contrary, this ideal has receded further into the background for all social classes.

8

Culture in the Mass Society

From time immemorial culture has been shaped by society. During medieval times it was an important facet of the power of the ruling classes. The increasingly magnificent cathedrals symbolized the greatness of the spiritual and temporal rulers and the submissiveness of the common people. During the Renaissance and the baroque period art and literature became the medium of social expression and the recreation of the aristocracy exclusively. The primary function of music and the theatre had become entertainment, and palaces were decorated with works of art for the aesthetic satisfaction they provided. The most successful artists, who had previously been anonymous craftsmen, now became famous men who worked mostly for princes. They were painters, architects, and sculptors such as Michelangelo, Leonardo da Vinci, Rubens or Bernini.

However, with the beginning of the eighteenth century, and even more so in the nineteenth, culture in Europe became the property of the new bourgeois class. Culture became *private*: books were printed in ever larger editions and found their way to private homes, whereas earlier they had been reserved for the libraries of palace and cloister. The same was true of paintings, which moved from the walls of churches and castles to the homes of industrial tycoons. Art was disseminated in the form of smaller canvases and lithographs so that it also suited the needs of the petty bourgeoisie. Music also changed to fit the requirements of a bourgeois audience. Liturgical music and concertos composed for the aristocracy were now replaced by chamber music and romantic songs appropriate to bourgeois salons.

In the homogeneous bourgeois society there was a clear choice of books, plays, musical compositions, and paintings. During the initial phase of the bourgeois world, up to the latter part of the nineteenth century, writers and artists were in complete harmony with their public—for example Walter Scott and Dickens, or Delacroix, Ingres and Constable. Then the most creative and daring artists began to turn against prevailing taste and their own public—or the bourgeois establishment rejected them. They became avant-gardists.

The period of avant-gardism extended largely from the 1890s to World War II, a period contemporaneous with the great era of the bourgeoisie and the beginning of its disintegration. This phenomenon can be interpreted from a social point of view: the more solidly established the bourgeoisie became, the more conservative its taste. And from an economic point of view: as art became more exploitable financially, the more it was controlled. This prompted writers, artists and composers to opposition, and they were strongly supported by the more radical factions within the bourgeoisie.

This created a tension through which art deepened, developed and assumed a commitment, despite the difficulties naturally encountered by the artists. It was the avant-gardism of the early part of this century that formed the nucleus of later development. The music of Stravinsky and Schönberg, the painting of Picasso and the cubists, the refashioning of literature by Joyce and Eliot, inspired a new generation of creative artists.

As late as the 1940s, books by writers such as D. H. Lawrence were persecuted, jazz was ridiculed as 'negro music', and the works of cubists and expressionists were laughed at. After the war opposition to new art forms became rarer—the last attacks were almost exclusively directed against permissive sexuality in art—and have virtually ceased now.

Mass culture has, to an ever greater degree, replaced bourgeois culture, and thus the situation of avant-gardism has changed.

Culture has spread enormously in the mass society, but simultaneously it has changed, influenced by the functions of the mass society. These functions are principally the new technological discoveries, the need for entertainment and relaxation and the growing centralization of society. This can be imposed for economic reasons: the bestseller market, million-dollar films, etc.—or for political reasons: censorship by right-wing dictatorships, state socialism, radio and television monopolies, and so on. Mass culture is formed by requirements of profitable mass production, standardization and bureaucratization. Culture is no longer dominated by creative individuals. 'Creativity tends to be transformed into production', writes French sociologist Edgar Morin, but he also maintains that this in itself is not necessarily a barrier to a high standard of artistic creativity. The potential of culture to reach as many people as possible certainly tends to give a flatness to the kind of culture offered, to industrialize entertainment, but at the same time carries with it a tolerance and willingness to accept virtually all new cultural forms. Whereas the cubists and *fauvistes* were ridiculed by the bourgeois public, Morin writes, an exhibition of the works of Salvador Dali can be a great success, and Jackson Pollock and the paintings of his group became expensive collector's items and museum exhibits only a few years after his début. But Morin ignores the fact that economic demand has a commercializing anti-artistic effect.

The mass society also gives the avant-gardist an entertainment value which renders him harmless and non-controversial. Marcuse maintains that in this way protest is made innocuous, protest which he calls 'the Great Refusal'.

> *The efforts to recapture the Great Refusal in the language of literature suffer the fate of being absorbed by what they refute.* As modern classics, the avant-garde and the beatniks share in the function of entertaining without endangering the good conscience of the men of good will. This absorption is justified by technical progress; the refusal is refuted by the alleviation of misery in the advanced industrial society. *The liquidation of high culture is a by-product of the conquest of nature, and of the progressing conquest of scarcity* [my italics].[1]

Daniel Bell also states that the tension between the permanent and the new, which existed in bourgeois society and was the basis of avant-gardism and experiment, has dissolved. 'There is no longer an avant-garde because no one in our post-modern culture is on the side of order or tradition. There exists only a desire for the new.'[2]

The entertainment function in mass culture has, of course, a positive value too, partly as relaxation and partly because it provides all people with an opportunity to appreciate culture. The old bourgeois society, claims Hannah Arendt, used culture for its own purposes and endowed it with social values. The social status attributed to culture excluded most classes within society. It is mere conceit to attack entertainment culture—upper-class fools who turn up their noses at entertainment are, in their hypocrisy and social snobbery, far more dangerous to real art than those who are entertained by mass culture. But at the same time, she warns that there is a definite danger since we live in a consumer society, and the demands of mass consumption controlled by economic factors can be ruinous to cultural development.[3]

As society influences man so the new mass culture shapes its public. 'Production creates consumption', as Marx formulated it. The struggle for increased equality between the sexes has its origins in the will to a greater freedom and tolerance, but it immediately suffers from various kinds of economic exploitation: the design of unisex clothes, family deodorants, and so on. The mass culture adheres to this economic pattern and creates products for everyone, indifferent to sex, age, education. The same book and film are familiar to all, newspapers must be as unspecialized as possible (daily papers, for instance, now contain an increasing amount of weekly magazine material), the same music is listened to by everybody and the same posters hang in all homes. The result, as an American sociologist sees it, can be that 'the social leveling belongs together with a standardization of taste and interests, which now finds its expression in the mass media, a standardization to which the mass media itself contributes.'[4]

The mass-media effect functions in such a way that the books, plays, films, or gramophone records which become hits are issued in larger editions, or have larger audiences, than ever before. On the other hand, the rate of change is increasingly rapid. It has been estimated, for instance, that the effective lifetime of a bestseller becomes ever briefer. In a comparative study of American bestsellers it was shown that in ten years the lifetime of a book on the bestseller lists has diminished by one-sixth.[5] As we have seen earlier, the lifetime of books generally has become much shorter, and classics, which more than other books are dependent on a long life, have, with a few exceptions, begun to disappear from the market.

There exists, parallel to the increasingly dominant mass culture, a more exclusive cultural form, often called high culture. This élite culture is defined differently in different circumstances, both positively and negatively. Occasionally what is meant is an art form created for a small coterie of specialists, while at other times it is the outer form of the product or event that is alluded to—a framed painting, an expensively bound book, attending a theatre première in a dinner jacket.

The conflict between mass culture and élite culture is one of the central problems in the changing of cultural patterns taking place in the mass society. This is further complicated by the fact that there is no clear contrasting relationship, but rather that mass culture, with its great economic resources and its tempting entertainment and re- laxation value, uses and simplifies the more exclusive art forms. Radical social analysts seek various methods of explanation and vin- dication but do not know how the ideal situation, the spread of authentic high-level culture to all people, can be achieved. Either the so-called entertainment value is defended as important, as with Hannah Arendt, or it is maintained that 'the higher culture' must be sacrificed on the altar of egalitarianism as Marcuse insists. Lucien

Goldmann implies that pure art has no value if it fails to make contact with the people, but at the same time he believes that no such contact is possible in our society. Marcuse considers that the actual technique and form of distribution abrogates the true essence of art; that is to say, art formulated

> as transgression and indictment. . . . The artistic alienation has become as functional as the architecture of the new theatres and concert halls in which it is performed. And here too, the rational and the evil are inseparable. . . . It is good that almost everyone can now have the fine arts at his fingertips, by just turning a knob on his set, or by stepping into his drugstore. In this diffusion, however, they become cogs in a culture-machine which remakes their content.[6]

Morin attempts finally, like Arendt, to question the authenticity of élite culture:

> Everything would seem to pit the culture of the educated against mass culture: quality as opposed to quantity, creativity against productivity, spirituality against materialism, aesthetics against merchandise, elegance against vulgarity, knowledge against ignorance. But before we question whether in fact mass culture is indeed what the educated see it to be, we must ask ourselves whether the values of élite culture are not dogmatic, formalized, fetish-like, if the cult of art is not merely a cover for a superficial intercourse with masterworks. All regeneration has been a rebellion against prevailing cultural norms. If today it is a rebellion against mass culture's norms, is it not also then a rebellion against the norms of élite culture?[7]

An important point of view that has not been aired in discussions of the position of culture in the mass society is the decline of its social status. Hannah Arendt touches on the problem by pointing out the social snobbery associated with art in bourgeois society. Snobbery implies, however, that art holds some value beyond the framework of economics and that it also provides positive rewards.

Both society and private persons supported (or opposed) art in bourgeois society, not just financially but also through a certain emotional and intellectual commitment. Public-commissioned art often inspired great controversy; exhibitions could achieve enormous public success; books should lie out on the salon table; art was frequently the subject of conversation and discussion, although all this usually occurred within a fairly limited circle.

When art was later introduced into the mass society it was done in a passive way, and art has often been exploited for both economic and political purposes. However, it no longer confers social status, no longer has any 'boast value'. This does not, of course, detract from the value of the spread of culture through the present-day media to all groups of people. But this is a problem for new creative art. It is not avant-gardism that is being spread but the work of artists who were avant-gardists many decades ago and have now been popularized. Avant-gardism possessed a strength and integrity which has been characterized as a refusal to compete, and thereby retained its freedom from economic manipulation.[8]

In the mass society, in contrast, the avant-gardist has become part of the system, even though he may not wish to be. He is subjected to economic pressure and is used, or meets, with benign indifference. He becomes a victim of the mass society's 'longing for the new'. A young poet who makes his début with the slogan 'Crush the damned cultural élite!' gets headlines and is immediately rewarded with a grant from the cultural élite, and it is equally difficult for other kinds of artists to evoke opposition or controversy with new art forms.

The rapid exploitation of art involves the risk of a flattening-out process, thus diminishing the influence of artists on society. The impressionists rediscovered nature. Cubism and functionalism transformed the external environment and changed people's way of seeing. Today artists live to a large extent isolated from social debate —except those who have chosen to use their art directly for political purposes—or their success is used by the mass media or for further financial exploitation in the form of 'Classics Illustrated', or Mumin trolls, Gatsby clothes, or Bonnie and Clyde fashions.

In the mass society there is a tolerance toward artistic expression precisely because the social function of art has diminished. It no longer functions as, in the words of Marcuse, 'transgression and indictment' or as 'the Great Refusal', but has been reduced to the level of entertainment or is regarded with benign indifference. It is enthusiastically rewarded with grants, and praised in the culture pages of newspapers, but it is isolated from social development. Therefore, radical new artists often search for other 'non-artistic' means to convey their message, that is to say, they write articles or controversial essays rather than novels, free theatre groups improvise their lines instead of sticking to the playwright's work, and artists utilize objects from the real world instead of creating them.

This is seen as a more effective method of opposing society and a way of remaining aloof from market forces. But a decisive difference has occurred: the message has become more important than the form or medium of expression.

It is an open question whether the radical message can be conveyed without a continual renewal of artistic form and expression: whether art can live isolated from society, or can function within the mass society on its own terms and as a central and influential part of it, and still survive as true art.

9

Sweden's Place in the World

When one analyses our modern society—herein called the mass, or service society—it becomes obvious that Sweden occupies not only a place in it but even possibly a leading position. Many of the predominant characteristics of the mass society are also typical of Sweden. Two major factors have contributed to this situation: the unprecedented economic development during the twentieth century, especially since the war, and the dominating position of various organizations in Swedish social life.

Having been a poor agrarian country until late in the nineteenth century, Sweden is now considered to be 'the world's richest country'. Sweden is the only country other than Japan, for instance, which, within a period of a hundred years (1865–1965), increased its total production ten-fold per individual. The particularly rapid growth during the 1950s and 1960s allowed for a unique rise in the material standard of living. What had previously been luxury consumption for the privileged few had become a self-evident part of the daily life of large numbers of people, represented by such things as cars, summer cottages, foreign travel, and television sets. In 1974 Sweden became the country with the highest ratio of television sets in the world, with colour television in 45 per cent of all households. During the 1960s only the USA and Canada had higher private *per capita* consumption, and according to a survey made in 1973 Sweden had the highest *per capita* GNP in the world, ahead of West Germany and the USA. Wages in Sweden are twice as high as those in Britain and 10 per cent higher than those in Finland.

Parallel to this development there is an increasingly strong tendency towards the centralization of society, in both industry and agriculture as well as public institutions. As early as the 1950s, fifteen farms per day ceased operation, and during merely a four-year period (1969–73) the number of private firms in industry and agriculture declined by one-fourth. At the same time the number of mergers increased five-fold. A similar trend exists within the very powerful cooperative movement where the number of associate branches diminished from 673 in 1957 to 204 in 1974. The goal for the 1970s is a further reduction to between 15 and 25 main associate branches, and in the 1980s to a *single* 'Storkonsum' (Great Cooperative). The number of sales outlets declined during the same period from 7,400 to approximately 2,700. In contrast, the number of department stores increased from 72 to 173.

In the social life of the country, this centralization can best be compared with the rapid urbanization that has taken place during this century. While 80 per cent of the population lived in the country at the turn of the century, 6 out of 8 million people now live in urban areas. This centralization is also reflected in the merging of municipalities. In 1952 Sweden was divided into 2,281 municipalities. Today these have been merged into 271 municipal blocks where all powerful representatives of the community are now paid municipal officials rather than elected politicians.

The most thoroughgoing social change lies in the increasing dominance of the public sector, one of the most characteristic features of the service society. In 1953 the national budget amounted to approximately 15,000 million kronor, by 1969 it was up to 70,000 million. From previously having accounted for about one-third of the GNP the public share increased to half during the same period—and to 60 per cent by 1972. The number of employees in the civil service has, of course, increased at the same rate. As we noted earlier, white-collar workers exceeded the blue-collar workers in the USA as early as 1956. This development was not so noticeable previously in Sweden but is occurring very rapidly now. During 1970 the number of people employed in State or municipal jobs was 1 million, the same as in industry. The greatest growth in the public sector took place during the 1960s when the State, which absorbed only 5 per cent of the total increase in work force in the 1950s, accounted for 85 per cent of this increase. The division between industrial workers and service personnel is also interesting, regardless of whether their employers were private or the State. Already in 1970 the number of persons employed in 'service production' was approximately 2 million, whereas 1.78 million worked in 'power and goods production'. It has been estimated that during the 1970s, of 400,000 new workers more than three-quarters will go into service production. During the 1963–73 period the number of people employed in commercial and industrial life declined by 243,000, while the public sector increased by 464,000.

The number of factory workers has declined not only in relation to white-collar workers, but also in absolute terms. In turn, the wages of industrial workers have risen much more rapidly than the salaries of office workers. During the 1960s the increases for the former group were 148 per cent for men and 196 for women, while the equivalent figures for male and female office workers were 121 and 161 respectively. This change, in conjunction with the spreading practice of a regular monthly wage rather than piece work even for labourers, has contributed to the levelling of social differences between factory worker and office worker. On the question of wage demands, for instance, the General Secretary of Swedish trade unions states: 'But, of course, we must not allow the pendulum to swing in the other direction, so that large groups of white-collar workers end up at the bottom with very low wages, while blue-collar workers become a new high-salaried aristocracy far above the average.' This statement may be supplemented with a remark by a representative of the Salaried Employees Organization: 'A change in the level of wages between worker and office employee groups has been taking place over a long period. Many office employee groups already have a lower pay than some trade union groups.'

The home and clothes, which previously demonstrated immediately the social differences between blue-collar workers and white-collar workers, clearly have much less importance now as social symbols. This change of attitude is reflected even within the trade unions. A union leader, from the Federation of Office Workers, includes even academics and professional people in this levelling process and says that 'the artificial trade-union separation of salaried employees and industrial workers contributes to the creation of un-justified demarcation lines and difficulties that hinder the academic from entering many areas of working life.' The unity between industrial workers and office workers was given its most advanced expression with the discussions held in 1974 between their respective unions concerning collective action in the 1975 wage negotiations, a virtually unthinkable constellation of forces a decade ago. (I should like to underline here that the description of the levelling of the social and economic differences between industrial worker and white-collar worker is an attempt to show the prevailing and characteristic *change* in the structure of the society. Of course, there are still very serious social differences between these two categories, especially outside the larger cities in purely industrial communities or company towns. But while these injustices are being eroded rapidly, at the same time new social injustices appear. This will be discussed further on.)

In addition, the trade union leaders paradoxically help steer development in the direction of a service society. 'Someone must consume what is produced', says the head of the trade-union research department, and maintains that since production requires fewer and fewer people, but nevertheless continues to rise 'too quickly' to be consumed, more Swedish citizens should be employed in community- or state-run services. He has estimated that 80 per cent of the population will be thus employed by the year 2000. This development is considered inevitable, but has, however, been criticized by economists from the private sector who do not believe that consumption will reach an 'absolute saturation point', but see the growth of the service society as a result of political manipulation, as further striving in the direction of bureaucratization and centralization.

A natural outcome of the development of a service society is the increasing influence of large organizations on Swedish social life. Expressed more succinctly, it could be said that class identity has been replaced by organizational membership. When these various organizations were built up at the end of the last century they were formed as popular movements in which powerless people joined together to gain through unity the strength to enforce their demands for justice. The trade unions fought for those without property, the cooperative movement for better and cheaper consumer goods, and the temperance movement for a healthier and more meaningful existence. The prevailing class conflicts sharpened the profile of these popular movements and gave them greater strength and unity.

With the achievement of many of their aims, and because the social conflicts became less sharply defined, the role of these organizations changed. They no longer stood outside the established society, but became themselves an important part of the establishment. Consequently, their power increased and instead of people joining the organizations in order to achieve some common goal, members were now recruited to strengthen the power position of the organizations themselves. One of the results of the increasing size and power of these (special interest) organizations was that individual members had much less influence, whereas the leaders of them gained more power than ever. Typical of this development is the way in which organizations tend increasingly to identify with their leaders.

The leader-controlled power of the organizations not only contributes to the centralization of society, but also to increasing influence in other areas, especially politics. The organizations have been used more and more as committees to which government bills are submitted for consideration on a variety of subjects and they have participated often in official reports. One finds an increasing number of organization functionaries sitting in Parliament, and they also occupy seats on the boards of directors of large and important institutions such as the Swedish Broadcasting Corporation. Lately representatives of the organizations hold board memberships in various branches of the civil service, and, in accordance with a newly submitted proposal, employees will have representatives, through their trade union organization, in the federal and municipal administrations.

In this way the leading functionaries of the organizations will have direct influence on political decision-making, the justification for this being that they represent a large body of people. These functionaries have never of course been given a mandate to represent industrial workers on the Board of the Department of Health and Welfare, for instance, and paradoxically therefore they have no responsibility to account for the position they adopt on such boards. In this way a small number of people have acquired a great deal of influence in areas where their views are unknown, and we cannot check on them in accordance with the normal democratic political process.

Olof Ruin, a political scientist with a socialist background who has studied this development, claims that Swedish social life today exhibits 'palpable corporatistic features' and defines corporatism as 'an integration in public decision-making—federal and municipal—of organizations based on special interests and professions rather than on opinions and ideologies'. He shows too how this change involves a decisive dislocation of the democratic balance:

> The political parties, to which all citizens must adopt a position during a general election, reflect the displacement and the distribution of opinion within the whole population. Our special interest organizations do not provide a comparable reflection of opinion. The 'weight' attached to their advice is not either always in proportion to the size of their membership.[1]

This crucial change in the democratic process is closely connected with the transformation of the class society to the service, or mass society. The new constellations of power, which the increased influence of special interest organizations in political questions involve, reflect a new social structure, or new class pattern. French sociologist Alain Touraine has coined the term, *participation dependent* to describe the new class divisions in a society he calls 'The Programmed

Society'. He too asserts that in western societies the conflict between capital and workers has been replaced by opposition between those who have the political and economic power, and those who are relegated to being 'dependent participants'—a term that is completely appropriate to my description of the ordinary trade-union member or consumer. From this it follows, according to Touraine, that the powerless citizen is no longer exploited so much as alienated, in a society that has replaced poverty in such a way that 'it seduces, manipulates and enforces conformism.'[2]

Western society has acquired a new power structure built upon technocracy and bureaucracy in which leaders of political parties, organizations, popular movements and, of course, large corporations have a common sphere of interest. This power structure displays largely the same features for the whole society, as J. K. Galbraith has observed in large corporations, to which he applied the term 'technostructure'. He means by this that large corporations are no longer controlled by the owners, or even the general manager, but rather by a ruling group of specialists who co-ordinate their knowledge and decisions. The reason for this change is that planning now is so technical, and information upon which decisions are made so vast, that no one person can be privy to all the necessary knowledge. But it is not only this—the decision-making group can easily replace private individuals, while at the same time no one person can be held responsible for the decisions:

> When power is exercised by a group, not only does it pass into the organization but it passes irrevocably. If an individual has taken a decision he can be called before another individual, who is his superior in the hierarchy, his information can be examined and his decision reversed by the greater wisdom or experience of the superior. But if the decision required the combined information of a group, it cannot be safely reversed by an individual. He will have to get the judgement of other specialists. This returns the power once more to the organization.[3]

This technostructure is doubtless to be found in the welfare state, just as in large corporations. It also exists within special-interest organizations, popular movements, state authorities, and political parties. This in turn means that political differences became less important—cooperation is achieved rather on the basis of common interests and technical grounds. Modern Sweden functions, as do other highly developed industrial countries, quite simply along the same lines as the ever larger centrally controlled corporations. The technostructure of a corporation can be compared with a new power structure in society. In a study on the division of power in Sweden, the problem is summarized thus:

> We now have members of Parliament, members of municipal government, leaders of popular movements and company directors who have mastered the administrative, planning and propaganda apparatus within their respective organizations, and in so doing they have, in practice, become as independent of voters or members as the General Manager of Volvo is of small shareholders. The alliance between elected representatives and the upper bureaucracy within the administration and popular movements is invincible.[4]

If one accepts this definition it shows further how little remains of the traditional class society in Sweden or other western welfare states (which of course does not mean that social injustice has disappeared). Instead of the classical pyramid with the lower classes at the base, the middle classes in the middle and the upper classes at the top, the division of power can be better illustrated by a cube, upon which there is a thin top layer representing the establishment. This is composed of owners of capital and industrial leaders, but only a fragment of them. Volvo's General Manager belongs there but none of Volvo's shareholders: the political leaders and the powerful leaders of the trade-union organizations as well as the directors of the Swedish Employers' Confederation; the leaders of the cooperative movement, the temperance organizations, large religious congregations and leading bureaucrats such as the general directors of the most powerful civil service departments etc. It does not matter that they have all kinds of political background from right to left.

We have already established that the differences between industrial worker and office worker are becoming increasingly vague. In addition, a wide variety of professions are included in the white-collar trade-union organizations; doctors, architects, and engineers, many of whom may occupy supervisory or managerial positions. This tends to make the traditional conflicts between employers' and employees' organizations increasingly illusory. The lines of battle have instead appeared *within* the organizations, where the leaders are isolated from the members. It has been a long time since the most influential trade-union functionaries were workers in the original sense of the word. When a worker is given a position of trust in the trade union he is quickly promoted to the white-collar level within the organization. It is equally common that functionaries come direct from universities and political organizations to top positions within the unions. Nor did it arouse any great surprise recently when a leading trade-union official left his post to become manager of a large private company—an arrangement which to all intents and purposes functions to the satisfaction of everybody concerned.

Cooperation across traditional borders involves the establishment of new power groups, among which the leaders of special interest organizations are included. Olof Ruin is thinking along these lines when he writes:

> The functionaries become part of an élite of decision-makers in the society. Close personal contacts are established within the élite. Shared points of view can be applied to problems of society. New loyalties can ensue horizontally, rather than vertically down to one's own organization.

Cooperation exists not only between persons, but at all levels of activity, especially perhaps on the economic plane. Joint projects between the State and private companies have grown increasingly common, and it is now not only the State which, for socio-economic reasons, takes the initiative. Recently it was reported, for instance, that Sweden's largest producers of textiles and a typical, conservative, family firm, wanted the State to become co-owner in the company. Even a large socialist cooperative oil company in Sweden does not hesitate to cooperate with the multinational Texaco Oil Company.

The former head of the Swedish Socialist cooperative movement has stated that he wished for: 'Additional cooperation with private companies in areas where the Co-op was too small, in order to provide the Movement with an opportunity to observe and influence.' The news that a consortium consisting of the temperance union (IOGT–NTO) and ten sports organizations had purchased 80 per cent of the multinational slot machine company Bally Bingo caused no violent reaction from the mass media. Similar cooperation has been discussed in political areas as well, even if only on a technical level, such as the negotiations held between *Aftonbladet* (the leading trade-union newspaper), *Dagens Nyheter* (owned by the Bonnier family, who are liberals and important in the publishing and finance world), and *Svenska Dagbladet* (the leading conservative paper) on technical cooperation.

Development continues to move in the direction of more intimate cooperation between the various capitalist groups, which tend to become increasingly larger and fewer. A recent study shows that the concentration of business in the hands of a very few companies continues at a rapid pace. During the period covered by the study, 1963–73, the average size of the larger companies had grown by no less than 40 per cent, whereas the growth rate over a preceding period of twenty years was only 18 per cent for these firms. The twenty-five largest corporations employed 37 per cent of the total number of Swedes employed in industry, as opposed to 28 per cent ten years earlier.

This development is considered satisfactory by all parties involved, or as the Socialist State Secretary of the Department of Industry expressed it: 'We need concentration and large corporations in order to meet competition from foreign companies.'

If one sees society as a post-industrial society, in which power has been transferred from rich capitalists to the new power structure—where many of the great capitalists are still found of course, but now in the company of leading politicians, organization officials and bureaucrats—this does not mean that the rest of the population is 'equal'. In the eyes of many the injustices are great, despite our statistically high material standard. A social scientist writes in the introduction to *The Class Society in Figures*:

> What then do these figures tell us? I believe they speak both of a relative and absolute need which is depressingly widespread. They tell of class divisions in so many areas of society that it could only be due to conscious exploitation. They make it clear that a great many people in this country merely exist rather than live; they sleep, work, consume and do very little else. That their existence is hard-pressed, difficult, not to say brutal, cold and monotonous. . . . How is it that so many of the injustices of the old privileged society have been allowed to survive in the new industrial state, along with all the inequalities *it* has created? How could we have avoided solving the simple problem of basic security when we now face the infinitely complicated conditions presented by advanced technology?[5]

The new classes can also be defined in another way. The service society has occasioned such great demands for productivity on those who work in industry (this is true of both white-collar and blue-collar workers) that in future it will not be inappropriate to speak of an A-team and a B-team—that is to say, those who can keep up with the highly accelerated pace and those who are rejected. Society simply cannot afford to have weaklings in production. It is more effective and expedient to provide them with reasonable compensation in the form of sick benefits or early pensions.

It is perfectly obvious that these people, without necessarily suffering any material distress, will form a new lower class. A Social Democratic political scientist sees, in the increasing influence of organizations in politics, the underlining and acceptance of the new class divisions:

124

It is absolutely clear that the increased power of special interest organizations on the labour market means an increased concentration of power for people during their working years, particularly those who have a steady job. When considerable influence on general social matters is exercised directly by the company, this means that power is transferred, from the arena where people have a common voice, to a narrower sector. We have a new graduated scale of voting rights, where one group is able to exercise their right to vote only once every third year [the period between general elections], whereas other groups possess additional voting rights in other institutions which deal with important social questions that actually affect everybody.

In this way the general elections become less valuable. What will happen to election-day interest when most people realize this, remains to be seen.

In future we should count on a class pattern much like the following system:

1) Wage earners with permanent employment
2) Entrepreneurs and other self-employed
3) Youths seeking jobs, other part-time workers, housewives
4) Pensioners
5) The sick and social outcasts

According to the principle of one man one vote, all citizens, regardless of which social group they belong to, have equal power on election day. The corporative pattern, toward which we are heading at full march, implies that groups 1 and 2 will have increased influence over and above their vote on election day. This situation can easily be compared with the graduated scale of voting rights that existed in the nineteenth century, where people with property, with established positions and higher incomes had voting privileges.[6]

In addition, the number of 'powerless' people in the future will increase quantitatively. It has been estimated that within the next ten years or so pensioners will comprise a third of the population.

Alain Touraine makes a similar division of classes based on French society. There is no specific poor working class, but instead the new lower class consists of workers in 'poor' industries, of the old, the physically or mentally handicapped, ethnic minorities and foreign labourers. 'The ruling class', on the other hand, is comprised of 'technocrats', 'bureaucrats' and 'rationalizers'.

There are many examples of the fact that the organizations no longer fulfil their original tasks and that individual members suffer a sense of powerlessness, and indeed not infrequently a feeling of opposition to their own leaders. The unauthorized mining strike in the north is the best-known example in Sweden. The situation was even more remarkable in this case since all three parties involved were representatives of the workers: the State owners, in practice the Social Democratic Government; the trade-union leadership; and opposed to these two forces, the striking workers. In a radio programme at the time a dock worker and a timberman were interviewed, and they both said much the same thing: 'The old trade-union movement is dead. Nowadays it belongs to the trade-union officials and bureaucrats', and 'There's no contact at all with the members. The higher bureaucrats have taken over. The trade-union officials have lost contact. They earn twice as much as a worker.'

We have seen earlier how free time in the mass society, despite the fact that it has doubled within a hundred years, is difficult to put to use in a meaningful way, especially when it comes to cultural activities. A study in Sweden has shown that leisure time is in fact extremely limited, notwithstanding the increasingly shorter working day. Two-thirds of all wage earners have five to seven free hours per weekday to use for their own personal activities. During this time all work in and around the home must be done first, which unquestionably reduces unspecified leisure time to a minimum. Many people have no opportunity to use the remaining time in any active way, a fact made clear by the information that approximately 30 per cent of the adult population 'have a reduced sense of well-being manifested by a general feeling of fatigue'.

The reality behind these facts, as it appears to a large number of people, has been described by a social researcher:

> When Johnny comes home from work—he works between 7 a.m. and 4:30—we eat dinner together. Then we play with the children and help each other to wash them and put them to bed. Then we watch TV of course.—But we're rather tired so we usually go to bed early.[7]

The enervating effect the mass society has on people is found to a high degree in Sweden, as in this description of 'workers with heavy and tiring jobs':

> We know that they take part in leisure activities to a far lesser extent than do other people—and this is especially true of cultural and intellectual activities which require active participation. . . . We know that persons with uninteresting and mechanical work, to a greater extent than others, are left to the passive consumption of the services of the recreation industry.
>
> Briefly: to the same degree that the highly rationalized and efficient production process reduces people to passive, powerless cogs in the machine, they are reduced to passive buyers of services supplied by the recreation industry and the mass media, which inhibits rather than

develops the individual's participation in the important affairs of common interest to everybody. They provide a certain entertainment and relaxation, but do not contribute to the individual's self-realization and integration into the society. Neither better education nor shorter working hours seem to provide a remedy.[8]

This statement, made by the manager of a large alpine hotel, shows that the enervating process does not only affect the least privileged persons in the society (even though he calls enervation 'activation'):

We must keep up with the times. . . . A modern alpine hotel cannot function the same way it did in earlier times. Then, the hotel provided food and room and allowed the guests more or less to look after themselves. Today we must be able to offer activities. We have photo weeks, fishing weeks, painting weeks and nature weeks for botanists and ornithologists. And of course keep-fit weeks both winter and summer.

Finally, in Sweden the situation, in so far as the adjustment of family life to the society is concerned, agrees exactly with the general situation described earlier. The large agrarian family has been completely transformed to the more mobile nuclear family unit and it has been observed that 'despite the housing shortage during the 60s, approximately 10 per cent of the population move every year. While the old Servants' Law was intended to hold the labour force on the land, the modern labour market policy is aimed at directing the work force to expanding areas and to re-establish workers elsewhere when factories are closed down. . . . The committee for housing service has concluded that the present urbanization of the country's population involves the development of a whole new pattern of life.' The social researcher quoted above summarizes the situation of today's family:

The family has lost almost all its function except the purely emotional. Once the source from whence we learned about work, society, marriage and life in general, the family is now limited to providing emotional satisfaction. . . . Along with the 'over-intimate' family, there exists a mass loneliness and alienation among people in society as a whole; this 'classless society without equality', without collective solidarity and group consciousness, where individuals, couples and families whirl about like lonely atoms.[9]

10

Culture in Sweden

We have seen now that development in Sweden is, to a very large extent a part of western service, or mass society, and that it is one of the most advanced countries in this respect. It is natural to assume then that the condition of culture in Sweden is much like the general view of culture pictured here. One could certainly have expected that the Swedish welfare society, with increased free time, a high standard of living and a high level of education, would have inspired a greater broadening of cultural activities. As we have seen, however, real free time has not increased all that much, the rise in the standard of living is essentially materialistic and for many does not include their total life situation, especially not their cultural life. In conjunction with this we will take a closer look at the significance of the rise in the level of education. The picture we then find will later be placed in relation to the total cultural position.

The most interesting aspect of cultural life in this context in firstly the reading of books, and secondly the closely related activities in the theatre, films and music.

Studies made of activities of this kind indicate that interest in them is very slight. In a questionnaire for a sociological survey, the question was put: 'Do you usually participate in any of the following activities? Go to the theatre, concerts, art exhibitions, read books, participate in study circles or courses?' Of the three alternative answers on the questionnaire, no, occasionally, or often, only 4 per cent answered 'often' and 48 per cent 'occasionally'. This negative result was further elucidated in regard to books in the L68 study on reading habits: of the total free time during a week, approximately half was devoted to 'mass media activities', that is to say, watching television, listening to the radio, reading newspapers, magazines and books. The amount of time devoted to reading books was 2–3 hours per week, and all types of book were included in this, textbooks, serious fiction and cheap news-stand literature.[1] Forty per cent, however, read books for less than one hour per week and had not read any books at all during the preceding year, and totally, the reading of books accounted for the least part of leisure 'mass media activities'.

Palpable differences were found in the educational level. Those with grammar school matriculation or higher education read 2–3 hours per week, which was accomplished mostly at the expense of television viewing time. This time was devoted almost entirely to the reading of magazines and books by 'established authors'. One of the most interesting findings was that, regardless of education, there was no difference in so far as the reading of popular or mass-market literature was concerned. 'There was no evidence in our data that cheap news-stand literature was read more extensively by people with only elementary education than those with higher education.'

Unfortunately the study gives no comparisons with earlier reading habits. The precursor of L68, a book study carried out between 1948 and 1952, does, however, indicate a certain change in the pattern. The survey asked whether the person in question had read any book during the past year. On this occasion there were 29 per cent who had not, compared with 40 per cent above. There is, however, no information as to what sort of books were read. The 1948 study also gives a general impression of fairly extensive readership among the young people of the time. In a study of male military conscripts in 1944, 34 per cent stated that they read books 'often' and 52 per cent 'occasionally'. (They also had 'seldom' and 'never' to choose from.) A study of gymnasium (high school) students, youths between the age of fifteen and twenty of whom the majority came from better-off homes, showed a change from detective magazines and the weekly press to more serious literature. These students had certain requirements and began to take an interest in poetry. Teachers' training college students who were interviewed at the same time had about the same tastes in reading as the gymnasium students. They read modern poets, and Selma Lagerlöf and Strindberg.

It is obvious that the choice of books was much more class-accented then than it is today. It was perfectly natural for the children of the bourgeoisie to change over to serious literature when they reached high school, while those children who had inferior school training and less, or no access to books in their homes read cheap romances, Westerns and detective stories. This is also confirmed in another survey carried out in conjunction with the 1948 book study which shows precisely the connection between the reading habit and access to books in the home, and vice versa. Obviously the situation in the 1940s was influenced by the much more limited access to libraries, and by the fact that the radio and gramophone, and of course TV, did not compete to anywhere near the same extent for those hours devoted to relaxation.

Class differences appeared in the L68 study in that book ownership and readership was more common among the inhabitants of areas generally regarded as socially superior, but more careful studies of the social background or class identity of readers were not made, as they had been in the 1948 study, probably because these differences were no longer so conspicuous. It is more interesting to observe just how the interest in reading *diminishes for all groups* when they reach their later school years. Between the ages of nine and twelve there is a considerable interest in reading, but this declines markedly between the ages of thirteen and fifteen. Interest is low among boys of fifteen compared with other leisure activities such as sports and music whereas it is higher among girls. The reading of books is lowest on the scale of interests for both boys and girls. For boys between fifteen and sixteen who live in areas that are considered most advanced socially, and which have the highest book-reading frequency compared with the other four areas investigated, leisure activities were ranked in the following order: Active in sports (2.53). Listen to music (2.29). Go to the cinema (2.27). Watch television (1.64). Read books (1.43). The reading of books accounted for even less of the leisure time of boys living in other housing areas. Among girls the interest was certainly higher, but the trend was the same.

The changes that can be noted from these statistics indicate that social differences continue to influence the interest in books, but far less since reading interest declined generally. As we have seen, this diminished interest is clearly noticeable as early as in the first year of gymnasium. The new and considerably broadened school curriculum has obviously not succeeded in increasing interest in reading books. An international study of schools in ten different countries, the IEA study (International Association for the Evaluation of Educational Achievement), revealed that in fact Swedish schools were not able to influence the reading interest of students when they had none to begin with, which often was because of their home environment. Since all schools are socially and qualitatively equal in Sweden, unlike those in Britain for instance, the result—that is to say the diminished interest in reading—is the same for all students.[2]

The lack of interest in literature is often discussed in terms of a failure of the Swedish school system. Gunnar Hansson, one of those responsible for the training of Swedish teachers, describes the situation as follows:

Swedish students in all grades have a much more negative attitude toward literature and literary studies than students in any other country. The girls are less negative than boys, but in general terms they all regard literature with indifference, as an uninteresting subject. This is true not only of the upper grades but also in the gymnasium, even though there is a variation among the different fields of study. . . . Many teachers give up the study of literature: according to the IEA material every fourth Swedish teacher of higher education says that they no longer teach literature, which is a shocking statistic. Compared with other countries, our upper-grades teaching seems to consist of the unstructured reading of modern literature, where the teacher makes no demands and has no great expectations of the students.[3]

Hansson has given as a reason for this continuing social differences. It has been shown that students from homes where the father has an unskilled job or profession have the poorest reading results. We have seen, however, that in the L68 sociological survey, reading interest has declined for all children regardless of home environment, which to some extent contradicts Hansson's interpretation.

Instead one must see it in the wider context that is to be found in the development of society as a whole. One important reason is certainly the high degree of efficiency and specialization required of society. A result of this is that Swedish teachers are given an increasingly 'narrow' training in an effort to train more teachers over a shorter period of time and that Swedish literary studies occupy a less important place among all the specialized subjects taught in schools. But, most importantly, behind it lie the centralizing and enervating processes taking place in society as a whole, with palpable effects even in education.

There is a revealing memorandum concerning the future of Swedish studies prepared by a team of researchers within the universities' registrar offices. It should be observed that this memorandum was made on the basis of a sharply reduced course in the history of literature that had been in effect for some years. The memorandum proposed that the teaching of this subject should be further adapted to suit the needs of the mass society. At the university, the prospective Swedish teacher should 'have read a number of textbooks concerning the various branches of commerce and industry', and future Swedish studies are to be 'a key subject within the humanities and like a *service subject*' [my italics]. The most important thing, according to the memorandum, is communication rather than literature. But as has been pointed out in a critical analysis of the memorandum, there is no definition of what is meant by communication. Underlying this is the view that 'Swedish technical language should be emphasized as the most important training in Swedish schools. And this is to be done largely at the expense of studies in the history of literature.' The brief time allotted to such studies and the declared aim of communication mean that, as the memorandum states, 'We sacrifice the chronological study of the history of literature, which has in any case been a chimera, since there were only five or six weeks allotted to the study of Swedish and general literature from early times until 1870.'

Similar critical views have also been expressed by two university teachers of Swedish. They maintain that the belief behind U68 (The Commission for Higher Education of 1968) that teaching should be integrated into the life of the society in general, has not become

> a fruitful reciprocal action between, on the one hand, the productive life of the society and, on the other, research and education. That which is most effectively served by the educational reform is a one-sided control of education by the established society and its institutions. . . . One need not add that the general subject of communication described in this way, and conceived on the basis of so static and historically false a model of communication, can serve no one other than the establishment. Swedish language studies will become an institution for the passive and repetitious acquisition of knowledge.[4]

A more personal comment from teacher and writer Kjell Sundberg places the teaching of Swedish in the context of education as a whole:

> Most assuredly the teaching of Swedish has collapsed. A whole world of education lies in ruins. I myself have experienced it as a teacher in the gymnasium and can testify that it is hardly possible to exaggerate the mess. It will be definitive too, when a new generation of teachers takes over, who know nothing but ruins. As a writer I also believe that the literary educated public, which was a product of our former school education, is melting away. But I don't doubt that there will be new generations of writers. The most fertile ground for us writers is not school, but the total life situation we have to pass through, to love, struggle, defend, decorate, see through. It is not so much the new growth of writers that is sabotaged by the school reform. It is the education of a whole nation. Earlier it was borne up by the bourgeois class. We do not want a return of that monopoly—but we do want a return of education![5]

Technocratic and productivity views have also been adopted in other branches of learning at the universities. This is particularly true of the humanities, where the situation is now considered to be so serious that the Humanities Research Council has carried out a study on the

deteriorating situation of humanism in Sweden. The trend is reflected in the creation of new professorships. In 1950 the number of
humanist professors was 79, natural science 54 and medicine 75.
In 1972, after the great expansion in higher education, the number
of humanists had risen to 115, natural science professors to 145, and
medical professors to 340. Although it is perfectly natural that the
natural sciences should be allotted more space, the proportionate
changes are unique in Sweden's history, and indeed in Scandinavia.
The lack of interest in history is especially noticeable, a fact that is
evident in the changed form of the history of literature, as I have
pointed out above. In 1972 Sweden had a total of 10 history professors, compared with 14 in Denmark, 20 in Finland and 23 in
Norway.

The features of centralization and the desire to force through
quick materialistic results are, then, apparent even in the realm of
higher education. Two post-graduate students maintain, in a critical
examination of U68, that 'without question the most important
changes within the organization of Swedish society during the post-
war period have been concentrated on the power structure. Step by
step, and with manifest consistency, the power functions have been
moved further and further up in the decision-making hierarchy.'
They write that U68 justifies its proposals consistently by stating
that education shall be designed on the 'basis of the needs of the
students and society and provide the students with knowledge and
proficiency, plus the crucial training that is *required for professional
occupations* [my italics] or further education.' In contrast to this are
the aims of the 1955 Commission on Higher Education, in which
there is no mention of the society's needs nor professional occupations, but merely an emphatic view that 'the most important thing is
that the student, in so far as possible, acquires a scientific and critical
way of thinking.' The two students summarize: 'The students are
turned into passive objects in the process of learning. The creative
aspects of education have to yield to short-sighted considerations of
efficiency.'[6]

Kurt Aspelin (a well-known Marxist writer and critic) has also
noted U68's mirroring of the society and the control mechanism that
is built into its proposals to increase the influence of the prevailing
power structure:

> The left-wing socialist criticism has already shown what we can expect
> from these reforms in higher education, which implacably will inte-
> grate the universities into the service of monopoly capital and the state
> bureaucracy. And are they not fundamentally the same as the 'reforms'

that are to improve the situation of the mass media? Who can fail to see that State press support, the tax on paper, the bureaucratization of television and its transformation to a single, giant, weekly magazine in living colour are quickly taking us to the point where 'free speech' has become nothing more than a pompous rhetorical phrase totally empty of any real meaning?[7]

The general characteristics that we were able to observe in the service society in Western Europe, and which are very evident in Sweden, are thus also to be found clearly outlined in teaching and education in general, and, of course, also in the teaching and study of literature. Society's improved standard of living for a large number of people has been of a material kind. Instead of being removed, the intellectual injustices have been fortified, or rather perhaps, that part of our existence in which spiritual values are the main consideration has been given a much more subordinate position. We have seen both from the L68 and IEA studies that social and economic status was not decisive in encouraging an interest in books. The status of spiritual values has fallen so low that they are considered no longer worthwhile pursuing other than for those with a definite special interest. Schools and universities see as their main task the creation of educated citizens as quickly and efficiently as possible; citizens who can rapidly be utilized in the production of further material goods.

It is perfectly natural that culture cannot be given much space in such a social pattern. Therefore, it will become more and more the concern of specialists, if, of course, it is not a part of the mass culture.

11

A New Concept of Culture

Up to the end of World War II culture in Sweden, as in other countries of the West, was largely reserved for the bourgeoisie of society; they went to the theatre, read books, listened to music and viewed art at exhibitions and in museums. Participation in cultural life had social status and meant, therefore, that even those people who were perhaps not primarily interested in art itself also wished to join in the activities that surrounded it. It was considered 'refined' to have read the latest books; one dressed up to attend the theatre, went to dinner afterwards, visited art exhibitions on Sundays and so on.

This socio-cultural pattern contributed effectively to excluding workers from a more extensive cultural contact. They had neither the knowledge, the money, the time nor the social security to take part in the cultural activities of the bourgeoisie. Early in the Swedish trade-union movement, however, there was a culture programme, manifested in 1912 by the founding of the ABF (the Workers Educational Committee) on the initiative of Rickard Sandler, who was later Prime Minister and Foreign Minister in a series of Social Democratic governments. The purpose of this [institution] was: 'through a free and voluntary unpartisan political and religiously neutral educational programme based on democratic principles, to train its members for the workers' movement and society and to make cultural values available to all citizens.' Activities were concentrated on education, lecturing, study circles and library activity. What was meant by cultural values was precisely the culture of bourgeois society, in the form of books, concerts, art, the theatre.

Gunnar Hirdman (Principal of ABF) could still write in the early 30s that it was necessary to combine education with cultivation, that it should be the goal of workers, when rudimentary knowledge had been acquired, 'to capture for the people a still greater share of the cultural values'. This idea of cultivation was derived from bourgeois culture, but the most important aspect of it is the quality of the culture itself and not the social background from whence it springs. Even if this should cause the working class to become more like the bourgeoisie, it is unimportant. The aim was to provide workers with the best culture available, not just to attain the bourgeois ideal, but to achieve 'a higher spiritual standard, greater spiritual riches, a more intense, a more manifold and deeper life of the mind'.

These cultural-political goals began to be achieved in Sweden on a large scale during the 1940s and especially after the war, with comprehensive activities in a number of areas.

The Social Democratic publishers Tiden and Folket i Bild began their revolutionary popular publishing venture. The magazine *FIB* (owned by the trade unions) competed successfully with the commercial weekly press, and a film company was started that was owned by a group of popular movements. An organization for the promotion of art distributed lithographs of major artists at low prices. The newspaper *Arbetet* (Work) started a Book Day, with readings by authors that became a prototype for similar arrangements throughout the country. The press, of all political colours, began to show an interest in cultural things even on the news pages, and the culture sections of papers were opened to public debate.

The increased spread of culture to larger groups of people also caused, however, an increase in commercialization. New 'markets' opened up for financial interests. Among others there was the popular series issued by Bonniers (a privately owned publishing house) in direct competition with the publishing activities of the workers' movement. The film and gramophone industries expanded and many less ambitious producers of books, magazines and music attempted to attract the new public. It was at least partly for this reason that the new Social Democratic Government began to interest itself in cultural matters. The Government was concerned to sustain quality while directing development. Apart from this, it was now considered that sufficient resources were available to provide for massive state-run cultural activities which would realize the goals of the 1920s and 1930s: to give all people an opportunity to enjoy culture. In 1947 a Government commission on music was set up and in 1948 similar commissions were sponsored to investigate the situation of books and art. In the field of literature there was a desire, as the Government phrased it, for 'a cultural rearmament whose purpose is to raise the educational standard of our people and give a dominant place to values of the mind'. The idea was 'to make art a cultural and social resource for all levels of society and all parts of our country'.

However, the various proposals made on the basis of the studies were, on the whole, never carried through because the idealistic, aesthetic definitions of culture, and the importance placed upon it in the 1920s and 1930s, which were retained in the directives for the commissions at the end of the 1940s, were less and less in tune with current social development. The first indication of this came in the Social Democratic Party's cultural political programme of 1952. There was little left of the idealistic view of culture contained in the writings of the party pioneers, but rather, for the first time, culture was seen as part of the social and bureaucratic context. The goal now was to create what was called a cultural environment: to pursue cultural politics was to be involved in politics of the whole social environment. A number of questions were taken up that hitherto had not been discussed in cultural-political terms, such as social planning, physical culture, the problems of working life and systems of organization. The organizational and economic conditions for culture also occupied a central place in the debate. The reason for this was that culture was seen, to a much greater extent than before, to be a part of the political pattern, and there was some anxiety that the rise of the material standard had not led to increased cultural activity. In 1964 Ragnar Edenman, then Minister of Culture, looked back on the previous year's cultural policies:

> Within the workers' movement we believed for a long time that increased welfare for the broad mass of people would automatically bring a growing cultural need and a rise in the level of culture. Today we are not so sure—one is rather more inclined to the belief that no such connection exists. . . . What is worrying is that mass culture's products flood over us in such a steady deluge. People do not choose themselves what to consume in this field.

No one was willing to accept the fact that cultural interest did not increase with improved material conditions. *Instead they began to question the traditional definitions of culture.*

In debates during the 60s progressive literary, art and music critics maintained that it was time to create a 'people's culture' *in contrast* to bourgeois culture, which they accused of élitism and snobbery. Here is a typical argument: 'There is a broad stream of writing by young authors of the 60s aimed at greater accessibility for the reader, a withdrawal from the esoteric, an attempt on the part of art and artists to function in an everyday society,' or, 'All the contempt that fills the cultural atmosphere is insufferable. The life of art, literature and music have been infected by snobbery since time immemorial.'

When a female Swedish writer died, of a similar type to Courts-Mahler or Netta Musket, one of our foremost critics wrote that her books, which are considered 'false, mediocre and artistically meagre', also expressed to an equally high degree 'a fresh, uncomplicated and joyful craftsmanship. She broke no new literary ground ... but she did attract many new readers and she gave them pleasure and material for day-dreams.'

The new values are not only valid for literature but for the whole concept of art in general, and it has been broadened to include all forms of human experience and creativity. In defence of American pop art, which gained such success during the 60s with its use of mundane objects, a Swedish radical critic, Torsten Ekbom, writes:

> Why is a Greek vase surrounded with almost religious reverence while a coca-cola bottle is thrown on the junk heap? What lies behind our frenzied idolatry, our mass-produced mythology? Does this mass culture consist only of evil, as some say? Is it not possible to see it from another perspective, a democratic point of view: a culture based on absolute freedom of choice, without pretentions as to what is good or bad, a culture suited to every conceivable level of experience? Is not this democratic cultural attitude more fruitful in the long run than aristocratic cultural ideas?

And Professor Ulf Linde uses as his point of departure the aesthetics of Marcel Duchamp's avant-gardism of the 20s: 'It is the *observer* who makes the paintings.' In another context he goes so far as to consider it reasonable to abolish art altogether: 'I am not convinced that a society such as ours necessarily needs art.... If a minority considers that man cannot live without meringue—for example—it does not necessarily follow that the society should encourage the production of meringue.'

The experience of the private individual is also used as a point of departure to defend a certain kind of music, often disparagingly described as banal: 'A theme of Haydn and a sentimental film melody from Hollywood function in exactly the same way on condition that we use them in exactly the same way. And as long as we are captivated by them or moved by them, it is impossible to say which is the most valuable.' Or Lars Forssell (a major Swedish poet), basing his argument on films to show that qualitative evaluation is a nineteenth-century invention and that prior to this judgements were based on personal taste: 'Every art form has begun where film began, that is to say, before value judgements. The main artery of literature begins with Homer, Aeschylus, Euripides *et al.* and not

with the aesthetics of Aristotle. A considerable amount of eighteenth-
and nineteenth-century literature, *Clarissa*, Dickens, *Wuthering
Heights*, Dumas, Balzac, etc. was read by everyone, high and low,
not because they knew it was good but rather because they themselves thought it was good.'

The broader concept attributed to culture during the 60s received
important support from sociologist Harald Swedner. Using as a
thesis the social composition of the theatre public he coined the term
'high culture' and showed that there were still people from the
upper middle class who participated in traditional culture activities.
In contrast to high culture he formulated a sociological, or perhaps
anthropological, definition of culture, that everything in fact that
man has engaged in is culture: 'all the concepts, values, activities,
habits, norms, skills, art forms, and so on which we share with other
people in our environment and which we pass on through upbring-
ing, education and intercourse between peers, and enhance from
generation to generation'.[1]

Swedner does not give a concrete description of the components of
high culture, but he does provide a social description of its function.
High culture is the 'cultural activity whose habitat is among
the educated upper class, within the bourgeoisie.' He shows how
workers, because of long tiring work, poor cultural background and
a lack of economic resources can only enjoy high culture to a very
limited extent. At the same time he asks whether it is really in the
interest of workers to involve themselves in such activity. He attacks
the popular educational institutions with the strange argument that
ABF and the whole of a long series of similar educational organizations together with the trade unions 'have served as some sort of
agents for high culture in the heart of a working-class environment.
It cannot be claimed that they have been particularly successful in
their attempts to sell high culture in the areas where they have been
active. One reason for this is certainly that here and there within
these organizations there have been *culture apostles with patronizing
attitudes* who have demonstratively committed some of high culture's
practitioners to oblivion and tried to summon to the forefront van
Gogh, Mozart and Ionesco. . . .'

Swedner doubts whether high culture has in fact anything at all to
give:

> many high culture activities are . . . a passive experiencing of something
> that does not engage. . . . High culture consists, among large groups,
> of a superficial prestige activity which insulates more than it engages.
> If mass culture, in the form of the weekly press, simple and uncom-

plicated film entertainment and much else, is called the opium of the people, then we should acknowledge in the same breath that high culture functions as the *opium of the bourgeoisie*, an escape from social and political realities.[2]

Formulations and definitions of this kind acquired great influence in Swedish culture politics, and with them Swedner created a contrasting situation between the traditional culture forms—institutionalized theatre, concerts, art exhibitions—which represented the upper classes, and the leisure activities of the workers. And in doing so he has arrived at a rejection of the traditional educational ideal of the popular educational organizations. He makes no attempt to define the quality of high culture but judges it to be automatically valueless, not on the basis of its content, but on the grounds of the social pattern it embodies.

One thus finds much unity in opposition to traditional cultural forms and in favour of a broadened concept of culture, including both political and social points of view, from writers on culture and culture politicians, from Social Democrats and from liberals. And those in charge of popular education make no attempt to defend the old ideal, but seek instead other ways to strengthen and secure their position within the culture bureaucracy.

There were warnings of the negative influence of mass culture, but they did not weigh heavily against the advocates of the broadened culture concept. Strangely enough little reference was made to the enormous technical development in the spread of mass culture. The mass media was mentioned of course, but most significantly, few saw any danger in this development. However, the new techniques and improved welfare caused a complete change in the spread of culture during the 60s. This was especially true of radio and television. The first TV test transmissions in Sweden began in 1957, and by the middle of the 60s over 2 million television licences had been issued, which means that Sweden had the highest ratio of TV sets *per capita* in the world after the USA. Not only were the radio and TV network expanded so that these media reached virtually every person in the country, but also sending time was lengthened and a new television channel added. The appearance of *Melody Radio* (a programme of popular music) in 1961 is indicative of the rapid spread of mass culture. Of a total of 16,000 hours of radio transmission time per year somewhat more than half were devoted to *Melody Radio* during the 60s.

The equally rapid spread of transistor receivers provided for a vast new dispersal of mass culture's new music, while the same was true of the new, inexpensive, easily distributed 45 and 33 rpm gramophone records.

Of course, these new media spread all kinds of culture, but obviously the superficial mass culture predominated. This was partly for patently commercial reasons, but the trend was the same on non-commercial radio and television. Those in charge saw it as their duty to give the people what they wanted. One of the heads of the Swedish Broadcasting Corporation maintained that in modern society 'radio has customers, and if the customers find that our store doesn't stock the goods they want then there's a risk that many of them will turn their backs on our store.' This argument was supported by the advocates of a broadened cultural concept, who claimed that every utterance must be judged at its own level: 'it is more honourable to compare Lill-Babs (a popular Swedish singer) with Eartha Kitt, and not with Birgit Nilsson' writes one radical journalist.

In this way mass culture was legitimatized much as it had been in other countries. Like Hannah Arendt, Edgar Morin, Herbert Marcuse and others, Swedish thinkers also tried to minimize the dangers, and sought a positive interpretation for the phenomenon. When Swedner claimed that traditional high culture had failed to reach outside the bourgeois class, then mass culture was provided with social justification too. Most important of all, this broad, socially founded definition was perfectly suited to a centralized bureaucratic society with a mixed economy. When a new cultural policy was to be formed, against the background of development and debate in the 60s, it was perfectly natural that this broadened concept of culture would provide the foundation for it.

The Social Democratic Party's Cultural Committee wrote in 1969 that an active cultural policy could not be isolated 'from environmental policy, family policy, from labour and social welfare policy or from social planning'. In an official report the cultural concept was broadened even more to include man's most fundamental activities:

> We do not see a lack of activity in the theatre, art, music or exhibitions as a sufficient sign of so-called 'cultural impoverishment'. It is hardly possible, for example, to describe people who are active in politics and trade unions, who fish, hunt and go berry picking, with a high degree of unity and interaction, as 'culturally impoverished', without being guilty at the same time of a gross under-estimation of the value of these people's lives. We would rather apply the term 'cultural impoverishment' to concepts which are associated with isolation, political poverty, alienation, powerlessness, etc.[3]

The question has been posed, however, as to whether it is possible to give everyone access to the culture that was previously reserved for the upper classes, in a society that has fundamentally changed by an extension of democracy and a rise in the standard of living for all hitherto neglected groups. Instead, culture becomes acceptable only as it is defined in its sociological context, while at the same time it is given a political mould. It has been pointed out how powerless the individual still is in society and how impossible it is for hardworking people to sustain the energy necessary to take part in cultural activities during their free time. The primary goal for culture-politics must be, therefore, to make society more democratic; only then will the proper conditions exist 'for, in any real sense, a free cultural life'. In other words, the basis of reasoning has been reversed. The motive is now no longer to make available to all the culture that was previously reserved for the privileged, but rather to use culture as an instrument of political manipulation.

The 60s were then a decade in which the final change in the concept of culture occurred. A variety of arguments were launched from many angles attacking the traditional notion of culture as art, literature, music, plays. In some cases these culture forms were considered rather a barrier to increased cultural activity for large new groups of people, who had at last gained a better standard of living. It was only within the Marxist left that art was seen as a way of changing and improving society and not as a more or less exclusive privilege of the few. It was maintained in these circles that art had a 'long-term strategic purpose . . . to sharpen the comprehension of reality and social consciousness, partly through motivational depth analysis and partly through formal and aesthetic analysis', in other words to see art as an active agent in the creation of ideas pertaining to criticism of the prevailing society, and as an expression 'of our relationship to nature and society'.

In the established cultural policy no such role was to be awarded to culture. When this was formulated in 1970 in the proposals of the Cultural Advisory Committee, the idea was that it would comprise 'environmental questions, education, club activities and the mass media'. In this way 'the artistic forms of expression', such as words, pictures, the stage and musical composition, were allotted a relatively obscure place. In more simple terms, it is possible to see the acceptance of the sociological concept of culture as a condition for making culture not only a part of society, but at the same time part of public administration. And with just such consistency the Cultural Advisory Committee has been turned into a department of the civil service, since 1974, and has become a part of bureaucratic and political life. (It should be mentioned here that the formulation of cultural policies during the 60s has, in principle, had the support of all the major political parties.) One of the results of this is that the popular educational organizations and study associations have acquired an important administrative role and thus an entirely different function from their original, purely educational activities.

12

The Novel in a Changing Society

A pervading theme in this work has been the importance of the novel for the book market. A modern book market is created with the novel, with independent writers, booksellers and publishers, and publishers' problems in the last few years are intimately connected with the crisis of the novel, both as an object of art and as an object of economics.

It is not the novel that creates the book market nor is it the book market that creates the novel, but rather both are products of society's development. As I have shown earlier, art became the focus of economic interests and was made private with the rise of bourgeois society. Literature, which had previously provided an expression of the power and interests of Church and aristocracy, was now given an opportunity to free itself and become independent—in so far as the new market forces allowed.

The first popular novels expressed the new individual feeling of self-awareness, such as Robinson Crusoe's ability not just to survive but to create a whole new existence for himself without other resources than his own two hands and his inventive genius, an existence where he not only supplied himself with the bare essentials of life but even managed, in adherence to his class, to acquire a personal servant, or the daring recklessness of Tom Jones, who demonstrated that it was possible for a poor boy to gain a higher social position and win a squire's daughter through his estimable moral qualities. Morality became a kind of central virtue for the new bourgeoisie, a substitute for noble birth and a complement to money. At the same time it fulfilled the need for a new system of norms specific to the group. The tone was first set by *The Tatler* and *The Spectator*, which also brought reasoned discussion to literature and thereby the pre-condition for the psychological novel. However, it was at a more emotional and romantic level that the new bourgeois morality was most successful; in books on love and virtue such as Rousseau's *La Nouvelle Héloïse* or Richardson's *Pamela*.

In the nineteenth century the novel developed over a broad spectrum, Dickens' entertaining and moralizing realism, the historical novel with its romantic and patriotic features, as in the works of Sir Walter Scott; Balzac's and Zola's bitter social criticism, the German educational novel, from Goethe to Thomas Mann, and the psychological novel from Stendhal to Dostoevski.

As we have seen earlier, it was only for a brief period that the novel was written in harmony with its readers. Soon it was to turn inward in analysis and contemplation, or to attack bourgeois society and its values. But this occurred the whole time *within* the system, the novel in all its different forms is always directed at the bourgeois reader.

Two features that existed in the very first first novels and have been characteristic of the genre through all its various periods are morality, frequently refined to psychological analysis, and realism, the description of reality. Lionel Trilling has even gone so far as to define the novel as a search for reality through the study of man and his manners. This 'moral realism' activated the readers, made them probe themselves. Trilling maintains that present development is moving toward greater realism at the cost of morality; that is to say, the ability to judge, to analyse. Reality crowds in on us, but we need both realism *and* morality to gain a proper perspective on the world we live in. The novel in its authentic form could provide this. It taught us to understand humanity. There is now a risk that the changes in society will mean the end of this form of the novel.[1]

On another level the novel is influenced by the conscious deformation of reality which began in the shadow of World War I and affected all the arts: cubism, surrealism and other forms of abstract painting, Schoenberg's use of the twelve-tone scale in music, the Dadaist disintegration of the language, the automatic writing of surrealism, and Joyce's technical experiments with the novel.

Art, as it developed during the second decade of this century and in the years between the wars, not only sought new forms of expression, but its purpose was also to destroy the old forms, as an extreme protest against society. It became intellectualized and in many cases completely cut off from all means of real communication. Post-impressionist art is, according to Hauser, no longer a reproduction of nature, but rather the rape of nature. He sees the break with old forms as the greatest change of style in the history of art since the Renaissance: 'the function of art being true to life and faithful to nature had never been questioned in principle since the Middle Ages. In this respect impressionism was the climax and the end of a development which had lasted more than four hundred years.'[2]

Thus, either realism is purified, which leads to reporting and literal descriptions of reality, or art becomes intellectualized and formalized, in either case there is no room for morality; the important thing is to avoid all sensual aestheticism and make a clean break with individualism and subjectivity.

At the same time as the forerunners of modernism broke with the traditional form of the novel, there were a number of very successful novels written between the wars by, for instance, Americans such as Faulkner, Hemingway and Steinbeck, and by Europeans such as Graham Greene, D. H. Lawrence, Joseph Roth, Franz Kafka, André Gide, and Ignazio Silone. With the exception of Kafka, who introduced the 'anti-hero' to fiction, they did not *develop* the novel but used it for realistic descriptions of their times or for escapist entertainment. It was not until after World War II that experiments with form were again taken up; this time in France by practitioners of 'the new novel' such as Robbe-Grillet, Nathalie Sarraut, and Robert Pinget. They finally gave up efforts at communication with the reader and transformed the novel into an anti-psychological and anti-subjective work. 'The new novel' has not brought a renewal of the novel form but has, on the contrary, led to a definitive cul-de-sac.

Behind these radical changes there are, of course, equally decisive changes in society. One can agree with Lucien Goldmann and see the initial appearance of the novel as 'a transference of daily life to a literary level in an individualistic society, which arises out of production for a market'. During the nineteenth century there was still a liberal market economy in which the individual was very important, and the novel pictured the conflict between 'individualism as a universal value' and the barriers that society simultaneously raised against the viability of individual development. When later, in the beginning of this century, 'the liberal competitive economy' changed into a 'monopolistic economy' the individual's importance was reduced and replaced by groupings such as 'institutions, the family, social groups, revolutionary groups, etc.' This transitional phase meant that the novel's main function as 'individual biography' was dissolved. Therefore, in the second period of the novel, which Goldmann counts from Kafka to 'the new novel', the search for a replacement of 'the problematic hero' was dropped and writers strove to write 'a novel dealing with the absence of subject, of the non-existence of any on-going search'.[3] In another context Goldmann has also characterized 'the new novel' as 'a veritable record of reification in a world where only objects act, where the time of man has passed, and where man himself has become a simple spectator, who has been reduced to his most abstract condition: an eye that observes and registers'.[4] In this way the novel has been deprived of all its traditional qualities, not least of which is criticism of the society, and has become a concept without content or function.

Another aspect of the novel's problem in our time is the change in language. During the period from the middle of the eighteenth century to the beginning of the twentieth the language of the bourgeoisie was a common denominator. Within this language there existed a frame of reference, of knowledge and readership that was a pre-condition for literature. The mass culture has changed these conditions: the mass media falsify and misuse language. The enormous development in knowledge has created a series of special branch languages, schools have not been able to keep up with the increased training requirements and have been forced to content themselves with seriously flawed teaching. George Steiner discusses this in an essay where he quotes a UNESCO report which states that almost half of all children in the world leave elementary school as 'almost illiterates'.

This language crisis has driven literature off in two directions, partly toward an increasingly private experimental poetry which functions as a kind of shield against the outer world, and partly toward extroverted, dramatic writing designed for the mass media, for a large public. But, Steiner says, there is no place in either of these forms for the traditional novel:

> 'The great novel' today is an art form, whose power and logic—one need only think of Solzhenitsyn's *The First Circle*—seems almost consciously old-fashioned. The novel embodies the linguistic conventions, the psychology, the sensibility, the rules for the erotic as well as the economic associations for the bourgeois culture that is just now dying. The classical novel was both a peak achievement and a typical element of this culture. Like many of its institutions and forms of expression, the novel can also survive over a long period, both in a sad and in a parodic way. But its vitality is no longer great.[5]

Writer Birgitta Trotzig (who has lived a long time in France) has also mentioned the language crisis as an important reason for the problem of prose. In a country like Sweden, with a continually greater concentration of power, where organizations and the economy tend more and more to steer our life-styles and way of thinking, people become de-personalized and passive. Advertising and the mass media 'neutralize man as a creative personality':

In the Sweden of the 70s there is very obviously a crisis in human expression, spontaneity, creativity and activity which permeates the whole society from top to bottom and expresses itself differently from one area to another. One of the problems is the occurrence of a very concrete language crisis. We totally lack a viable spoken language: we have, and will continue to have, a language of the ombudsman, a parody of the old upper-class language of power. It is strange and disturbing to see this tradition—the forms of expression of power and authority—which our speaking habits have adopted with masochistic servility—and not the vigorous and expressive speech of the people. . . . Our general frame of language then can be characterized as the opposite of inspiring: it is singularly inhibiting. And with such a background there is no reason to expect a flow of . . . young writers as the normal state of things. One can only wait and hope for the exception to this rule, for those who have perceived the framework of the language, not as a tool to be used out of necessity after a few modifications—but who makes a frontal attack upon it in order to break it down.

And these persons write, in Sweden, not prose, but poetry [my italics].[6]

Sven Delblanc, another leading Swedish novelist, has pointed out 'the corruption of the language' through a lack of feeling for historic tradition. The political commitment of the 60s has also created an indifference to the craftsmanship in works of fiction that makes the labours of a serious novelist so difficult:

We are incredibly short of traditions and lack a literary language with the smallest common denominator. The great Biblical tradition disappeared with Vilhelm Moberg. His majestic Swedish was spacious enough to embody both lyricism and epic power.

We writers must struggle with the corruption of political language and the decay of usage in newspapers. We must invent the language anew each time we write a book.

The problem of the language, as it pertains to the novel, was illustrated recently in a graphic way when a major Swedish publishing house was forced to suspend a competition of first novels. Although there were 180 entries none were considered sufficiently qualified to be awarded a prize. One of the jury members gave as the major reason the deterioration of the language: 'The most frightening thing is the deplorable Swedish, influenced by the usage of politicians, civil servants, bank managers, and certain journalists.'

An important reason why the novel no longer functions as the main literary instrument of our time has to do with an acute awareness of the Third World. The increasingly importunate picture of need and poverty and of threatening catastrophe, brought to us via the mass media, makes the psychological and moralistic novel an unserviceable instrument for many writers. If one wishes to penetrate to the very essence of an event in a concentrated way one uses poetry or writes non-fiction directly from reality.

In the 6os there was a breakthrough for new prose. Instead of novels, authors wrote report books, sociological, ethnographic and political documentaries. The frontier between fiction and reality was transgressed and dissolved. Authors such as Norman Mailer write ruthlessly subjective reports, Truman Capote writes a non-fiction novel about two condemned murderers, Alberto Moravia forsakes the novel for reportage or didactic plays, and the anthropological studies by Oscar Lewis of impoverished Mexicans are published not only as a research paper but as a penetrating study of the human condition. In Sweden there is a similar transformation in the work of erstwhile fiction writers such as Göran Palm, who writes reports on the Third World or on a factory that manufactures telephones, Sara Lidman, who is *engagée* in Vietnam and Africa and Sven Lindqvist, who uses the realities of China and Latin America as the basis of his literary work.

An original method of combining the traditional form of the novel with non-fictional reportage has been used by Tom Wolfe, who created the term 'new journalism'. For him the reportage is a new art form where the most important prose written in America today is by journalists. He notes the disintegration of the novel, a literary form that has destroyed itself by drifting away into idea novels, Freudian novels, surrealistic novels, Kafkaesque novels, rather than continue within the genre's most fertile area: dealing with the society, the social scene, manners and morals, quite simply, with the life of man. Those books that Wolfe claims have replaced the novel in our times are descriptions of a subjective reality. They are written by journalists like George Plimpton, who trains with professional football players and then writes about them, like Hunter Thompson, who lives with the motor-cycle marauders, Hell's Angels, and Gay Talese, who gains the confidence of the Mafia in order to write about it. Wolfe points out the difference between Thackeray and Balzac and our present-day novelists: 'There is no novelist who will be remembered as the novelist who captured the Sixties in America or even in New York, in the sense that Thackeray was the chronicler of London in the 1840s and Balzac was the chronicler of Paris and all of France after the fall of the Empire. Balzac prided himself on being 'the secretary of French society'.[7]

149

The traditional novel does not function for writers in the Third World either. So far no African has successfully written, or perhaps wishes to write, an important novel, whereas, however, plays and poetry are forms of expression with which they have often been successful. In a situation where the essential thing is survival, or to establish a new identity, the novel is too long-winded and indirect a form. The literary language of the prison and concentration camp is poetry, Nadezhda Mandelstam has said, in her account of Soviet camp life, in *Hope against Hope*. Pier Paolo Pasolini makes a similar observation in his preface to Alexander Panagoulis' (the Greek resistance fighter's) book of poetry in which he writes: 'Torture made a poet of him.'

Another interesting observation was made by Per Wästberg, who claims that in South Africa a kind of shorthand prose has developed, in the few newspapers that dare print it, a genre 'practised by many young Africans—the short, personal causerie or sketch which reflects haste, the temporary respite before the paper is confiscated in a raid'. An English critic has tellingly remarked about the Nigerian novelist Chinua Achebe, that the civil war in Nigeria caused him to give up prose: 'he was hurt into poetry.' Achebe himself has called attention to the didactic element in the Third World: 'A novelist must be a teacher.' Another prominent African writer, Ezekiel Mphahlele comments on his remark:

> In independent Africa literary practitioners do not commonly make statements on aesthetics. When they do, it is to emphasize that now that Africa is rid of colonial rule, there needs to be a shift in imperatives. And so we see fiction, and poetry and drama turning their focus on social manners, political upheavals, the individual's relationship to political and economic power, the neo-colonial subversion of national goals, and so on.[8]

Wole Soyinka, also from Nigeria, has stated that the aim of a writer should be total surrender to the 'eternal values, justice, freedom and human dignity', a goal that means that literature at the present time does not function at all other than parenthetically and at a low level.[9] The South African writer, Nadine Gordimer, from her perspective, sees a growing impossibility for white authors to write:

> I believe that so far as white writers are concerned they will have less and less to write about, within South Africa, as the inside view of the total society they live in becomes more and more restricted for them. Culturally, the South African white population inclines to a test-tube existence. . . . Art, in this situation, is in danger of becoming an embellishment of leisure.[10]

The isolation from real problems, which Nadine Gordimer so obviously feels in white South Africa, is unquestionably an additional reason behind the problems of the novel even in more general terms. Balzac, Zola, or the Swedish proletarian writers, lived in the environment they wrote about, or were a part of it themselves, at the same time as they achieved a certain distance from it. When it comes to Third World suffering, those who write about it are visitors who can observe from the outside and write a report, but not know how a person there feels and thinks. And for those who live in the middle of it there exists no possibility of detachment to observe and write.

The same situation is true of the richer countries. The relating of information about how people live is done clinically by the extremely effective mass media. The writer is deprived of an important part of his work, to expose, or 'to be the chronicler of his times'. In this way psychological description loses its roots in reality and becomes thin or unreal. Bernard Bergonzi has pointed out that the lack of, or limited, experience of present-day novelists has caused their books to become more and more alike. They begin with ready-made patterns of the type: lonely, sensitive girl in the suburbs with sexual problems; middle-aged couple with marital problems; the middle-class Jewish novel; students in revolt, and so on, 'and interpret their own experiences, which they believe to be unique, in accordance with these formulas'. This in turn means, Bergonzi says and claims the support of critic Edmund Wilson, that reviewers also fall into the same clichéd thinking when they judge these novels.[11]

German critic Walter Jens gives a more positive interpretation to the same phenomenon, the lack of experience and the competition for facts from other media. He maintains that the novel is freed from 'the banality of the obvious' and that this liberation means that it no longer needs to be entertaining or dependent upon a foundation of reality. Now it can be 'art and nothing other than art'.[12] In fact, with this statement Jens confirms the curtailed function of the novel in our society.

It is apparent from the situation of the proletarian novel of today just how important it is for a writer to live in a society in the centre of a conflict that is palpable and of comprehensible proportions, where he feels that his portrayals actually serve a function. The workers' struggle for human rights, which was first described from a bourgeois point of view and then later by young working-class writers, has been one of the most vigorous areas of novelist literature. In a society where the demarcation lines between blue-collar and white-collar worker are being erased and where the problems of the under-privileged are no longer solely economic, the proletarian novel has difficulty functioning. Swedish writer and critic Artur Lundkvist asks justifiably if there is really a need any longer for the workers' novel. Workers 'are no longer the important bearers and promoters of social change.' Lundkvist also calls attention to the conditions of the Third World, as the problem that overshadows all else: 'In the present situation, how is it possible to feel that it is either urgent or inspiring to depict the class struggle or write special novels about workers? Would it not be necessary to restrict one's consciousness almost to a point of blindness, to deal with problems which were neither current nor relevant, to run the risk of being a case for a kind of artificial respiration?'

Another thing that reflects the change of reading habits is the gradual disappearance of the serial, withdrawn initially from the daily papers and now, more and more, from the weekly magazines. It was precisely this form of publishing that provided the basis of the novel's popularity and, as we have seen, not merely a self-evident element but the most 'selling' element in the paper. (As late as 1890 the newly founded *Strand Magazine* increased its circulation from 200,000 to 400,000 by publishing Conan Doyle's tales of Sherlock Holmes.)

The importance of the serial began to decline immediately after World War I, parallel with the threat to the central position held by the novel. This was shown primarily in that it was now unusual for important writers to write for newspapers, but most of all through a decline in the quality of the novels published. The term 'serial novel' became during this time a definition for romance or adventure at a low literary level. After World War II the serial novel disappeared from the daily press and has, with some exceptions, vanished also from the weeklies during the last few years. According to editors of newspapers and magazines this has been due to a decrease in demand. There is no reason to believe either that any other than economic factors have been responsible for the disappearance of the serial, the same factors that motivated its introduction in the first place.

It was non-fiction that usurped the place of serials: 'The accepted reason in Fleet Street was that non-fiction extracts and series put on more circulation than novels', was an English comment, a view unquestionably shared by most newspaper publishers throughout the western world.[13]

There is every reason to believe that the accelerated pace of life and the lack of reading time are contributing factors in the disappearance of the serial. Furthermore the big television series, such as *The Forsyte Saga*, can be regarded either as a continuation of the serial novel or as a replacement for it.

We have thus noted how the novel, seen from various angles, such as form, content, and language, no longer functions as the dominant means of literary expression. The changes in society, both in regard to the western world and its relations with, and knowledge of, the rest of the world, have affected the position of the novel in a decisive manner. This should furnish an answer to the usual question as to whether the novel is dead or not. It is not of course, but it no longer has a crucial or central function in literature. The novel will be one among many artistic forms in the future and in all probability not the most important. Fifty years ago novelists devoted all their time to the writing of novels. Today they frequently choose to mix many forms and media—reportage, drama, radio or TV productions and fictional prose—or else they reject the novel entirely when they feel it is inadequate or unsatisfactory.

The novel will also become less important as entertainment, or rather already has become so, since it must compete with many other media and because we have less and less time for reading.

13

The Economics of the Novel

On 26 November 1880, publisher Thomas Longman gave his wife a pair of diamond ear-rings. With this he celebrated one of the most important days in his life, namely, the publication of a novel, Benjamin Disraeli's *Endymion*.[1] The diamond ear-rings were a symbol that his happiness was not only of a literary character, but also financial, two qualities that he himself certainly never separated.

The gift shows how important a novel was for a publisher, even for one such as Longman who had a large publishing house with a varied type of publishing. He had paid Disraeli the highest fee ever paid up to that time for a novel, £10,000, a sum large enough for the author to be able to live off the interest. For the publisher the deal looked like this: sales of the original edition in three volumes brought him about £1 per copy, with a retail price of 31s 6d. Ten thousand sold copies earned him approximately £10,000. Production costs can be estimated at £2,000, advertising, etc. at £200–£300. This meant a loss of a little more than £2,000, but at the same time the publisher owned the copyright. This was exploited by issuing a single-volume 25,000-copy edition within two years at 6s per copy, which should have produced a profit of about £2,000. In addition to this there were all the foreign editions—in America 5,000 copies were sold 'in a few hours'[2]—and there were further English printings, both in collected and cheap editions, all of these without any additional fee being paid to the author. Longman paid high stakes this time, but it is also part of the game that if he had sold an additional 5,000 copies of the first edition he would have gained a £4,000 profit.

I have mentioned earlier the huge printings novels could attain during the latter half of the nineteenth century—between 10,000 and 40,000 copies for the novels of Dickens, George Eliot and Dumas—but even small editions could bring a good profit. The reasons were the stability of the currency value, a homogeneous readership and incredibly low costs for distribution, marketing and administration. And also, book prices were high—one and a half guineas for a 'three-decker'.

Gettmann reproduces a number of estimates in order to show the finances of a Victorian publisher. (I reprint them here slightly more concentrated and with a mark-up figure added. The so-called 'mark-up' in the estimates is a traditional rule of thumb to indicate how many times publishers multiply their production costs to arrive at the retail price. It is clear from the rising value of the sum that production costs become a smaller part of the book price.)

TABLE 1. *Trollope:* The Three Clerks, *1857. 3 volumes of 320 pp. each*

Price: 31s 6d	*Printing:* 1,000		*Mark-up:* 5.8
		Receipts (948 sold)	*Profit*
Production costs	£272		
Advertising	63		
Author's fee	250		
	£585	£675	£90

TABLE 2. *Mrs. Linton:* Christopher Kirkland, *1885. 3 volumes of 320 pp.*

Price: 31s 6d	*Printing:* 1,000		*Mark-up:* 8.6
		Receipts (648 sold)	*Loss*
Production costs	£183		
Advertising	173		
Author's fee	250		
	£606	£520	£86

The publisher who issued these books, Bentley and Colburn, often had to pay large sums of money for advertising, and thereby the loss shown in Table 2, where advertising costs are almost as high as production costs. As is apparent, the money spent on advertising did not help the sales. Table 1 shows that the publisher's profit was reasonable, despite the high fee paid to the author, and the small sale. The large profits came with even a modest increase in sales, 3,000 copies, for instance. The income in Table 1 would then rise by almost £1,300 and no further overhead would be incurred other than possibly an additional £300 in production costs. The profit then would be £1,000. Bentley alludes to this in a letter: 'It is therefore in the sale after 1,500 that I begin to look for my profit.'

The publication of a book shows, however, a profit in principle of £100 or more after 1,000 sold copies, from 2,000–5,000 copies £200 to £500, and for 5,000 copies a profit of £1,000. These figures are for three-volume novels. As I mentioned above, it became increasingly common towards the end of the century to issue cheap editions in a single volume at a price of 6s. The printings could be around 20,000 copies and the profit for the publisher in this case would be approximately £1,000.

That Bentley's fairly modest operation was a financial success is shown by the fact that on his death in 1895 he left £86,000, quite a fortune in today's money, roughly £2 million. (Oddly enough another Victorian publisher, George Routledge, left exactly the same amount at about the same time.)

In the nineteenth century the predominant items for the publisher were production costs and authors' fees, and occasionally advertising costs. These costs, of course, are seen in relation to the net price the publisher received from the retailer. The discounts at the time were generally around 25 per cent but could vary greatly—the large lending libraries, particularly Mudies, had very high special discounts. They usually paid 15s for a 31s 6d novel; a discount of over 50 per cent. On the other hand, sales to the lending libraries were extremely important to the publishers, Mudies for example bought 3,000 copies of *Endymion*, which in this case, however, proved to be far too many.

Administration costs were insignificant in contrast; this can be seen from the wide margins within which the publishers operated. Bentley, for instance, lowered the price of three-deckers in 1853 by two-thirds to 10s 6d, and for two-volume novels from 21s to 7s without changing either the quality of the books or the bookseller's discount. He was not able to print any large editions either, although certainly he must have counted on increased sales. The sensitivity of prices at the time was, however, apparently not so great since Bentley's effort to increase his sales failed and he was forced to return to the old prices, which other publishers had calmly retained. These prices remained unchanged for the next forty years.

As we have seen, authors' fees could also vary greatly. The royalty system became more general near the end of the nineteenth century and publishers gladly juggled with the fees. Royalties could vary from 6 to 40 per cent of the retail price. Tables 1 and 2 on p. 155 show examples of 'normal' fees. I have mentioned much higher author's fees earlier on. (£250 was not bad—at current value roughly £5,000, and virtually no taxes to pay.) In general terms, however, fees were extremely low—during the eighteenth century and the beginning of the nineteenth payment often consisted only of a number of free copies of the author's book. As late as 1898 Cassell could pay as little as £25 for Conan Doyle's *A Study in Scarlet*.

All this must be taken into consideration when judging the estimates of the time, along with the stable currency, the long sales period at full price and the low costs for interest rates, rent, and wages.

The situation was similar in Sweden. Book prices were considerably lower, but the main item in the price estimates was production costs and occasionally authors' fees, while other costs were very low. Right into the first decade of this century, when Bonniers had a turnover of more than half a million kronor, the number of employees in the office and stockroom was only about ten, and the offices occupied four rooms which also functioned as a small stockroom. In 1910 the salary for an office girl was approximately 2,000 kronor per year (about £100). This meant that salaries for ten office employees amounted to 20,000 kronor a year, or little more than 3 per cent of a turnover of 600,000 kronor, or, with the publication of fifty books per year, 400 kronor (£20) per book. Rent was even less significant, usually, as in Bonniers case, the publisher owned the building, and with an interest of only a small per cent and a stable currency, it was more of a capital investment than an expense. (Compared to the British standard of life, Richard Dimbleby writes in his memoirs that in 1913 £500 per annum was enough to keep a family on a comfortable level including a daily help, a maid, a gardener, nanny and a car.)

A few estimates, based on available material, give a fairly good idea of the finances of a publishing house, despite the rounding off of figures and certain calculated guesses, in the publishing of 'normal' books; larger more expensive works are excluded. As can be seen from the tables, the publisher's incomes, and occasionally the author's, could be considerable. (There is not sufficient material available for the earliest years on the financing of smaller editions, but it must have been similar to the English example.)

These three estimates provide examples of extremely successful editions, which of course was not always the rule, but which produced such huge profits for the publisher, in this case Bonniers, that

TABLE 3. *Henry M. Stanley:* Through the Dark Continent, *Bonniers, 1878. 792 pp., 2 volumes*

Price: 12 kronor *paperback* 16 kronor *hardcover*	Printing: 5,000		Mark-up: 4

		Receipts (4,500 sold)‡	Profit
Production costs*	15,000kr		
Author's fee (est.)†	5,000		
Advertising	500		
	20,500kr	40,500kr	20,000kr

* In this case 25 per cent of gross paperback selling price.
† Unknown, but according to K. O. Bonnier the English publisher had 'high expectations'.
‡ Since the book was a success, a good estimate is 4,500 copies sold. All copies are reckoned at the paperback price and the bookseller's discount is estimated at 25 per cent.

TABLE 4. *Fritiof Nansen:* Across the Polar Sea. *Bonniers, 1897. 34 booklets*

Price: 65 öre *per booklet* = 22:10kr.	Printing: 6,000		Mark-up: 4

		Receipts (5,500 sold)‡	Profit
Production costs*	33,120kr		
Author's fee†	30,000		
Advertising (est.)	1,000		
	64,120kr	85,085kr	20,965kr

* Estimated as 25 per cent of gross price.
† 'We paid a fee of 30,000 kronor—considered very chancy at the time.'
‡ Since this was an 'impressive success' it is assumed that 5,500 copies were sold at full price. Booksellers' discount estimated at 30 per cent.

fortunes could quickly be amassed on such success. It should be noted that in two examples above the authors' incomes were greater than the publisher's. Here, as in the English examples, no other costs have been included, nor were they significant. It is also interesting to see the similarity of profits. 20,000 kroner was about £1,000,

TABLE 5. *Verner von Heidenstam: Karolinerna. Bonniers, 1897. 708 pp.,* 2 volumes

Price: 9 kronor *paperbound* 12 kronor *hardcover*		Printing: 8,000	Mark-up: 4

		Receipts (7,000 sold)†	Profit
Production costs*	18,000kr		
Author's fee	16,000		
Advertising (est.)	1,000		
	35,000kr	47,250kr	12,250kr

* 25 per cent of gross paperbound selling price.
† 7,000 copies were estimated to have been sold at full price; this book was also a big success. The booksellers' discount has been estimated at 25 per cent and all sales are calculated in paperbound copies.

which was a typical profit for a 5,000-copy edition. No further profits were noted either, if they existed. Often there were copies in stock that were sold at full price, even though this could take some years, and then too, successful books were often issued in cheap editions, as was Disraeli's *Endymion*. *Karolinerna* was issued in booklet form in five editions in 1914 and sold for 3.75 kronor per booklet and 6.25 in hardcover. There was also a cheap illustrated edition at 1.50 kronor and a hardcover at 4.25. Since then it has always been on Bonnier's backlist, with the latest edition, the thirtieth, printed in 1969, at 14.50 kronor.

Writers were often paid fees also, although they could never amass fortunes like the more successful publishers. One good-selling Swedish fiction writer earned between 600,000 and 700,000 kronor from the twenty-five novels and collections of short stories he published from 1920 to 1960, a sum almost exactly equal to the salary of a university professor for the same period. But of course, fairly large printings were essential for earnings of this size, which in this particular case meant sales of 10,000 to 20,000 during his most successful years, plus the fact that a couple of his books became 'minor classics' with steady backlist sales.

The value of the currency remained stable and wages stayed low in Sweden until after World War I. The economy did not change much between the wars either: in the early thirties wages in Sweden were actually lowered for a few years by as much as 20 per cent.

An office employee's salary was approximately 3,000 kronor per year in 1918 and 4,000 by 1923, the level at which it remained until the 40s! In 1945 it was 5,000 kronor per year. Then the first real rise in living standards occurred and was followed by inflation in a sharply rising curve: 1950—8,500, 1954—13,000, 1959—16,000, 1965—22,000, 1970—30,000 and 1973—38,000 kronor: trebled within twenty years!

This development is, of course, reflected in book prices. A number of estimates from the publishing house of Wahlström & Widstrand provides a graphic illustration of this. In all cases the booksellers' discount has been calculated at 40 per cent. All costs are real but rounded off to the nearest kronor. Production costs include typesetting, printing, paper, cover design, printing blocks and in some cases translation. All books are paperback. It may be of interest to note that the technical costs predominate in the first estimates. Paper costs, for instance, were high—in Table 6 they were 600 kronor, printing was 1,068 kronor, binding 191 kronor, while other items included in production costs amounted to only small sums, such as cover design 30 kronor, and type block for cover 15 kronor. In addition to this there was the translation cost of 300 kronor.

TABLE 6. *Mercy-Argenteau:* En kejsares sista kärlek (*An Emperor's Last Love*). *W & W, 1916. 278 pp.*

Price: 5:50 kronor	*Printing:* 1,750		*Mark-up:* 4.2
		Receipts (1,300 sold)	*Profit*
Production costs (*1:31kr per copy*)	2,300kr		
Advertising	330		
Author's fee	168		
	2,798kr	4,290kr	1,492kr

Slightly more than two-thirds of the edition was sold, bringing a fair profit. Production costs in this case were more than one-third of receipts if the whole edition had been sold. On the other hand, the author's fee was insignificant, approximately half the cost of the translation.

The following estimates show how unchanged the financing of publishing was up until the inflation that started with the Korean

War. A novel in 1943 cost almost exactly the same to produce as a novel in 1918!

TABLE 7. *Frida Steenhoff:* Filippas öden. *W & W, 1918. 243 pp*

Price: 7:25 kronor	Printing: 1,750	Mark-up: 4.8
	Receipts (700 sold)	Loss
Production costs		
(*1:50 per copy*)	2,600kr	
Advertising	1,100	
Author's fee	500	
	4,200kr	3,150kr	1,050kr

TABLE 8. *Eugène Sue:* En riddarbragd. *W & W, 1925. 220 pp.*

Price: 4:25 kronor	Printing: 2,250	Mark-up: 6.6
	Receipts (1,500 sold)	Profit
Production costs		
(*0.67 per copy*)	1,500kr	
Advertising	150	
Author's fee (*out of copyright*)	—	
	1,650kr	2,550kr	900kr

It can be seen from the estimates just how stable the economic situation remained for publishing even during the period between the wars. That is to say, book prices increased at a slow rate which, of course, was due to a slow rate of interest in costs. This meant that publishing was profitable even on a small scale and that small editions could earn a fair profit and large editions a considerable profit.

In Table 6 the sale of two-thirds of the edition brings a profit equal to half the invested capital. In Table 7 the sale of half the edition regardless of its small size would have returned a profit if the cost of advertising had not been so extraordinarily high. This shows how important it was to be economical even on a small scale. This situation is largely unchanged twenty years later in Table 9 (1938). There was a loss here too, of course, even though more than half the

Price: 9:50 kronor	Printing: 3,300		Mark-up: 5
		Receipts (1,750 sold)	Loss
Production costs			
(*1:90 per copy*)	6,000kr		
Advertising	1,500		
Author's fee	3,700		
	11,200kr	9,975kr	1,225kr

edition was sold, but here again advertising costs were abnormally high. This particular case was an American bestseller, which it was hoped would sell in a very large edition. This explains the—for a translation—unusually high author's royalty. The loss was not so great, however, that it could not be covered when the remaining copies were later sold at sale prices.

Administration costs appear first in Table 12, 1963. As we have seen, the costs for personnel, rent, mail, and telephone were insignificant at the beginning of the century, even for a publishing house as large as Bonniers. The same was true of Wahlström & Widstrand. In 1914 the staff consisted of two owner-managers, P. K. Wahlström and Otto Widstrand, both their sons, a stock man, a cashier, a bookkeeper, three people who received and handled orders, a delivery man who also took care of packing the books, two errand boys and an errand girl. The six members of the office staff had 200 to 225 kronor per month and the errand boys and girl had 7 kronor per week each, that is, for the whole staff of nine approximately 13,000 kronor per year. How much the two partners and their sons paid themselves is not known, but the sons probably had little more than the office personnel. A professor's salary in the 20s and 30s was approximately 8,000 kronor per year. A reasonable estimate then would be total costs for salaries of around 40,000 kronor per year, with the publication of forty titles a year, and 1,000 kronor per book. The turnover is not known but a qualified guess would place it between 300,000 and 400,000 kronor. Administration costs then, were approximately 10 per cent.

The staff and costs remained much the same up to 1937, when, besides the new manager and owner, there were his assistant, a production manager, a secretary and three office girls, a stock man and three packers. Those who worked fairly independently had salaries of about 4,000 kronor per year, the office girls 3,000 and packers 1,500 kronor, for a total of approximately 21,000 kronor. If we estimate that the two directors had around 20,000 kronor each, the annual costs, including rent, office material, etc., could hardly have exceeded 50,000 kronor, still with the publication of forty titles per year.

Production costs had not increased greatly either: approximately 1.75 to 2 kronor per book for a normal printing of 3,000 copies. This too is reflected in the price of books, which remained still under 10 kronor.

Table 10 shows that 1,500 copies sold out of a printing of little more than 2,000 produced a good profit in 1943—over 6,000 kronor, that is to say, two office girls' salaries or 15 per cent of the total administration costs. In the 50s costs began to rise, as can be seen in Table 11. The price of books is now almost double what it was ten years before. The table illustrates a successful book, a sale of

TABLE 10. *Viveka Starfelt:* Porträtt av shinglad flicka. *W & W, 1943.* *234 pp.*

Price: 8:50 kronor	Printing: 2,250		Mark-up 6.5
		Receipts (1,500 sold)	Profit
Production costs			
(*1:33 per copy*)	3,000kr		
Advertising	500		
Author's fee	1,500		
	5,000kr	11,475kr	6,475kr

TABLE 11. *Margit Söderholm:* Möte i Wien. *W & W, 1951. 274 pp.*

Price: 15:00 kronor	Printing: 8,450		Mark-up: 8.8
		Receipts (8,000 sold)	Profit
Production costs			
(*1:77 per copy*)	15,000kr		
Advertising (est.)	5,000		
Author's fee	15,000		
	35,000kr	72,000kr	37,000kr

8,000 copies with a decent profit, in this case a bestseller, however, and not a normal edition. Comparison with Tables 3 and 4 shows at the same time that at the end of the nineteenth century a sale of only 5,000 copies could return a profit of 20,000 kronor, a considerable sum of money at that time.

TABLE 12. *Dorothy Baker:* Cassandra på bröllopet (*Cassandra at the Wedding*). *W & W, 1963. 232 pp.*

Price: 23:50 kronor	Printing: 3,300		Mark-up: 5.4
		Receipts (2,000 sold)	Profit/Loss
Production costs (4:33 per copy)	13,000kr		
Author's fee	3,500		
	16,500kr	28,200kr	11,700kr
Administration costs*	13,000		
	29,500kr	28,200kr	−1,300kr

* Advertising is included. Determined as 100 per cent of production costs.

From Table 12, the beginning of the 60s, onwards, administration costs are included as a special item. In the 50s general overhead costs began to rise very rapidly. Exact figures are no longer available but they certainly amounted to approximately 0.5 million on a turnover of 2 million, or 25 per cent of the total turnover. In the early 60s administration costs had become as high as production costs, that is to say 100 per cent, and their percentage continued to increase rapidly. Administration costs at Wahlström & Widstrand in 1963, including fifteen employees, rent and salaries, amounted to 1.8 million kronor! The number of titles issued that year was close to a hundred, but the number of employees had only increased by four since 1937. These administration costs, which cannot be attributed to separate books, are divided proportionately among all published titles, as a percentage of the production costs. (Advertising and other marketing costs are included in this figure.) As can be seen from the tables these general overhead costs increased from 100 per cent of the production costs in 1963 to 160 per cent in 1974; this happened even though production costs themselves increased tremendously during this time. (An office girl's salary rose as we have seen, from approximately 20,000 to 38,000 kronor.) This is a simple yardstick to show how 'handling costs' increase the cost of production.

It is these administration costs, of course, that have caused the rapidly rising book prices—and also a sharp decline in profits. During the 60s it became virtually impossible to publish a book in an edition of 3,000 copies. As can be seen in Table 12, two-thirds of the edition was sold and yet still brought a small loss. Table 14 shows that only five years later a book printed in 4,000 copies, of which three-quarters were sold, incurred a considerably greater loss—although book prices rose by 4 per cent during this brief period. As we have seen, the reason for this is the rapidly spiralling administration costs. Then too, the price increases are at least partly illusory from the publisher's point of view—although not from the customer's—because of the new value added tax.

Tables 13 and 15 show how large a printing was necessary to ensure a comparable profit to that earned during the period between

TABLE 13. *Jan Fridegård:* Hemkomsten. *W & W. 1963. 250 pp.*

Price: 23:50 kronor	*Printing:* 8,380		*Mark-up:* 9
		Receipts (7,000 sold)	*Profit*
Production costs			
(2:60 per copy)	22,000kr		
Author's fee (16⅔%)	27,300		
	49,300kr	98,700kr	49,400kr
Administration costs (100%			
of production costs)	22,000		
	71,300kr	98,700kr	27,400kr

TABLE 14. *Jörn Donner:* Världsboken. *W & W, 1968. 259 pp.*

Price: 32:50 kronor (incl. 11.11% VAT)	*Printing:* 4,320		*Mark-up:* 6.6
		*Receipts** (3,000 sold)	*Profit/Loss*
Production costs			
(4:90 per copy)	20,000kr		
*Author's fee (16⅔%)**	15,000		
	35,000kr	52,600kr	17,600kr
Administration costs (125%)	25,000		
	60,000kr	52,600kr	−7,400kr

* VAT deducted.

TABLE 15. *Desmond Bagley:* Guldberget (*High Citadel*). *W & W, 1968.* 250 pp.

| Price: 33:50 kronor (incl. 11.11% VAT) | | Printing: 8,400 | Mark-up: 8 |

		Receipts* (7,000 sold)	Profit
Production costs (4:16 per copy)	35,000kr		
Author's fee (average 10%)*	21,500		
	56,500kr	126,000kr	69,500kr
Administration costs (150%)	52,500		
	109,000kr	126,000kr	17,000kr

* VAT deducted.

the wars, something like 8,000 as opposed to 2,000 and virtually the whole edition would have to be sold at full price. It is common knowledge that of the many thousands of novels issued each year there are very few titles which achieve sales approaching this figure.

In 1974 the situation had worsened further. Table 16 shows that a printing of 10,000 copies, of which 90 per cent must be sold, was necessary to yield a decent profit. Table 17 shows that not even a printing of 5,000 with 80 per cent sales at full price was sufficient to bring a profit. Administration costs had risen to 160 per cent of production costs and book prices, including increased VAT, are almost 50 per cent higher than six years earlier. To publish a novel in an edition of 3,000 copies and sell 2,000, which was good business in the 40s and the break-even point in the 60s became impossible in 1974, despite the fact that the price had doubled within ten years. An edition of 3,000 copies was therefore impossible to publish at

TABLE 16. *Victoria Holt:* De tusen lyktornas hus (*House of the Thousand Lanterns*). *W & W, 1974.* 295 pp.

| Price: 49:00 kronor (incl. 17.6% VAT) | | Printing: 10,500 | Mark-up: 10 |

		Receipts (9,000 sold)	Profit
Production costs (5:04 per copy)	53,000kr		
Author's fee (average 10%)	41,650		
	94,650kr	225,000kr	130,350kr
Administration costs (160%)	84,800		
	178,450kr	225,000kr	45,550kr

anything like an appropriate market price, while at the same time it was relatively difficult to sell 2,000 copies of a novel by a young Swedish writer or a translation of a serious foreign novel.

TABLE 17. *Swedish novel. 1974. 270 pp.*

Price: 47:00 kronor (incl. 17.6% VAT)		*Printing:* 5,000	*Mark-up:* 8.3
		Receipts (4,000 sold)	*Profit/Loss*
Production costs (5:64 per copy)	28,200kr		
Author's fee (16⅔%)	26,640		
	54,840kr	96,000kr	41,160kr
Administration costs (160%)	45,120		
	99,960kr	96,000kr	−3,960kr

TABLE 18. *Swedish novel. 1974. 188 pp.*

Price: 44:00 kronor (incl. VAT)		*Printing:* 3,000	*Mark-up:* 7
		Receipts (2,000 sld)	*Profit/Loss*
Production costs (6:33 per copy)	19,000kr		
Author's fee (16⅔%)	12,000		
	31,000kr	42,840kr	11,840kr
Administration costs (160%)	28,000		
	59,000kr	42,840kr	−16,160kr

A few comparisons from other countries provide a wider perspective of current development. In Britain, where wages are among the lowest in all western industrialized countries, and where until recently book prices too have remained remarkably low, a profit and loss statement for a book in the 50s looked like this:[4]

TABLE 19. *Novel. 1956. 288 pp.*

Price: 15s	*Printing:* 3,000		*Mark-up:* 3
		Receipts (2,350 sold)	*Profit*
Production costs (5s per copy)	£780		
Advertising	120		
Author's fee	160		
	£1,060	£1,075	£15

Philip Unwin, who published it, described it as an example of a book that was 'moderately successful', but pointed out that no administration costs were included. This estimate is in line with the Swedish example from the 40s, with the exception of the low book price, apparent from the low mark-up.

Book prices and costs too were still low in Britain in the early 60s. The same publisher does not include any administration costs at that time and still manages to show what he calls a 'reasonable profit' for a book with relatively modest sales.[5]

TABLE 20. *Travel book. 1960*

Price: 12s 6d		Printing: 5,000	Mark-up 4
		Receipts (3,119 sold)	Profit
Production costs (3s per copy)	£680		
Advertising	90		
Author's fee	160		
	£930	£1,300	£370

The mark-up is a degree higher than the preceding estimate and the book shows a fair profit with a sale of barely two-thirds of the printing—still the ideal pattern for a book calculation.

If one compares it with a contemporary Swedish estimate, Table 12, where sales amounted to the same percentage of the printing, the difference in the result lies in the fact that in Sweden it had now become necessary to include the rapidly rising administration costs, an expense not mentioned in Philip Unwin's statement. The situation in Britain today is much more like that of Sweden in the middle of the 60s, with rapidly rising book prices, and although the mark-up should be somewhere between 6 and 7, it has become increasingly difficult to earn a profit on such small printings.

Comparing the Swedish estimates of the 70s with those in America one finds a marked similarity, but then again there are other great similarities between these two countries, especially in regard to wages and high handling costs. The difference is that book prices are still somewhat lower in America. This is partly because there is no VAT and partly because the potential market for a success is so much greater that the printings can be many times larger and therefore publishers are able to risk a marginally lower price. However, the prices are now rising very close to the level in Sweden. Here is the financial statement for a publisher who invested in a young writer who achieved success with his second book.[6]

TABLE 21. *First novel*

Price: $7.95	Printing: 5,000		Mark-up: 4.5
		Receipts (2,200 sold)	Loss
Production costs	$8,775		
Advertising, etc.	2,875		
Author's fee	5,000		
	$16,650	$8,800	$7,850
Administration costs	5,500		
	$22,150	$8,800	$13,350

When a writer has received good reviews his next book has considerably better sales chances, and the size of the printing is increased substantially, which gives the following result:

TABLE 22. *New novel by the same writer*

Price: $7.95	Printing: 30,000		Mark-up: 8
		Receipts (23,000 sold)	Profit/Loss
Production costs	$28,000		
Advertising, etc.	22,250		
Author's fee	23,700		
	$73,950	$92,800	$18,850
Administration costs	20,400		
	$94,350	$92,800	− $1,550

The publishing house lost 13,350 dollars on the first novel but went on to publish the second book. Table 22 shows that the investment in the second book was over 70,000 dollars, part of which went on an expensive advertising campaign costing more than 20,000 dollars. Despite the large investment and excellent sales, and the fact that the second book's price was kept up even though the printing was six times as large, publication brought a loss to the publisher. However, the well-developed mass market took good care of the book subsequently, as much perhaps because of the extensive advertising as the reasonably good sales and positive reviews. The publisher succeeded in selling the book to a book club and a paperback publisher. They paid 10,000 and 75,000 dollars respectively, shared in the USA between author and publisher, in this particular case 60:40. Therefore, with the issuing of this novel the publisher earned an additional 34,000 dollars, which provided a profit of 20,000 dollars on the publication of both books. The author, on the other hand, earned an income of 75,000 dollars on the second book alone.[7]

The estimates show how, during the 60s, it has became increasingly difficult to publish general literature at a profit. In Sweden this resulted in a publishing crisis. This is clearly apparent in L68 studies, which provide a summary of the situation during the late 60s.

About 1,000 titles published in 1966 by typical 'bookseller publishers' were investigated. The serious fiction category comprised prose, poetry and 'entertainments' which, however, did not include mass-market literature. (The figures in the studies were affected to some extent by the fact that one-quarter of the books included in the serious fiction category consisted of poetry.)

Serious fiction accounted for the greatest number of small printings. Forty-four per cent were published in editions of less than 3,000 copies—if we subtract the poetry (10 per cent) 34 per cent remains—while the non-fiction share amounted to 15 per cent.

Of these fiction titles almost half had sold less than 1,000 copies each, while the number of titles produced in such small printings amounted to only 9 per cent of the whole (in this case poetry!). Which of course means a tremendous amount of unsold stock.

The researchers comment on the studies: 'Of those titles which showed a loss or an insignificant profit, the majority were fiction, most of which were books of poetry.' In contrast it was shown that 'a number of novels and short stories, primarily of an entertainment character, sold in very large numbers. Without their contribution the publication of serious fiction in 1966 would have been unprofitable.' (There was also mention, of course, of the problems involved in the publication of other categories of books, but this is irrelevant in the present context.)

The decline of fiction in the western world is also reflected in publishing statistics. Although these statistics also include mass-market books and simpler kinds of entertainment literature—a type of book which is apparently on the increase—it is evident that there is a definite proportionate reduction in publication since World War II.

If a comparison is made between the years 1961 and 1968, in

accordance with the statistics of UNESCO, the results are as follows (figures for 1961 in parenthesis):

The percentage share for fiction was, in the USA (31.9) 20.1, in Britain (34.6) 28.2, in France (38.8) 26.6, in West Germany (24.2) 16.6, and in Sweden (32.2) 26.9 per cent. These figures can be compared with those in the East European countries, countries which are not so technically advanced as the West and where the 'time' problem is not so acute. In 1961 equivalent figures were 13.5 per cent, and this had *increased* by 1968 to 15.9 per cent. In addition to this there is no mass-market literature in these countries, which of course also influences the picture. It should be observed, however, that the total number of fictional books increased in all countries, but that the increase in other categories of books was considerably greater, particularly in the social sciences, natural sciences and technology.

In Britain there were forewarnings of a publishing crisis in 1974 which caused a reduction in the number of titles published compared with the preceding years. The number of titles published in 1974 was 7,852—the lowest figure since 1967 and a reduction of almost 20 per cent compared with the previous year. One of the three categories of books that showed a slight increase was fiction. This does not, however, influence the long-term development, and especially not of the serious novel. The increases both in Sweden and Britain most certainly lie within the realm of simple entertainment literature. There are no reliable figures to go by but the strong sales increases of both B. Wahlström in Sweden and Mills & Boon in England would seem to imply this (compare with p. 91). We know that the number of titles published in Sweden of mass-market paperbacks rose between 1965 and 1970 from 462 to 562, that is, 100 titles, although the total number of published titles did not increase. Mills & Boon, who are the world's largest publishers of romantic fiction, have increased their sales (partly through mergers it is true) from 27 million volumes in 1972 to 40 million in 1974. Their books are translated into a number of languages including those of Scandinavia.[8]

The decline of interest in good fiction is also apparent from the change in press reviews. L68 shows the following in a survey dealing with the years 1956 and 1968. (It should be made clear here that 1968 was a somewhat misleading year. Political literature was more predominant than usual.) The study concludes that newspapers, in so far as serious fiction is concerned, 'even in the case of the well-known writers have reduced their space to some extent'. A study of *Dagens Nyheter* (Sweden's largest morning daily) 'indicates that a large portion of serious fiction is allotted relatively less space than previously. This is especially true of translations; an appraisal supported by a similar observation regarding *BLM* (leading literary magazine). It is probably true of Swedish fiction as well.' An estimate of the scope of the culture pages in *Dagens Nyheter* and the share thereof of literary reviews reveals 'that the latter have increased their space much less than the extension of the culture pages as a whole, and that the culture pages have not entirely kept up with the rapidly expanding total size of the paper'.

The reality behind the statistics can be illustrated by the seriousness with which publishers and writers in the West view the present situation of the novel. Clearly they are anxious about its future, both from a literary and financial point of view.

In an article surveying the future of the novel and its financing in the USA, John P. Dessauer claims that overproduction and the bestseller psychology inhibits the development of the novel and that non-fiction will come to dominate the market.[9] Growing commercialization means that many novelists will never have an opportunity to develop. Twenty or thirty years ago novels sold better than any other type of book, whereas now there are more other books filling the bestseller lists. Certainly there is an increase in the publication of novels, but the sales of novels by unknown or less well-known writers is steadily declining. Booksellers, especially the larger chains, will not take any risks. Most of them will not buy first novels at all, and many will not stock novels which do not seem to promise 'above normal' sales. The result is that first novels barely sell 2,000 copies, most of which are purchased by libraries. Even more serious, Dessauer claims, is the fact that novels that earlier sold reasonably well, perhaps 8,000 to 20,000 copies, no longer sell either. One publisher has this to say about the present situation: 'fiction is either big or dead.' In consequence, book prices rise rapidly and publishers find themselves in a vicious circle. The fiction books that sell best are 'mysteries, science-fiction, Gothics'.

In another article a number of American publishers were interviewed (representing Macmillan, Farrar, Straus & Giroux, Harper & Row and Harcourt Brace Jovanovich), who expressed similar views. 'Serious fiction sells less well than serious non-fiction, and therefore fewer serious first novels are published now', one of them says.[10] People certainly read stories, but they are mostly historical novels or romances. They also claim that there are fewer bookshops and their stocks poorer—they only take in books that sell quickly. One publisher maintained that the competition from news drives out books, that is to say, what was earlier conveyed by art has now been taken over by other more superficial media. Another believed that people had quite simply lost the habit of reading. A third verified the above estimates: the sale of 3,500 copies of a novel means a loss of 7,000–10,000 dollars, 'on condition that one hasn't paid out too much for advertising'.

In Britain the situation of the novel is considered so alarming that a state subsidy was provided to start a book club, 'The New Fiction Society', because those responsible for culture were so worried about 'the seeming decline in fiction'. The authorities do not believe the problem is primarily due to a lack of good new novels, but rather the declining interest of readers.[11] The expectations of success for this venture are rather modest obviously since those in charge of it appeared to be relatively satisfied with 1,000 members after six weeks and hope for 10,000 within three years, in spite of the fact that the club offers subsidized books by such attractive writers as Lawrence Durrell, Richard Adams and Beryl Bainbridge.

Statements by British publishers further illustrate the problem. Two publishers, Wildwood House and Quartet, began ambitiously in 1973 to publish good fiction at reduced prices, paperbacks that would fill the gap somewhere between hardcovers and low-priced paperbacks. They reported a year later that they were no longer able to continue publishing novels, although they had received a great deal of support from booksellers. They had, however, both succeeded with non-fiction and were now going to restrict their publishing activities to this field exclusively. The sale of novels remained around 1,000 copies and one of the publishers maintained that the reason was one of principle: 'I think the credibility of contemporary fiction is very low.'[12]

One of Britain's foremost editors, Anthony Godwin, a few years before his untimely death, actually moved to the USA, claiming that British publishing houses could no longer afford to publish serious novels, and that books at ordinary prices are read less and less and become increasingly expensive, not even bestsellers sell well any more: 'The normal bestseller today sells 15,000, which is ridiculous. Margaret Drabble, Edna O'Brien, Eric Ambler—they're the three of of our best-selling authors. As writers they're household names. Yet they sell only 15,000. Just 15 years ago authors of comparable status would have sold at least 35,000 in hardback.'[13]

The situation is even worse in Britain for translations. At a symposium on the publication of German books in English, a publisher stated that four different translations of German novels had sold an average of 500 copies each, which produced a loss of £1,200 per book in direct costs. Production costs per book were £1,700 and sales brought in only £500. According to a representative of Penguins this is also true of paperbacks, especially the translation of poetry. A series of modern European poets had, as late as 1967, sold 3,500 copies per book per year, but by 1973 sales were down to a maximum of 500 copies.[14]

The difficulty in selling serious fiction is also a familiar problem to booksellers. In an interview one bookseller said: 'The books reviewed in the Sundays are rarely asked for in this shop. Fiction, apart from you-know-who, is seldom asked for, and yet our turnover is up ... intelligent new fiction is priced out of existence.... Even the paperbacks don't want to risk their money on it.'[15]

Experience is exactly the same in Germany. In an article on the book market the situation was described thus: 'It has become a familiar quotation in the book trade: "only not novels, you can't sell them."' A bestseller can certainly bring very large profits, but the majority of novels remain unsold. The publishers react to this by being extremely restrictive in publishing new fiction; this is particularly true of the smaller publishers who cannot afford expensive marketing costs, which are a prerequisite for reaching readers.

A survey of the bestseller lists in Germany over a period of ten years shows a concentration toward fewer and fewer books which, by way of compensation, have sold in ever larger editions. The normal printings of 4,000 to 6,000 copies have been reduced to 2,000 to 3,000. This means that publishing is divided into two classes, a few books which produce large profits and many books which bring losses. The 'sound middle zone' of the past is disappearing rapidly. The risk is that books that cannot be issued in large editions will not be published at all in the future.[16]

This is also confirmed by the fact that the literary publishing houses are cutting back on their operations. Luchterhand has reduced the number of new books in their literary series by half, and Rowohlt has done the same with their equivalent series, Das neue Buch. The same tendency has been reported from Molden, Fischer and Bertelsmann.[17]

Publishers in Germany speak much the same way about the situation as their colleagues in Britain and America. A representative for Kiepenheuer & Witsch says: 'The situation for German book publishing is changing. More readers are now interested in scientific and theoretical works than in fiction.'[18] Even a publisher of bestsellers such as Willy Droemer complains that 'there is less interest in novels and other fiction nowadays, perhaps because books are not as good as they used to be. In any case, the large novels are not so good and don't sell in Germany or the USA.'[19]

In a survey of the future of the book market in Germany, H. M. Ledig-Rowohlt, part-owner of a large literary publishing house, answers the question regarding the future situation: 'Terrible . . . the pleasure in being a publisher is disappearing. Interest has swung toward non-fiction, and so many sensational things are happening to draw the attention of people today away from things of the imagination. When one sees this, then there is no longer any place for a publisher of my kind. . . . It has become more and more difficult to make new discoveries. For example, when my father started publishing Hemingway, he was still barely known then, even in America. . . . It is going to be very difficult to publish avant-garde literature in the future, a publisher can only do it if he earns a profit, but if he has losses then he can't take the responsibility, for his own sake or for the sake of his employees. Even middle-form literature by writers like Muriel Spark and Edna O'Brien no longer sells. Where earlier you could sell, with some difficulty four, five, six thousand copies, you can now sell only two to two-thousand-five-hundred. Actually one should quit the business. . . . My brother once said to me that it's not the novel that's dead, it's literature.'[20]

German publishers, like their British and French colleagues, have been forced to merge with larger financial groups and must search for other kinds of literature to subsidize serious fiction. S. Fischer and Droemer Knaur are financed by a large book club, as is Rowohlt which is also partly owned by *Time-Life*. Ullstein belongs to the Springer newspaper empire. Hanser survives by the publication of medical journals, Luchterhand by legal journals and State publications. Hoffman and Campe have a magazine publishing company behind them and Suhrkamp lives off its theatre publications.

Finally, a statement by a Swedish publisher, George Svensson, who has been responsible for the publication of foreign fiction at Bonniers since 1930:

Sales were even better at that time than later [the end of the 30s]. Writers such as Hemingway, Steinbeck, Remarque, James Hilton, Bromfield, Vicki Baum easily reached printings of 20,000 copies, and sales were made entirely through bookshops. Then the climate deteriorated rapidly for hardcover editions. The explanation is rather simple. To begin with, foreign books were reviewed much more often during the 30s and 40s, and not in the superior manner that later became so common, especially in the case of books that it was believed could be dismissed as entertainment.

In the 40s the cheap series appeared. The first book club started in 1942, the popular book series, in 1945. They took over part of the buying public.

At last, in 1957, Sweden got paperbacks in Swedish. First the Aldus books with a fairly modest selection. Then much more extensively the Delfin books in 1960. One got more used to the demand for inexpensive books. Then television arrived and the whole development in the field of recreation, all of which made for competition with books.

Naturally there are books other than novels that are, or have been, important to the publishing houses that publish general literature. Travel books, biography and memoirs have, of course, been very important financially to publishers in growth and development since the nineteenth century. The success of Stanley's travel books has already been mentioned, as well as the books of Sven Hedin.

Bentley and Colburn were as much specialists in travel books and biographies as they were in novels. But the printings were not especially large in normal editions of these genre. Travel books were the least rewarding for the publishers and most of them sold under 1,500 copies. Biographies and memoirs could rise to some thousands of copies, but most printings even for these were around 1,000 or less. But the conditions for these books were much the same as for novels, they could be very successful occasionally and bring very good profits.

The similarity between these books and novels was that they were simple and quick to produce and that the sales period was usually very short: they could return the invested capital the same year, or at least within a few years of publication. But from the financial point of view the novel was unbeatable. It required very little labour from the publisher, in principle the manuscript was ready for production when it was sent in. If the writer had been successful previously there was already a public which guaranteed a certain number of sales. And besides this, unlike memoirs, biographies and frequently travel books, the publisher could count on new manuscripts coming in regularly from the same writers, often for years, and likewise on the steady reprinting of earlier books.

The importance of the larger collected works and series for the finances of publishing houses has not been discussed here. They were and still are, of course, of great importance. But financially they function in another way in that they require long-term investment and show eventual profits only after an equally long period.

It is difficult to generalize about the various types of books issued and it is not relevant to this analysis of the publishing crisis. Large collected works and encyclopedias, if they are successful, can finance the general publishing activities of a publishing house for a certain time and in doing so conceal, sometimes even from the publishers themselves, that general literature, which is the main publishing activity, no longer pays for itself. When these larger works no longer sell, the publisher incurs losses and must close down—unless a similar new work has begun in good time. At the same time, the publication of the larger works and technical literature requires so much of the publisher in terms of capital and editorial resources that there is always a risk that the house will give up the publication of general literature and become a specialist publisher—of encyclopedias, hand-books, textbooks, and so on.

14

Closing the Books

I have tried to show that the publishing crisis is a deep structural crisis and not merely a temporary difficulty founded on over-production, rising prices and the general economic situation. The crisis has its roots in the decisive changes taking place in western industrial society, in which the Swedish example is indicative of what is bound to happen in the other highly developed European states. In America this development has been going on for a long time, since, in many important ways, the social and economic structure has been unlike that of Europe. Foremost is the fact that there has never been a bourgeois, culture-sustaining class, but from the beginning literature has been formed in accordance with the requirements of mass society: wide dispersal of a few books, using the same techniques of distribution as for other consumer goods. There has not been a homogeneous social class that provided a distinct market for published books, but rather it has been necessary to reach the presumptive buyers by using every means available. Therefore a distribution system for books of the European type has never been built up: a commission-based book trade spread throughout the whole country with the same, virtually complete, assortment of new books. Instead the book market has been dominated by powerfully marketed cheap books or centralized book clubs where the publisher decides the choice of books.

Changes in society are slow and their course complicated, and they have been only lightly sketched here. But the transformation to the service society, which began during the years between the wars and accelerated in the rapid economic development of the 60s, has now come so far that it is the dominant type of society in Sweden. Material welfare has come more and more into the foreground, whereas culture has received a relatively obscure place and become bureaucratized as well as centralized, like many other social functions. In the process the humanistic elements of culture and particularly serious fiction, have had to give way to professional knowledge, technology and specialization. The dream of education for the people and culture for all has been transformed into an efficient educational technocracy where the purpose of knowledge is the highest possible productivity for society.

This is all too apparent from the value placed on culture by politicians. At the universities subjects such as philosophy, history and literature have stagnated, while natural science and technology move forward. Specialized vocational selection occurs earlier than ever in schools, and basic proficiency in the mother tongue is becoming progressively poorer. In the West the amount governments spend on culture is insignificant compared with what Eastern Europe spends for instance. A typical political evaluation of culture can be discovered in the change in the cultural concept that has the support of all the political parties and larger organizations in Sweden. The so-called sociological concept of culture, culture in the broadest sense of the word, is touted and provides the basis for centralized manipulation of culture.

The service society also has a negative effect on reading habits. Increased leisure time certainly involves a shorter work day, but not an increase of free time comparable to the reduction of working hours. The accelerated pace of work has a tiring and enervating effect on more and more people, while the ever increasing flow of information makes it difficult to select what is important. The rising availability of consumer goods further diminishes the time that could be devoted to cultural activities.

Culture is not only relatively uninteresting from a political point of view, it is also unimportant economically. The frenetic recreation industry finds it more profitable to sell travel and hobby articles rather than books. This industry also gains support from the growth ideology adopted by industrial countries, which is aimed at quantity consumption and not its quality.

Our housing patterns too have a negative influence on cultural activities. Because more and more people live in the suburbs of large cities they are isolated from each other and from association with culture. Families and friends do not gather together to read aloud or to join in study circles unless it is for some sort of specific practical training. On weekends and holidays those people who can, leave their homes either to go to the country or to visit friends. Their time is spent in cars, with their hobbies, with friends and very seldom in reading.

Culture no longer has any important social status, as it did during the bourgeois period. To attend the theatre, the opera, an art exhibition, a concert, and to have read the latest books was a clear demonstration of power and wealth or social standing, whether one enjoyed doing these things or not. The new rich often displayed their wealth in cultural areas, as patrons of the arts, book collectors or music enthusiasts. Today this kind of ostentatious display usually manifests itself materialistically in the acquisition of luxury houses, yachts, aeroplanes, clothes.

At the same time the changes in society and new technological developments increased the possibility of contact with culture, particularly for the underprivileged people in the society. Television and radio has brought music, the theatre and films directly into the home in wealthier countries. And in Sweden, live theatre also has been made available to more people than ever before, and at reasonable prices. But this has occurred on mass society's own terms, which has meant centralized control of what was offered to the public and a limited choice both of quality and variety.

Bourgeois society had its definite, often moralistic values; there is considerably more tolerance in the mass society. The limits of the acceptable have been stretched successively: this is not only an indication of a more liberal attitude but also of greater indifference. Most of all, however, it indicates that art no longer serves the central function in society it once did.

Instead, the difficulty for art today is to gain attention in the swelling stream of information and influences. In the mass society it has been more difficult for books to reach an audience and to adjust than it has been for other art forms. Both plays and music, for instance, are easily and cheaply distributed through the modern media. (The première of Ingmar Bergman's production of *The Magic Flute* on television was seen by two to three million people, at a cost of a couple of kronor per viewer!)

The financial situation for serious writers has improved considerably, at least in Sweden. But the writer has also become more isolated from reality. For this reason many have sought other forms of expression: they have gone to TV and radio, become journalists, and turned to political writing, since in these fields they have a much better opportunity of contact with their readers.

A successful writer may experience his isolation thus:

We have an élite culture completely without a popular foundation, free-flying in the atmosphere of society like one of the flying islands in Swift's tale of Laputa. The people are directed to commercialized scrap literature, while simultaneously their aesthetic creative powers become crippled. . . . The established élite art is converted into an exclusive order . . . with secret signs, a secret language and values that only apply within the confines of the order.[1]

Or a critic's view of the situation of literary books:

> The general impression one gets . . . is the picture of a dutiful little lifeboat, packed full of serious fiction, being towed by a huge freighter filled with large gift books, handbooks on everything, books on the occult and mysticism, science-fiction, detective stories and historic pap.[2]

The position of fiction writers today is the result of the conditions imposed by the mass society, either to be steered through the centralized distribution channels or to remain more or less unnoticed. This situation has been poignantly described by Swedish writer Birgitta Trotzig:

> The writer's problem and the life-problem of everybody is the social situation, which appears more and more threatening—the increase in the concentration of real power in a few power groups, the increased pressure and efforts towards the manipulation of life-styles and ways of thinking by these organizations in their struggle to retain and broaden their sphere of power, their markets . . . in this situation the real power, the actual law of gravity, tends to transform, in so far as possible, the private, socially conscious and living personality into an isolated individual, in the truest sense of the term. . . .
>
> The expression of this de-personalization and enervation, this neutralizing of a man as a creative personality which our society, with a variety of means, subjects children and adults to (in advertising, in the mass media's tendency toward diluted, innocent, idyllic information in the directing of life-styles via consumption toward inexpensive, simplified quasi values, quasi activities)—becomes the individual's sense of isolation from others in a mechanized, impersonal world of material things.[3]

The author Jan Myrdal sees the writer's position from a similar angle. Not only does he feel the influence of the mass society, but he sees these pressures as a manifestation of conscious manipulation. In a comment to the State Culture Fund he writes:

> . . . the greatly increasing need for grants for writers is connected with the politically determined, already completed, liquidation of Swedish publishing and bookselling operations. That these 'support actions' are intended to make us 'parallel' to current economic development is also mirrored in the fact that the administration of writers and artists is being transferred more and more to the jurisdiction of the Labour Marketing Board.[4]

This belief is confirmed in the discussions recently carried out in Sweden concerning society's rights to authors' works. In a directive for a study centring on these problems, it was pointed out that there is a general interest in the work of individual writers and that there were great 'practical difficulties' involved in using these rights if it is necessary to ask the permission of the person who owns them, that is to say, the writers. But most of all it was emphasized that such rights should be seen 'in a broader social and general cultural-political light' and that some instrument should be created to level incomes between various writers.

It was stated that while some writers earn absurdly large incomes, often from the general public's use of their work, there are others who receive an unjustly small financial reward for what they write. The point seems to be that writers should hand over their copy-rights to society, which may then freely use them, in return for a reasonable fee regardless of how they are used.

Such a view is based to a great extent on the acceptance of the belief that in a centralized society there is generally so little contact between writers and their public that society must give writers financial support, and in turn has the right to control the use to which their work is put. This development will most certainly con-tribute to a further shielding of writers from their readers and lead to the 'parallelization' with general social development that Myrdal fears—apart from the threat it poses to freedom of speech!

The role of the literary writer and the literary book in society can best be seen in relation to Escarpit's two circuits: *the cultivated circuit*, which distributes books to people who are actively interested in literature, frequently intellectual and educated but no longer limited to a particular class; they are defined rather by their interests than by their social background. The other is *the popular circuit*, whose literature and distribution apparatus is directed toward those who are not habitual readers and to those with a life-style and work situation that makes it difficult for them to read regularly.[5] (The term 'the cultivated circuit' is an unhappy choice. It should instead be called 'the specialized circuit', since it does not pertain to a specific social class but to a small group with special interests.)

Escarpit points out just how exclusive the cultivated circuit is. Pub-lishers, booksellers, readers, critics and often writers belong to the same circle. Also it tends to become increasingly narrow because the publisher selects a certain type of manuscript to be published, the bookseller chooses from the publisher's list and the limitations of critics and readers further tighten the circuit.

Escarpit has not placed his theory in a social context and therefore it drifts rather vaguely in the air. But if such an analysis is made his terms become eminently applicable. The cultivated circuit then becomes a result of the mass society's 'rejection mechanism'. All the culture forms that are unsuitable to the popular circuit are isolated together in the other circuit. It is perfectly natural therefore that writers who do not reach a large public feel increasingly isolated. It is also common, as we have seen, that printings of their books actually decline. The writer can count on increasing financial support in Sweden from various organizations which will enable him to live, but it becomes more difficult for him to reach readers through his books, or indeed even to have them published. There are two patterns of reaction against this: either to work in other media than books, or to further isolate himself from the institutions the mass market has to offer.

The latter has resulted in the forming of writer co-operatives and stencil publishers. Birgitta Trotzig proposes just a solution:

> But if reality then cannot be encouraged, even by artificial respiration, to function in the desired direction? . . . If the gulf between the official language and the secret inner monologue has already become too great? Well, in that case perhaps the publishing houses can survive a few more years in a kind of pseudo existence by serving up Böll in Nobel sauce and Solzhenitsyn in the beard of Imperial Russia—but sooner or later they will have to do as the bookshops do, sell paper napkins. . . . . The solution is to do things ourselves. The age of the village leagues, the political cells, the mimeograph, is here . . . We'll MEET AT THE MIMEOGRAPHS!

Similar points of view are becoming current in the USA. A young writer who has published two books has formed a collective for the publication of serious fiction. He gives the following reason:

> The publishing industry can no longer support quality fiction. . . . There are still of course accident-novelists of quality who also have mass market appeal . . . while serious fiction in its slow discourse with culture most often finds its initial public among the happy few. At the same time that publishing has been starving out serious fiction, the genre has experienced a resurgence of vitality and inventiveness. What we currently have is a mass market industry that cannot afford to produce small, reasonably priced editions of quality fiction.[6]

But the consequence will be a further shrinking of the cultivated circuit to a vicious circle. Writers will prefer to write for 'the happy few' than to enter the increasingly impossible struggle to join the 'popular circuit'.

This isolation does not only change the economic situation of writers and publishers. In an earlier chapter I have shown how the literary novel has begun to turn inward. Until the 50s these novels still functioned as an important part of the cultural debate, now writers find it more difficult to influence the general public at all, including the public in the shrinking cultivated circuit.

This is caused to some extent by the altered role of critics in society. They have undergone the same development as authors. During the nineteenth century the critic was a judge of taste, a guide, radical or conservative, a George Brandes or a Sainte-Beuve, with a great deal of influence and power within the homogeneous milieu. It was not without reason that Sainte-Beuve was called 'the Emperor'. Soon the critic was given a special section in the newspaper, the literary pages, from which he could direct taste and the course of literature.

The critic also played an important part in the cultural-political struggle, whether or not he was conservative or radical. The position he adopted, his praise or condemnation, sharpened, defined and stimulated the development of literature.

A natural consequence of the shrinking of the cultivated circuit is the diminished influence of the critic. Not only are there fewer reviews, but their importance has declined both in terms of the general debate and in their influence on the sale of books. The critic no longer writes primarily for the public since it has become more and more difficult to reach in the mass society, but rather for his colleagues and writers—the latter are often also critics. It is symptomatic of current reviewing of most theatrical and musical life in our society that critics are dealing with performances that are over and done with when the reviews are published, namely, those performances that are given on TV and radio. The critic addresses himself exclusively to those who have written, directed or performed the work.

In an interesting essay a Swedish literary sociologist has discussed the changed role of the critic in the mass society. He regards the cultural pages as:

> a place where the literary establishment itself decides the subjects of discussion. It is here the criteria of judgement are formed that are current for the present, but they are not accepted with confidence nor do they fulfil any social need. . . . The cultural pages have also changed rapidly during the 60s, to become a kind of correspondence section for the conflicting opinions of the intelligentsia on all kinds of matters . . . (it concerns) a growing isolation and insignificance and capitulation in the face of the third and extreme instance: the consuming mass public.[7]

A legacy of the critic's lack of contact with the reading public is the development of a literary activity which in many cases exists only for the critics. There are already a number of very good writers who receive excellent reviews, but whose books are confined to a closed system with few readers, and they have virtually no hope of a breakthrough in the future. In the USA, for instance, there are Walker Percy, William Gass, John Cheever, John Barth, or in England Margaret Drabble, Brigid Brophy, Penelope Mortimer and Colin Wilson.

They are often candidates for prizes, they may have an occasional book taken by a club or even filmed. but generally they fail to break through into the popular circuit. Instead of their public increasing, the printings of their books are reduced. The final result may be that they no longer have their books published at all or that they stop writing. These writers are regarded by many as 'difficult' or 'boring' and are called 'academic'. An American publisher expresses it this way:

> The Novel, particularly the literary novel, has lost touch with its audience . . . serious writing [has turned] inwards alienated and often obscure, it leads booksellers to ask 'where are the good reads of yesteryear'?[8]

Another American publisher has similar views about the writer's contact with readers:

> . . . good writers have become less informative and we have had a more solipsistic kind of writing: it is the difference between Ibsen and Shaw in the theatre, and Pinter and Williams.[9]

The cultivated circuit's main distribution channel is the bookseller with a full assortment. We have seen how the bookseller in the nineteenth century, from first having taken part in the production of books and sometimes even operating as a lending library, became a purely retail dealer in the sale of books. This was in tune with nineteenth-century economic development, with the striving for specialization at different levels of trade.

The commission book trade reflected the society of the time. Its function was to keep all newly published books in stock. In principle every bookshop was to have the same assortment of books no matter where it was located in the country. This was an obvious requirement, since it was the bourgeoisie who bought books and the social structure was the same in every large community throughout the country, although naturally the number of persons composing it varied. (The changed market situation for books can also be explained by the changes in the social structure of the mass society, outlined on page 122. In the old class society the upper middle class was an easily defined and accessible target group for the book trade.

If one sees the social structure more as an 'establishment cube', the power stratum is of course easily defined, but those in it are not more interested in culture than other people. Therefore, in the mass society the majority of people become *potential* readers, but it is difficult and expensive to reach them—crassly put, it entails an expensive nation-wide advertising campaign instead of merely placing a book in the display window of a bookshop.)

Therefore the situation for the traditional book trade became ever more difficult when mass society began to replace bourgeois society. Instead of a uniform sale to a relatively limited class of book buyers with a steady demand for many books, suddenly there is a mass-media-influenced demand for *one* book. It does not require a fairly restricted number of widely spread, well-stocked bookshops to fulfil this need but rather a vast number of sales outlets stocked with just this book.

In the cultivated circuit's narrowing circle the position of book-shops becomes ever more precarious. Its expensive service, trade knowledge and stockholding, protected by fixed book prices and limitations on the establishment of new shops, from the bourgeois epoch, is countered by declining need. The purchase of books over a broad spectrum of subjects is no longer the pattern of a specific social class but merely the requirement of a few enthusiasts, much the same situation as with modelling hobbies or stamp collecting. In future we can also count on booksellers having similar types of shops—specialist shops for poetry or drama, or East European literature, or simply serious fiction—which will replace bookshops that carry a wide assortment of books. It seems unlikely that there will be many of them; in a mass-market system they will represent a greatly reduced demand.

What will happen is that the majority of bookshops will adjust to the popular circuit. This has already occurred to a large extent in the western world, with the Montanus chain in Germany, the French FNAC shops and the Book Supermarkets in Sweden, shops that sell cheap paperbacks and have a limited selection of the most popular hard cover books, supplemented by similar mass-market products like gramophone records and posters.

Here too America has formed the pattern. Since Americans have never had a bourgeois class with homogeneous reading habits, they have never had a need for bookshops with a full assortment of books. A quotation here shows that current development is even affecting the relatively few well-stocked bookshops that do exist. The future of bookshops is judged as follows in a recently published survey:

Books by unknown writers or books containing unpopular opinions would vanish first. Some in fact are disappearing from the bookstores now. The trend is toward fewer stores, many of which stock exclusively fast-moving books ... bookclubs with their limited and often vulgar offerings are increasing in size.[10]

Escarpit considers the popular circuit generally to be the publication and distribution of so-called news-stand literature. Here too the definition can be broadened and placed in its proper social and economic context.

We have seen how popular literature has bourgeoned in the western world. In addition to this it has become more socially acceptable—or rather opposition from intellectuals has declined—particularly in Sweden, through the emphasis placed on the sociological concept of culture, which has meant that even libraries are now stocking this popular literature. The studies in L68 on reading habits showed that this cheap literature was not being read exclusively by 'culture-poor groups' but 'to an equal extent by well-educated groups with high incomes'.

The same result was arrived at by British sociologist Peter Mann. He pays particular attention to the turnabout that has occurred in the last few years:

When I wrote my first study of the readers of romantic fiction in 1969 ... practically no one in the world of books mentioned them in conversation. ... Many thousands were avidly bought each month by enthusiastic readers all over the world, and many public libraries bought them in large quantities for their eager readers. But in spite of the large readership for romance, the genre was still regarded as something not to be discussed in polite circles. ... Since 1969 romantic novels have been written about much more, they have been talked about on radio and television and much of the prejudice against them has gone. These eminently unrespectable books have at last become 'respectable'.[11]

Mann's study shows that in Britain too there is a wide readership for these books even among the higher social groups and at various levels of education.

It has been shown here that popular literature is not in itself a product of the mass society. However, mass society and mass culture are conducive to the spread of these books. The high material level of society has not directed taste towards a higher quality of books, instead popular literature has been revalued since it is eminently suited to the new social structure.

As a supplement to popular literature—which from the beginning is directed at the popular circuit and has its own special channels of distribution—there are also some books which have their origins in the cultivated circuit. This kind of breakthrough is rare and can only occur under certain circumstances and on the mass society's own terms.

The simplest way to achieve this is that a book planned for the cultivated circuit—a bookshop book in ordinary hardcover design and at going prices—is turned into a bestseller. Often it is a novel, but it can also be from some other branch of general literature such as memoirs, biographies or travel books. Very occasionally external circumstances can combine to create the extraordinary attention that is essential; a literary prize, for instance, or some sensation connected with the author, or that the subject of the book is of interest to the mass media. As noted earlier, a good review is not in itself sufficient to arouse interest in a book, it must be of such character that the self-perpetuating mass-media effect is brought into play, that is to say, the review—not the book!—attracts the attention of the press, radio and possibly TV so that they become interested in the writer and thereby create self-generating publicity around him.

Certain literary prizes have a built-in automatic triggering effect that functions as a selecting mechanism: the effect of the Nobel prize is well known, as is the effect of the Goncourt, Renaudot or Medici prizes in France. The Goncourt prize is so important that book customers often don't bother to ask for the book by its title but for the 'Goncourt book'. But this does not mean, however, that the author is automatically established. With the next book he or she can return to an obscure existence within the cultivated circuit. Indeed, a prize-winning book can disappear completely from the market after a few successful years. Books by Nobel prize-winners such as Agnon, Andric, or even Sjolochov, are very difficult to find outside their native countries.

The usual way of creating a bestseller is that the publishers themselves produce publicity around certain selected books. This only works with a very few books written by writers whose person the mass media may be interested in. The publisher's own efforts in the form of advertisements, bookshop displays and so on are no longer sufficient to create a bestseller since it is impossible to reach the popular circuit by normal advertising procedures. The advertisement that was adequate in bourgeois society to inform the traditional circle of customers no longer functions in the newspapers of the mass society.

It should be emphasized here that the creation of a bestseller has very little to do with the quality of the book. Often they are good books, occasionally of an extremely high literary quality.

I have touched earlier on the development towards a few books yielding exceptionally large returns. The chapter on the economy of the novel has, for example, shown that it is essential for a publishing house that publishes general literature to have a certain number of bestsellers: books selling 10,000 to 20,000 copies. But the necessary bestseller does not in the long run support the literary book. The publisher's impatience quickly grows with the writer who doesn't manage the breakthrough, and frequently the income from the bestsellers is not sufficient to cover the cost of all the other books, or the publishing house becomes so absorbed in creating new bestsellers that it loses interest in other books published by them. There is a risk of a kind of moral wear and tear on the literary editor at a publishing house. The constant demand for success often impinges on the demand for quality. There is not sufficient time to build an author up slowly over a period of years. As a result enthusiasm can be cut off too early or be transferred to more superficial books. In an American analysis this is expressed as follows:

> The bestseller psychology places too much emphasis on a few big books to the detriment of all the rest.... Costs including guarantees to authors are skyrocketing. Publishers are talking glumly about the prospects of new and first novels. Editors fear that a growing commercialism will cut short the writing careers of some promising new talent.[12]

Here is an even more illustrative example of the same thing, a description of the development in the German book market, in which most publishers will surely recognize themselves:

> There is a development taking place in the German publishing business ... where the larger publishing houses are concentrating more and more on the 'bestseller' idea ... a typical remark in German press circles is that the literary publisher has developed into a cold calculating creator of products.... In Germany a book is regarded as a bestseller when it reaches a printing of 30,000 copies or more, but it is not really counted as such unless it reaches sales of six figures.... The bestseller wave, which seems really to have swamped the large German publishing houses, has created a new pattern of communication from these publishers to the booksellers and the public. Earlier there was a term used in the German book trade called *Schlager*. Quite simply, it meant books that sold well. At that time German publishers managed adequately by advertising in *Börsenblatt* [German book-trade journal], sending out the odd prospectus and sending

review copies out to the press, and in generally building upon the book's literary qualities, the publisher's reputation and the interest such factors could produce. Today much more is required. . . . The whole programme of development used by German publishers is a faithful copy of American methods. They have learned to invest large sums in advertising in the daily press, as they have learned to treat books like other marketable goods. They have learned to use all the means at their disposal, not least of which is to recruit the author into the process. Terms like public relations and sales promotion have become everyday expressions for publishers and now even 'show effect' is being used.[13]

Bestseller publishing requires very good finances, great influence in the mass media and wide contacts. All these things favour the forming of large publishing houses and the closing down of smaller ones. Such a trend is in line with business development generally in industrial countries. In the USA, Britain, France, Germany, and Sweden as well, most of the medium-sized and smaller publishing houses are already owned by large corporations.

Those publishers who are not bought up by the larger concerns are themselves forced to try to issue bestsellers. Norwegian publisher Henrik Groth has said that 'the publisher of today has forgotten how to read the letters of the alphabet—he can only read numerals', and Klaus Piper, head of a traditional general literature publishing house in Germany has this to say: 'Books like *The Day of the Jackal* and *The Odessa File* my father would never have published.'

As a result literary publishers are now often replaced as heads of publishing houses by economists. It is perfectly natural then that the latter should judge the publishing of books from an economic standpoint, an attitude that can hardly favour the publication of serious literature. These publishing houses also tend to become large corporations and must be run like large corporations. This statement was made in a survey of European publishing operations during the past few years:

In comparing a publisher with a factory manager he expresses in a nutshell changes which since the sixties have been turning European book publishing into European book industry. The individual publisher's decisive role in the market has disappeared, and the old-fashioned style of English gentleman among publishers is virtually dead. In their place we find as almost everywhere on the economic scene giant market operators, networks, holding companies.[14]

An important aspect of success in the popular circuit is control of distribution. The larger publishing concerns have shown interest earlier in owning chains of bookshops such as the leading Doubleday chain in America, Collins which owns the Hatchard chain in Britain and Hachette which dominates the field both in bookshops and news-stands in France. The normal bookshops, however, belong to the cultivated circuit and as such no longer have any great appeal for the larger publishers. In contrast, however, the new type of boutique which sells a small selection of books together with other goods, such as paper and records, like the German Montanus chain, is well suited to the popular circuit. A similar chain has been built up in Sweden over the last few years, the so-called Bokman shops, which carry a mixed assortment of goods with books accounting for only one-third of the turnover. It is logical then that Bonniers, who sold their conventional bookshops some time ago, have recently acquired 50 per cent of the stock.

The form of distribution best suited to the mass society is, however, the book club. It fills all the requirements for the distribution of books to people who are tired and stressed, who have difficulty making their own selection, who are influenced by the mass media to notice a small number of books, who have little spare time and who find it convenient to have a book automatically delivered to their home. The accepted passivity of the members is perhaps best illustrated by the success of the so-called package book clubs like Lademan's in Denmark and Bra Böcker in Sweden. These clubs send out a package, usually containing three books, from which the members are not allowed, and obviously have no wish, to make a choice.

The increasing dominance of the book clubs in the distribution of general literature, particularly novels, is manifest in all western industrial countries. The idea originated in the USA and has spread throughout Europe since World War II. It has been such a great financial success that book clubs now control a large part of the book market, in some cases as multi-national companies, and generally speaking it is the income from their operations that increasingly subsidizes publication within the cultivated crcuit. In the USA the effect can be determined directly from the licensing fees paid by the clubs to the original publishers (Table 22, p. 169). It has been estimated that an average loss for the publisher within the cultivated circuit of approximately 7 per cent is transformed to a profit of approximately 7 per cent through income from licensing fees or subsidiary rights to the publisher.

In Germany, where 45 per cent of the total book sales are made through book clubs, the publishing of general literature is completely dominated by Bertelsmann who have built up a book club that has over 3 million members in Germany, and approximately the same number in the book clubs that this concern partly or wholly owns in Holland, Austria, Switzerland, Spain, France and recently in Brazil, Mexico, Argentina, Columbia and Venezuela. Bertelsmann finances directly, by buying part ownership in other publishing houses, or indirectly through the purchase of not less than 90 per cent of the book-club books from publishers outside the company, a large part of the German fiction offerings. The other large German book club, the Holtzbrinck group, follows a similar pattern. From a modest beginning it grew after the war to approximately 1.4 million members. This company has bought shares or controlling interest in a number of German literary publishing houses such as S. Fischer, Droemer, and Rowohlt. The group has also acquired multi-national interests through subsidiary companies in France, Spain, and Holland.

In France one of the leading publishers, Presse de la Cité—the second largest publisher after Hachette—started a book club operation jointly with Bertelsmann, now a great success with more than a million members. In Britain W. H. Smith, which owns many of the railway news-stands, started a book club together with the American Doubleday company; this publisher in turn dominates book club operations in the USA.

In Scandinavia during the 60s the book clubs began to gain control of the market for general literature.

In Denmark Lademann and Gyldendal have approximately 600,000 members between them. The best-known book clubs in Norway are owned by the four largest publishers of general literature and have a membership of approximately 300,000. And in Finland membership is probably about the same, around 300,000.

The development of book-club sales in Sweden have followed the international trend, at about the same speed and in conjunction with the other changes in Swedish society. During the 50s book-club sales were still largely to the cultivated circuit. Svalan was the only large book club at the time and the majority of its 20,000 to 40,000 members bought most of their books in the regular bookshops.

Near the end of the 50s direct selling by the book clubs increased noticeably and during the 60s it grew tremendously with a turnover of more than 15 million kronor per year.

During the publishing crisis at the end of the 60s and early 70s Svalan proved to be decisive to the financial survival of Bonnier's publishing house and today more than half of this publisher's turnover of approximately 150 million kronor comes from wholly owned book clubs. Besides this Bonniers is the largest shareholder in Månadens Bok (Book of the Month Club) which was fashioned on its American counterpart and was an immediate success when it began in 1973. Book club operations probably now finance completely all other publishing activities so that within a decade this conventional literary publishing house, whose activities were formerly aimed at the cultivated circuit, has gone over almost entirely to the popular circuit —a remarkable change.

The other major publishing houses now also have their own book clubs or are partners in one of the larger clubs. Altogether, then, about 700,000 people buy books through book clubs. This means that if every member bought books for 200 kronor per year the total would amount to almost 150 million kronor, and would account for approximately 30 per cent of the total sales of general literature. (The Swedish Publishers' Association estimated 1973 sales to be approximately 520 million kronor in consumer value.) A realistic prognosis for the remainder of the 70s is a 50 per cent increase in sales. This would mean that almost half of all general literature will be sold through book clubs, a situation that already exists in Germany.

It should be clear then that the situation for general literature and especially the novel is very serious. The situation of writers becomes more and more difficult because of their isolation and poor returns. The ability of small literary publishers to survive as independent firms is lessened and the interest of larger publishers in serious fiction is becoming increasingly subject to short-term considerations. This means of distribution is reduced to a few very powerful channels, and, most serious of all, public interest in a broad literary offering is diminishing.

There are certain mechanisms within the mass society which favour the popular circuit and which are difficult to counter: simplification, passivity, the influence of the mass media, and as a result, often low prices. Opposed to this is the cultivated circuit's negative circle, which is completely dependent on a badly functioning market economy. According to Escarpit the relatively comprehensive offering required by the cultivated circuit is directed towards 'an insufficiently broad consumer base, and the steadily renewed demand leads to a system based on successive selections, within the cultivated circuit to waste and compulsory unproductiveness.' In other words, more is written than there are people who have either the time or the desire to read it. Opposed to this is the threat of the popular circuit to literary quality: 'The lack of socially adjusted producers, the surrender of the initiative to the distributor, the infinite and anonymous demand of a public that remains unknown but which consumes . . . [leads] on the one hand to a wearing and mechanization of the literary forms, and on the other to an alienation of the cultural life of the masses.'

Is there any solution? Escarpit claims that it lies in the possibility of breaking out of the cultivated circuit to enter the popular circuit. He suggests a variety of possibilities: book clubs, quality paperbacks and libraries. All these three channels are important. One example is the Book-of-the-Month-type club which offers new books, predominantly novels in original hardcovers at reduced prices. However, even though these books are often of a high literary quality the selection is narrow and this kind of operation tends to encourage the original publisher to concentrate on a certain type of book, where experimentation and daring are avoided.

Quality paperbacks have, in any case, not managed to break through to the popular circuit in Scandinavia, but rather offer a good inexpensive alternative to hardcovers for the traditional bookshop customers. But sales have stagnated. Publishers have neither succeeded in capturing a new public nor have they found new distribution channels for books. In the areas where the main languages are English or French they have had more success. Escarpit mentions Penguin books. In spite of this, however, most of these books appear to be sold through bookshops to the 'cultivated circuit'.

Unquestionably the libraries have been most successful. But despite this success development in this area also is moving towards popular books of the mass culture. By allowing demand to decide selection and availability, the lending of books in libraries has moved in the direction of more bestsellers, or towards writers of the popular circuit. In principle, if a book sells well it is purchased in large numbers by the libraries, whereas if it sells poorly only a few copies are bought. In this way the libraries follow the general development within the mass society (cf. also p. 171 and Mann's information on the large library purchases of Mills & Boon's 'romances').

Will the non-factual book, and I mean primarily here the novel, play a central role in the future? We have already seen that its importance has declined, that there are other ways of informing, of illustrating society, of portraying people. Hauser speaks of 'the film age'. Others have mentioned a revival of the theatre, as George Steiner, for instance, who claims that the novel now lacks vitality. He maintains that it is not possible to draw demarcation lines between the various techniques of 'representation', such as theatre, films, television and radio: 'A society with fewer private libraries and a declining number of readers . . . can definitely be a society with numerous movie screens, arenas and theatres.'

The period of the novel in our culture has been extraordinarily short compared with that of drama. The latter has also been shown through a number of different periods to be a medium for the whole of society—from the aristocracy to the farm worker, from the bourgeoisie to the parlour maid. The theatre is suited to modern techniques including those of the mass society. It is therefore reasonable to assume that it will have considerable cultural influence at the expense of the novel.

Even though the novel no longer occupies the same central position in our culture it is an irreplaceable part of it. But the novel can only survive and flourish with a reasonably broad offering, if it is to reach its public in a natural way. To keep it from being isolated it must be given powerful support by society. No section of the cultivated circuit will in the future have the potential to give the novel the support it requires, neither writers, publishers nor booksellers. It is perhaps logical, but hardly satisfactory, that those cultural forms such as the theatre and films, which are better suited to the mass society, have already received considerable government aid in many countries while the book has so far had to go without. An immediate and sizeable contribution by society is needed in order to preserve and continue to develop the literary book—as much for the sake of society itself as for the book.

Notes

1. *The Reading Public and the Book Market*

1. Royal A. Gettmann, *A Victorian Publisher, A Study of the Bentley Papers*, Cambridge 1960, p. 29
2. Ian Watts, *The Rise of the Novel*, Penguin, London 1957, 1972, pp. 38ff.
3. Arnold Hauser, *The Social History of Art*, Routledge & Kegan Paul, London 1951, p. 541
4. Q. D. Leavis, *Fiction and the Reading Public*, Chatto & Windus, London 1932, p. 131 and Richard D. Altick, *The English Common Reader. A Social History of the Mass Reading Public 1800–1900*, Chicago 1957, p. 231. In an appendix there is a table of printings and editions of books, magazines and newspapers which is of great interest
5. Hauser, p. 541
6. Quoted from S. H. Steinberg, *Five Hundred Years of Printing*, Penguin, 1974, p. 239
7. This figure is from Dr. Johnson but has been doubted and corrected to 5,000. See Altick, p. 47
8. F. A. Mumby & Ian Norrie, *Publishing & Bookselling*, Jonathan Cape, London 1974, pp. 138ff.
9. Philip Wallis, *At the Sign of the Ship. Notes on the House of Longmans 1724–1974*, Longmans, London 1974, p. 17
10. Quoted from Gettmann, p. 29
11. Mumby, p. 191
12. Quoted from Gettmann, p. 7
13. Cf. Mumby, pp. 138, 155
14. Hauser, p. 548
15. Quoted from Arthur Waugh, *A Hundred Years of Publishing. Being the Story of Chapman & Hall*, Chapman & Hall, London 1930, p. 132
16. Quoted from Gettmann, pp. 4f.
17. Quoted from Gerald Gross (ed.), *Publishers on Publishing*, Grosset & Dunlap, New York 1961, pp. 35 and 64
18. Cf. Gettmann, pp. 80, 82, 113ff.
19. David Keir, *The House of Collins*, Collins, London 1952, pp. 161ff.

20. Jean Mistler, *La Librairie Hachette de 1826 à nos jours*, Hachette, Paris 1964, pp. 49, 81f.
21. See Albert Ward, *Book Production, Fiction, and the German Reading Public 1700–1800*, Oxford University Press, Oxford 1974
22. Quoted from Peter de Mendelsohn, *S. Fischer und sein Verlag*, S. Fischer Verlag, Frankfurt 1970, p. 15
23. Gottfried Bermann Fischer, 'S. Fischer und sein Verlag', from Almanach, *Das fünfundsiebzigste Jahr*, Frankfurt 1961, pp. 9ff.
24. Charles A. Madison, *Book Publishing in America*, McGraw-Hill, New York 1966, pp. 23ff., and p. 64
25. Quoted from *Publishers on Publishing*, p. 58
26. Quoted from Madison, p. 157
27. Hauser, p. 715
28. S. Fischer, 'Der Verleger und der Büchermarkt', from *Das 25. Jahr*, S. Fischer Verlag, Leipzig 1911, p. 26
29. S. Fischer, *Bemerkungen zur Bücherkrise*, privately printed, Leipzig 1926, pp. 216ff.
30. Asa Briggs (ed.), *Essays in the History of Publishing*, Longmans, London 1974, pp. 25ff.
31. Gottfried Bermann Fischer, *Bedroht-Bewahrt, Der Weg eines Verlegers*, S. Fischer Verlag, Frankfurt 1967, pp. 403f.

2. The Disintegration of the Reading Public

1. Cf. Watts, pp. 39, 46, 330; Mumby, p. 201 and Wallis, p. 65
2. Quoted from Gettmann, p. 164
3. Cf. Leavis, pp. 33f.
4. Cf. Erich Auerbach, *Mimesis*, Anchor Books, New York 1957, pp. 434ff.
5. Briggs, pp. 182ff.
6. Keir, pp. 219f.
7. Steinberg, pp. 354ff.
8. Cf. Louis James, *Fiction for the Working Man, 1830–1850*, Oxford University Press, London 1963, and Altick, p. 267 and pp. 288ff.
9. Leavis, pp. 163f.
10. Hauser, pp. 834f.
11. Leavis, pp. 49f.
12. Leavis, p. 35
13. Donald Sheehan, *This was Publishing*, Indiana University Press, Bloomington 1952, pp. 28ff.
14. Madison, pp. 24, 51, 69, 77, see also Frank L. Schick, *The Paperbound Book in America*, R. R. Bowker, New York 1958, pp. 50ff.
15. Gross, p. 62
16. Leavis, p. 29

3. The Development of the Book Market in Denmark, Norway and Finland

1. Aleks. Frøland, *Boger, Bogsalg, Boghandlere*, Forening for Boghandvaerk, Köpenhavn 1969, pp. 19, 90, 112ff.
2. Lauritz Nielsen, *Gyldendal gennem 175 aar*, Gyldendal, Köpenhavn 1945, p. 47
3. Harald L. Tveterås, *Den norske bokhandels historie*, Olso 1964, vol. 2, p. 11
4. Cf. Sigurd Evensmo, *Gyldendal og Gyldendøler*, Gyldendal, Oslo 1974, pp. 40ff.
5. Cf. Harald L. Tveterås, *Den norske bokhandels historie*, vol. 2, pp. 139, 152, 197, 201, 322
6. Cf. Nils Kåre Jacobsen, *Bak kobberdørren, Gyldendal Norsk Forlag 1925–1975*, Gyldendal, Gjøvik 1974, p. 30
7. Cf. Evensmo, pp. 348, 355f.
8. Jacobsen, p. 129
9. Cf. Ola Zweygbergk, *Om bokförlag och bokförläggare i Finland*, Helsingfors 1958

4. The Swedish Book Market

1. Sven Rinman, *Svenska Bokförläggareföreningen 1843–1887*, Stockholm 1951, p. 21
2. Cf. Elisabeth Tykesson, *Rövarromanen och dess hjälte*, Lund 1942, pp. 123ff.
3. Rinman, pp. 21, 45ff.
4. Henrik Schück, *Den svenska förlagsbokhandelns historia*, Norstedts, Stockholm 1923, pp. 444ff.
5. Schück, pp. 337ff.
6. Rinman, p. 256
7. Bonnier, vol. III, p. 144
8. Cf. K. O. Bonnier, *Bonniers En bokhandlarefamilj I–V*, Albert Bonniers förlag, Stockholm 1930, 1931, 1956, part IV, p. 240 and Carl G. Laurin, *P. A. Norstedt & Söner*, Norstedts, Stockholm 1923, p. 33

5. Sweden: the Publishing Crisis. A Case Study

1. References to the various Swedish sources can be found in the Swedish edition of this book. It may though be of interest for English readers to know that the State Commission of 1968 (L68) has published a summary in English in *Boken*, Stockholm 1974

6. Perspective from Abroad

1. Bo Bramsen, *Bogens vilkor i Danmark*, Det Danske Bogmarked nr

21, 1973. Cf. also the report on the current situation of the Danish book trade by the same author, *Bogens vilkor*, Köpenhavn 1973

2. Hans Hertel, *Det litteraere system i Danmark*, A commentary included in the Danish translation of Robert Escarpit, 'Sociologie de la littérature', *Bogen og laeseren*, Köpenhavn 1972

3. Hertel, pp. 283f.

4. Wulf D. von Lucius, 'Wachsende Märkte für das Buch?' *Börsenblatt für den Deutschen Buchhandel*, nr 14, 1973

5. Gerhard Schmidtchen, 'Lesekultur in Deutschland 1974'. *Archiv für Soziologi und Wirtschaftsfragen des Buchhandels XXX, Börsenblatt für den Deutschen Buchhandel* nr 39, 1974

6. Cf. *The Bookseller*, 8 April 1972, *Publisher's Weekly*, 30 September 1974 and *La Quinzaine Littéraire* nr 201, 1975

7. See *Children's Reading Interest*, Evans and Methuen, London 1974 and the survey by the National Council of Women

8. Lucien Goldmann, *Recherches Dialectiques*, Gallimard, Paris 1959, pp. 64–101

7. The Mass or Service Society

1. Daniel Bell, *The Coming of Post-Industrial Society*, Basic Books, New York 1973

2. Ralf Dahrendorf, *Class and Class Conflicts in Industrial Societies*, Routledge & Kegan Paul, London 1959

3. André Gorz, *Stratégie Ouvriére et Néo-capitalisme*, 1964. Here quoted from Bell p. 151

4. See J. K. Galbraith, *The New Industrial State*, Houghton Mifflin, Boston 1967 and *Economics and the Public Purpose*, Houghton Mifflin, Boston 1973

5. Herbert Marcuse, *One-Dimensional Man*, Routledge and Kegan Paul, London 1964

6. Marcuse, pp. xiif.

7. David Riesman, *The Lonely Crowd*, Yale University Press 1950, 1953

8. Bell, p. 129

9. Alvin Toffler, *Future Shock*, Pan Books, London 1972, p. 25

10. Marianne Frankenhaeuser, *Overstimulans*, Department of Justice, Stockholm 1973, p. 58

11. *Dagens Nyheter*, 24 May 1974

12. Edgar Morin, *L'Esprit du Temps*, Editions Bernard Grasset, Paris 1974, p. 13

13. Toffler, p. 159

14. Cf. Sebastian de Graza, *Of Time, Work and Leisure*, New York 1962, pp. 66 and 78, and Nels Anderson, *Work and Leisure*, London 1961, pp. 53 and 60

15. Staffan Burenstam-Linder, *The Harried Leisure Class*, Columbia University Press, New York 1970, p. 95
16. Burenstam-Linder, p. 20

8. *Culture in the Mass Society*

1. Marcuse, p. 7
2. Daniel Bell, 'The Cultural Contradictions of Capitalism', from *Capitalism To-Day*, ed. by Daniel Bell and Irving Kristol, Basic Books, New York 1970, p. 35
3. Hannah Arendt, *The Crisis in Culture, Between Past and Future*, London 1961
4. Toffler, pp. 153ff.
5. Leo Bogant, *The Age of Television*, quoted in Edgar Morin, *L'Esprit du Temps*, Paris 1968, p. 42
6. Marcuse, p. 65
7. Morin, p. 21
8. Dwight Macdonald, 'A theory of Mass Culture', from *Mass Culture*, ed. by Bernard Rosenberg & David Manning, The Free Press, New York 1957, p. 63

9. *Sweden's Place in the World*

1. Olaf Ruin, *Svenska Dagbladet*, 29 May 1974
2. Alain Touraine, *The Post-Industrial Society*, Wildwood House, London 1974, p. 9
3. John Kenneth Galbraith, *The New Industrial State*, p. 75
4. Gustaf Olivecrona, *Svenskarna och deras herrar*, W & W, Malmö 1974, p. 13
5. Nordal Åkerman, *Klassamhället i soffror*, Prisma, Lund 1973, p. 10
6. Agne Gustafsson, *Svenska Dagbladet*, 31 May 1974
7. Åke Daun, *Förortsliv*, Lund 1974, p. 52
8. Bertil Gardell, *Dagens Nyheter*, 1 March 1974
9. Kerstin Vinterhed, *Dagens Nyheter*, 25 September 1973

10. *Culture in Sweden*

1. 'Läs- och bokvanor i fem svenska samhällen', *SOU* nr 20, (L68), Stockholm 1972, p. 10
2. Alan C. Purves, *Literature and Education in Ten Countries*, Uppsala 1973, pp. 21 and 24
3. Gunnar Hansson, *Dagens Nyheter*, 30 May 1974
4. Bertil Hertzberg and Brigitta Holm, *Dagens Nyheter*, 30 April 1974
5. Kjell Sundberg, *Vi vill ha bildningen tillbaka*, Vår Lösen nr 5, 1974, p. 231

6. Fredrik Berglund and Marie Bergom Larsson, *Dagens Nyheter*, 15 June 1973
7. *Aftonbladet*, 27 May 1974

11. *A New Concept of Culture*

1. Harald Swedner, *Om finkultur och minoriteter*, Uppsala 1971, p. 64, (The original essay was published in 1965)
2. Swedner, p. 69
3. Agneta Lundahl, *Fritid och rekreation*, Stockholm 1971, p. 66

12. *The Novel in a Changing Society*

1. Lionel Trilling, 'Manners, Morals and The Novel', from *The Liberal Imagination*, The Viking Press, New York 1950
2. Hauser, p. 930
3. Lucien Goldmann, *Towards a Sociology of the Novel*, Tavistock, London 1975, p. 13
4. Goldmann, *Recherches Dialectiques*, pp. 64–101
5. George Steiner, *Kultur und Post-Kultur*, *Merkur*, November 1971
6. Birgitta Trotzig, *Vi möts vid stencilerna*, *Sydsvenska Dagbladet*, 8 August 1973
7. Tom Wolfe, *The New Journalism*, Harper and Row, New York 1972
8. Ezekiel Mphalele, 'The Function of Literature at the Present', *Transition* nr 45, 1973
9. Interview in *Transition* nr 42, 1973
10. Nadine Gordimer, '98 Kinds of Censorship', unpublished, Stockholm 1974
11. Bernard Bergonzi, *The Situation of the Novel*, Macmillan, London 1970, pp. 24f.
12. Walter Jens, *Deutsche Literatur in der Gegenwart*, Deutscher Taschenbuch Verlag, Munich 1964, pp. 118ff.
13. R. H. Langbridge, 'The Fiction Serial in Eclipse', *The Bookseller*, 1 September 1973

13. *The Economics of the Novel*

1. Briggs, p. 172
2. Cf. Gettmann, pp. 141 and 164
3. The bookseller's discount varied but was usually 20–25 per cent at this time
4. From Gettmann p. 124. The figures are in much more detail in the original example

5. Philip Unwin, *Book Publishing as a Career*, Hamish Hamilton, London 1965, p. 160
6. From *Publisher's Weekly*, 5 August 1974
7. See also Dan Lacy, 'The Economics of Publishing', from Roger H. Smith (ed.), *The American Reading Public*, Bowker, New York 1963, pp. 55f.
8. Peter Mann, *The Facts about Romantic Fiction*, London 1974
9. John P., Dessauer, 'Some Hard Facts about the Economics of Fiction', *Publisher's Weekly*, 5 August 1974
10. Peter S. Prescott, 'The Lot of the Writer', *Newsweek*, 2 February 1974
11. See *The Bookseller*, 9 September and 2 November 1974
12. *The Bookseller*, 6 July 1974
13. *The Sunday Times Magazine*, 23 September 1973
14. *The Bookseller*, 2 June 1973
15. *The Bookseller*, 21 September 1974 and *Neue Zürcher Zeitung*, 25 August 1974
16. Dieter E. Zimmer, Aspekte einer Kulturkrise, Merkur 1971
17. *Die Welt*, 12 October 1974
18. *Publisher's Weekly*, 21 October 1974
19. *Publisher's Weekly*, 16 April 1973
20. Dieter E. Zimmer, ibid.

14. *Closing the Books*

1. Sven Delblanc, *Den Fkamliga Kosten*, Uddevalla 1973
2. Nils Gunnar Nilsson, *Sydsvenska Dagbladet*, 25 June 1974
3. Birgitta Trotzig, *Sydsvenska Dagbladet*, 1 August 1973
4. *Dagens Nyheter*, 28 August 1971
5. Robert Escarpit, Sociologie de la Littérature, pp. 85ff.
6. Ronald Sukenick, '*Author as Editor and Publisher*', *The New York Times Books Review*, 15 September 1974
7. Arne Melberg, 'Till kritikern', *Bonniers Litterära Magasin* nr 4, 1974
8. Dessauer, ibid.
9. Interview with William Jovanovich, *Newsweek*, 25 February 1974
10. *Newsweek*, 25 February 1974
11. Mann, ibid.
12. Dessauer, ibid.
13. Fleming Fiurendal, 'Erhvervet uden nåde', *Det Danske Bogmarked* nr 45, 1973
14. *The Times*, 1 October 1974

Index

ABF, 135
Achebe, Chinua, 150
Adams, Richard, 173
Addison, Joseph, 13, 14, 22, 32
administration costs, 156, 162–9
advertising costs, 155–69
African writers, 150
Aftonbladet, 123
Agnon, Shmuel Yosef, 188
Åhlén & Åkerlund, 79
Åkerlund, Erik, 79
Aldus, 176
Algeria, 31
Almqvist, C. J. L., 69, 70
Almqvist & Wiksell, 39n
Almqvist & Wiksell/Gebers, 84
Ambler, Eric, 173
American Publishers' Association, 38
Andersen, Charles John, *Lake Ngami*, 76
Anderson, H. C., 61
Andric, Ivo, 188
The Annual Register, 27
Arbetet, 136
Arendt, Hannah, 111, 112, 113, 141
aristocracy, as the reading public, 13, 17
Aschenhough, 39n, 62, 63, 66
Aspelin, Kurt, 133–4
Athenaeum, 28
Atterbom, P. D. A., 69
Auerbach, Erich, 46
Austen, Jane, 60
Austria, copyright, 23
authors, equality of income, 182; financial and social position, 22–7; payment, 21, 23–4, 26, 35, 36, 48, 63, 154–69; unknown, 169, 172
avant-gardism, 110–11, 114, 138

backlists, 30, 55
Bagley, Desmond, *High Citadel*, 166
Bainbridge, Beryl, 173

Baker, Dorothy, *Cassandra at the Wedding*, 164
Baldwin, James, *Tell Me How Long the Train's Been Gone*, 90
Balzac, Honoré de, 19, 29, 45, 46, 59, 70, 139, 145, 149, 151
Bang, Herman, 34
Barth, John, 185
Baum, Vicki, 175
Beadle, Erastus, 56, 57
Becker, *World History*, 77
Bell, Daniel, 98, 99, 102, 111
Bellman, Carl Michael, 76
Bentley and Colburn, 155–6, 176
Bergman, Bo, 78
Bergman, Ingmar, *The Magic Flute*, 180
Bergonzi, Bernard, 151
Berlingske Tidende, 60
Bernini, 109
Bertelsmann, 39n, 42, 174, 192
bestsellers, 53, 162; and the development of the novel, 172; in Germany, 41, 174, 189–90; in United States, 38, 55, 112; introduced to Europe, 41, 57–8; lifetime of, 112; purchased by libraries, 194; and the quality of the book, 188–90
Bibelhistorie (Gyldendal), 61
Bible, 28, 36, 49
La Bibliothèque des Chemins de fer, 31
La Bibliothèque Romans Etrangers, 31
La Bibliothèque Rose, 31
biographies, 176
Björnson, Björnstierne, 34, 62–3; *Magnhild*, 62–3
The Black Fritz, 69
Blanche, August, 70, 73
BLM, 172
Bodley Head, 43

207

Seneca, *Ethics*, 35
serial stories, 16, 18–19, 45, 60, 152–153
servants, and the reading public, 16
service society, 98–108; reading habits, 179; in Sweden, 116–27
Shakespeare, William, 50; *Hamlet*, 21
Shaw, George Bernard, 34, 76
Sheffield Public Library, 16
Shelley, Mary, *Frankenstein*, 29
Sherlock, Bishop, *Letter from the Lordbishop of London*, 44
La Siècle, 19
Silone, Ignazio, 146
Siwertz, Sigfrid, 78
Sjolochov, 188
Smith, W. H., 30, 31, 50, 192
Smollett, Tobias, 51, 59; *History of England*, 21
Social Democratic Party (Sweden), 136, 137, 141, 142
social mobility, 102–3
Söderberg, Hjalmar, 78
Söderholm, Margit, *Möte i Wien*, 163
Söderstrom, Werner, 39n, 66
Solzhenitsyn, Alexander, 183; *The First Circle*, 147
Sophocles, 30
South African, novels, 150–1
Soviet Union, education in, 101
Soyinka, Wole, 150
Spark, Muriel, 175
The Spectator (1714), 13, 14, 18, 32, 59, 69, 144
Spiller, Robert E., 37
Springer, 42, 175
Stagnelius, Erik Johan, 69
Stanley, Henry M., *Through the Dark Continent*, 76, 158
Starfelt, Viveka, *Porträtt av shinglad flicka*, 163
State Commission on Literature, 1968 (Sweden), 83, 85, 86, 88, 91, 130, 131, 134, 170, 171, 181, 187
Steele, Sir Richard, 13, 32
Steenhox, Frida, *Filippas öden*, 161
Steinbeck, John, 54, 146, 175
Steiner, George, 147, 194
Stendhal, 145; *Le rouge et le noir*, 29
Sterne, Lawrence, 22, 29, 51; *Sentimental Journey*, 69
Stiernhielm, Georg, 67
Stockholm, 68
Stone, Irving, *A Sailor on Horseback*, 162

Stowe, Harriet Beecher, *Uncle Tom's Cabin*, 80
Strand Magazine, 152
Stravinsky, Igor, 110
Strindberg, August, 77–8, 129
subscription publishing, 22, 24–5
Sue, Eugène, 19, 59, 60, 70, 75; *En riddarbragd*, 161
Suhrkamp, 175
Sundberg, Kjell, 132
Svalan, 192
Svea, 75
Den Svenska Argus, 69
Svenska Dagbladet, 123
Svenska Familje-Journalen, 77
Svensson, George, 175
Sweden, book clubs, 192–3; culture, 128–34; development of book market, 67–83; economics of the novel, 157, 158–67, 170, 171; publishing crisis, 84–91; society, 116–27
Sweden's National Literature, 79
Swedish Broadcasting Corporation, 120, 141
Swedish Lyric Poets, 79
Swedish National Price and Cartel Office, 84, 85
Swedish Publishers' Association, 73, 84, 86, 90, 193
Swedner, Harald, 139–40, 141
Swift, Jonathan, 22, 80; *Conduct of the Allies*, 44; *Gulliver's Travels*, 22

Tacitus, 30
Talese, Gay, 149
Tammi, 66
The Tatler, 13, 18, 59, 144
Taylor, Gordon Rattray, *The Doomsday Book*, 90
technocracy, 101–2
technostructure, 121
Tegnér, Esaias, 69; *Fritiof's Saga*, 73
television, 104, 130, 140, 153, 176, 180, 184, 188
The Terror of Spain, 69
textbooks, *see* school books
Thackeray, William Makepeace, 31, 49, 65, 76, 80, 149; *Vanity Fair*, 49
Third World, 150–1, 152
Thompson, Hunter, 149
Thomson, N. H., 70–1
Thomson group, 43
Thrale, Mrs, 15

210